# Other Books and Se[

*1901-1907 Native American Census Seneca Ottawa, Peoria, Quapaw, and Wyandotte In Territory)*

*1932 Census of The Standing Rock Sioux R. 1924-1932*

*Census of The Blackfeet, Montana, 1897- 1901 Expanded Edition*

*Eastern Cherokee by Blood, 1906-1910, Volumes I thru XIII*

*Choctaw of Mississippi Indian Census 1929-1932 with Births and Deaths 1924-1931 Volume I*
*Choctaw of Mississippi Indian Census 1933, 1934 & 1937, Supplemental Rolls to 1934 & 1935 with Births and Deaths 1932-1938, and Marriages 1936-1938 Volume II*

*Eastern Cherokee Census Cherokee, North Carolina 1930-1939 Census 1930-1931 with Births And Deaths 1924-1931 Taken By Agent L. W. Page Volume I*
*Eastern Cherokee Census Cherokee, North Carolina 1930-1939 Census 1932-1933 with Births And Deaths 1930-1932 Taken By Agent R. L. Spalsbury Volume II*
*Eastern Cherokee Census Cherokee, North Carolina 1930-1939 Census 1934-1937 with Births and Deaths 1925-1938 and Marriages 1936 & 1938 Taken by Agents R. L. Spalsbury And Harold W. Foght Volume III*

*Seminole of Florida Indian Census, 1930-1940 with Birth and Death Records, 1930-1938*

*Texas Cherokees 1820-1839 A Document For Litigation 1921*

*Choctaw By Blood Enrollment Cards 1898-1914 Volumes I thru XVII*

*Starr Roll 1894 (Cherokee Payment Rolls) Districts: Canadian, Cooweescoowee, and Delaware Volume One*
*Starr Roll 1894 (Cherokee Payment Rolls) Districts: Flint, Going Snake, and Illinois Volume Two*
*Starr Roll 1894 (Cherokee Payment Rolls) Districts: Saline, Sequoyah, and Tahlequah; Including Orphan Roll Volume Three*

*Cherokee Intruder Cases Dockets of Hearings 1901-1909 Volumes I & II*

*Indian Wills, 1911-1921 Records of the Bureau of Indian Affairs Books One thru Seven;*
*Native American Wills & Probate Records 1911-1921*

# Other Books and Series by Jeff Bowen

*Turtle Mountain Reservation Chippewa Indians 1932 Census with Births & Deaths, 1924-1932*

*Chickasaw By Blood Enrollment Cards 1898-1914 Volume I thru V*

*Cherokee Descendants East An Index to the Guion Miller Applications Volume I*
*Cherokee Descendants West An Index to the Guion Miller Applications Volume II (A-M)*
*Cherokee Descendants West An Index to the Guion Miller Applications Volume III (N-Z)*

*Applications for Enrollment of Seminole Newborn Freedmen, Act of 1905*

*Eastern Cherokee Census, Cherokee, North Carolina, 1915-1922, Taken by Agent James E. Henderson*          *Volume I (1915-1916)*
                                                   *Volume II (1917-1918)*
                                                   *Volume III (1919-1920)*
                                                   *Volume IV (1921-1922)*

*Complete Delaware Roll of 1898*

*Eastern Cherokee Census, Cherokee, North Carolina, 1923-1929, Taken by Agent James E. Henderson*          *Volume I (1923-1924)*
                                                   *Volume II (1925-1926)*
                                                   *Volume III (1927-1929)*

*Applications for Enrollment of Seminole Newborn Act of 1905 Volumes I & II*

*North Carolina Eastern Cherokee Indian Census 1898-1899, 1904, 1906, 1909-1912, 1914 Revised and Expanded Edition*

*1932 Hopi and Navajo Native American Census with Birth & Death Rolls (1925-1931) Volume 1 - Hopi*
*1932 Hopi and Navajo Native American Census with Birth & Death Rolls (1930-1932) Volume 2 - Navajo*

*Western Navajo Reservation Navajo, Hopi and Paiute 1933 Census with Birth & Death Rolls 1925-1933*

*Cherokee Citizenship Commission Dockets 1880-1884 and 1887-1889 Volumes I thru V*

## Other Books and Series by Jeff Bowen

*Applications for Enrollment of Chickasaw Newborn Act of 1905*
*Volumes I thru VII*

*Cherokee Intermarried White 1906 Volume I, II, III, IV, V, VI, VII, VIII & IX*

Visit our website at **www.nativestudy.com** to learn more about these
and other books and series by Jeff Bowen

# CHEROKEE INTERMARRIED WHITE 1906 VOLUME X

## TRANSCRIBED BY
## JEFF BOWEN

NATIVE STUDY
Gallipolis, Ohio
USA

Originally published:
Baltimore, Maryland
2014


Reprinted by:

Native Study LLC
Gallipolis, OH
*www.nativestudy.com*
2020


Library of Congress Control Number: 2020917307

ISBN: 978-1-64968-079-2




*Made in the United States of America.*

This series is dedicated to
Jerry Bowen
the Brave and the Strong.

# DEPARTMENT OF THE INTERIOR

## Commissioner to the Five Civilized Tribes

Muskogee, Indian Territory, March 9, 1907.

NOTICE IS HEREBY GIVEN that the undersigned, the Commissioner to the Five Civilized Tribes, has been designated by the Secretary of the Interior, as the official to make and approve appraisals of the value of improvements upon land in the Cherokee Nation which were made prior to November 5, 1906, by white persons who intermarried with Cherokee citizens prior to December 16, 1895, and who have the right under the Act of Congress approved March 2, 1907 (Public 180), to sell improvements.

NOTICE IS FURTHER GIVEN that former claimants to citizenship by intermarriage who have made permanent and valuable improvements on lands of the Cherokee Nation and who claim the right to sell the same under and by virtue of said Act of Congress of March 2, 1907 (Public 180), must appear before the Commissioner to the Five Civilized Tribes prior to April 1, 1907, and designate the land upon which are located the improvements which they claim the right to sell by virtue of said Act; and if any such intermarried citizen shall fail to appear before the Commissioner to the Five Civilized Tribes prior to April 1, 1907, it will be considered that he makes no claim to the benefits conferred by said Act. Such appearance and designation of improvements must be made before the Commissioner at his office in Muskogee, Indian Territory, at any time between Monday, March 11th, 1907, and Saturday, March 30th, 1907, inclusive, or at any of the following named places between the dates named at which places the Commissioner will have a representative to receive said designations and hear testimony relative thereto:

Bartlesville, Ind. Ter., Monday March 18th, 1907, to Saturday March 23rd, 1907, inclusive.

Tulsa, Ind. Ter., Monday March 25th, 1907, to Saturday March 30th, 1907, inclusive.

Claremore, Ind. Ter., Monday March 18th, 1907, to Saturday March 23rd, 1907, inclusive.

Nowata, Ind. Ter., Monday March 25th, 1907, to Saturday March 30th, 1907, inclusive.

Vinita, Ind. Ter., Monday March 18th, 1907, to Saturday March 23rd, 1907, inclusive.

Pryor Creek, Ind. Ter., Monday March 25th, 1907, to Saturday March 30th, 1907, inclusive.

Tahlequah, Ind. Ter., Monday March 18, 1907, to Saturday March 23rd, 1907, inclusive.

Sallisaw, Ind. Ter., Monday March 25th, 1907, to Saturday March 30th, 1907, inclusive.

Designations must be made in person by the intermarried white claimant, or in case proper proof is made that he is physically unable to appear, by some adult member of his immediate family, or in case proper proof is made of the fact that the intermarried white claimant is physically unable to appear and has no adult member of his immediate family, by a person holding a properly executed power of attorney; provided, that in every case the designation must be made by a party familiar with the character, ownership, location and value of the improvements to be designated. At the time of said designation the testimony of any competent person will be taken by the Commissioner as to the location, character and value of said improvements.

No former intermarried white claimant will be permitted to designate improvements upon more land than he would have been entitled to take in allotment for himself had he been admitted to citizenship. If any intermarried white claimant has made a tentative selection of a full allotment he will not be allowed to designate improvements upon other land.

NOTICE IS FURTHER GIVEN that if any citizen of the Cherokee Nation entitled to select an allotment shall claim that the improvements on land tentatively selected by a former intermarried white claimant, or held by him, do not belong to said intermarried white claimant, or makes any adverse claim to said improvements, or to the right of the intermarried white claimant to sell said improvements under the Act approved March 2, 1907 (Public 180), said citizen must appear before the Commissioner to the Five Civilized Tribes either at Muskogee, Indian Territory, prior to April 1, 1907, or at one of the places above designated and within the dates above designated and make formal complaint before the Commissioner to the Five Civilized Tribes of his contention. At Muskogee, Indian Territory, between March 11th and March 30th, 1907, inclusive, and at the other places herein named during the hearings at said places as herein fixed, plats will be open for inspection showing the location of tentative allotments made by former claimants to citizenship by intermarriage and all other land on which such claimants claim improvements, so far as indicated by the records of this office.

All persons interested should take careful note of the limitation of time herein provided for, within which designations and complaints may be made, and that they must be made by appearance before the Commissioner.

**TAMS BIXBY,**
Commissioner.

This particular notice concerns the appraisals of improvements on properties held by Cherokee intermarried whites. You would have found notices like this throughout the Nation to bring in people to finalize the allotment question, of who belonged and who did not.

## DEPARTMENT OF THE INTERIOR,

### COMMISSIONER TO THE FIVE CIVILIZED TRIBES.

---

In the matter of the application for the enrollment of
ALBERTIN HAMPTON as a citizen by intermarriage of the Cherokee
Nation.

## D E C I S I O N

THE RECORDS OF THIS OFFICE SHOW: That at Fairland, Indian
Territory, July 9, 1900, Albertin Hampton appeared before the Commission to the Five Civilized Tribes, and made application for the
enrollment of himself as a citizen by intermarriage, and for the
enrollment of his wife, Jane E. Hampton, et al. as citizens by
blood of the Cherokee Nation. The application for the enrollment of
the said Jane E. Hampton et al. as citizens by blood of the Cherokee
Nation has been heretofore disposed of, and their rights to enrollment will not be considered in this decision. Further proceedings
in the matter of said application were had at Muskogee, Indian
Territory, September 3, 1902, October 14, 1902, and January 2, 1907.

THE EVIDENCE IN THIS CASE SHOWS: That the applicant herein,
Albertin Hampton, a white man, was married, in accordance with
Cherokee law, January 20, 1874, to his wife, Jane E. Hampton, nee
Thomas, who was at the time of said marriage a recognized citizen
by blood of the Cherokee Nation, and whose name appears on the approved partial roll of citizens by blood of the Cherokee Nation,
opposite No. 195; that since said marriage the said Albertin Hampton
and Jane E. Hampton have resided together as husband and wife, and
have continuously lived in the Cherokee Nation. Said Albertin
Hampton is identified on the Cherokee authenticated tribal roll of
1880, and the Cherokee census roll of 1896, as "Bert Hampton", an
intermarried citizen of the Cherokee Nation.

IT IS, THEREFORE, ORDERED AND ADJUDGED: That in accordance with
the decision of the Supreme Court of the United States, dated November
5, 1906, in the case of Daniel Red Bird et al. vs. the United States,

N.C.M.                     - 2 -                    Cherokee 58.


under the provisions of Section twenty-one, of the Act of Congress
approved June 28, 1898 (30 Stat., 495), Albertin Hampton is entitled to enrollment as a citizen by intermarriage of the Cherokee
Nation, and his application for enrollment as such is accordingly
granted.


                                        _____
                                              Commissioner.

Dated at Muskogee, Indian Territory,
this   JAN 18 1907
       _____


The above is an accepted decision of the Commissioner to the Five
Civilized Tribes. The Attorney for the Cherokee Nation had fifteen days
after the date of Commissioner's decision in which to protest.

W.W.HASTINGS.
ATTORNEY

H. R. VANCE.
SECRETARY.

OFFICE OF

Attorney for the Cherokee Nation,

MUSKOGEE,I.T.      January 18, 1907.

The Commissioner to the Five Civilized Tribes,

Muskogee, Indian Territory.

Sir:

Receipt is acknowledged of the testimony and of your decision enrolling Albertin Hampton, as a citizen by intermarriage of the Cherokee Nation. Time for protesting said decision is waived and I consent that said person may be placed upon the schedule immediately.

Yours very truly,

W. W. Hastings

Attorney for Cherokee Nation.

The above is a notice of the Attorney waiving the time for protesting the Commissioner's decision (on the two previous pages) concerning Albertin Hampton's application and consenting to place the applicant upon schedule immediately.

# INTRODUCTION

The *Cherokee Intermarried White*, National Archive film M-1301, Rolls 305-307, are found under the heading of Applications for Enrollment of the Commission to the Five Civilized Tribes. The genealogical value of this series concerning the relationships between many Cherokee tribesman and their marriages among another race is very important and virtually a treasure trove of information long sought after. While on the other hand what these cases are really about are the efforts of many to attain Cherokee land allotments. Referenced from the Supreme Court Decision, Cherokee Intermarriage Cases – 203 U.S. 76 (1906).

This collection of Intermarried claims involves two hundred and eighty-eight separate cases with a variety of scenarios from the divorced to the widowed to the deserving to the deceptive. During these times there were many that wanted what was rightfully only the Cherokees. You will see each case will be headed by the title from the first folder as an example: *Intermarried White I, Trans from Cher. 34*, the transfer number is the Dawes Commission number from the claimants spouse.

These cases are fascinating because of the generational bloodlines that can be verified by documentation rather than just word of mouth. From Kent Carter's book, *The Dawes Commission*, "The tribe also, continued to oppose the enrollment of whites who had married into the Cherokee tribe. That controversy dragged through the U.S. Court of Claims and then the Supreme Court, which finally ruled in favor of the tribe on November 05, 1906. The court upheld the Cherokee citizenship laws that denied rights to any white who had married into the tribe after November 1, 1877. It also upheld an 1839 law which stated that anyone who moved out of the nation lost their citizenship unless they were readmitted. The applications of 3,341 persons were rejected as a result of this ruling, and the allotment clerks were forced to undo a great deal of their work. With the issue finally settled by the courts, the commission was able to send the first schedule of Cherokees by intermarriage, containing fifty-five names, to the secretary of interior on June 10, 1907. Eventually only 286 people were enrolled as intermarried whites----far fewer than the number put on the rolls of the Choctaw and Chickasaw tribes, which had much more liberal laws on rights based on marriage." [1]

---

[1] The Dawes Commission and the Allotment of the Five Civilized Tribes, 1893-1914 by Kent Carter, pg. 121

In Cohen's Handbook of Federal Indian Law he states, "In the *Cherokee Intermarriage Cases,* the Supreme Court considered the claims of certain white persons, intermarried with Cherokee Indians, who wanted to participate in the common property of the Cherokee Nation. Such persons were permitted by tribal law to be tribal citizens with limited rights in tribal property. The tribe had also provided for the revocation of citizenship rights of a white person who intermarried with a Cherokee if the Cherokee spouse were abandoned or if a widower or widow married a non-Cherokee. The Court found that the Cherokee Nation had authority to qualify the rights of citizenship which it offered to its "naturalized citizens. Such tribal action defeated the claims of the plaintiffs:

The laws and usages of the Cherokees, their earliest history, the fundamental principles of their national policy, their constitution and statutes, all show that citizenship rested on blood or marriage; that the man who would assert citizenship must establish marriage; that when marriage ceased (with a special reservation in favor of widows or widowers) citizenship ceased; that when an intermarried white married a person having no rights of Cherokee citizenship by blood it was conclusive evidence that the tie which bound him to the Cherokee people was severed and the very basis of his citizenship obliterated."[2]

An important footnote that Cohen published within his pages for the above paragraph also needs to be studied. He noted, "Under Cherokee law white persons intermarrying with Cherokees before 1875 were tribal citizens for most purposes, including allotment of tribal land, but had no interest in tribal funds except those funds derived from tribal lands. A Cherokee law that became effective in 1875 provided that whites marrying Cherokees had no rights to tribal property but could obtain full citizenship by the payment of $500 to the tribe. In 1877 the tribe provided that no intermarried citizen could obtain any rights to tribal land or funds."[3]

During many years of study this author has found cases that should have been been accepted, especially with the particular documentation presented. All in all the outcome of the decision made should have rendered a different result. Also there have been many that numb the mind as to how they their cases were even considered. The years have given many the hopes that their ancestors were one of those that had a decent claim and an honest consideration. Like any time in history there are political struggles

---

[2] Felix S. Cohen's Handbook of FEDERAL INDIAN LAW 1982 ED. pgs 20-21.
[3] Felix S. Cohen's Handbook of FEDERAL INDIAN LAW 1982 ED. pg 21 footnote16.

and the human factor that points out man is not perfect. These pages were transcribed with the wish that another person somewhere along the line will find their relation from the past and give them the answers long hoped for.


Jeff Bowen
Gallipolis, Ohio
*NativeStudy.com*

**Cher IW 267**

◇◇◇◇◇

Cherokee 5885

DEPARTMENT OF THE INTERIOR,
COMMISSIONER TO THE FIVE CIVILIZED TRIBES.
Muskogee, I. T., January 4, 1907.

In the matter of the application for the enrollment of John M. Smith as a citizen by intermarriage of the Cherokee Nation.

John M. Smith, being first duly sworn by Frances R. Lane, a Notary Public for the Western District of Indian Territory, testified as follows:

By the Commissioner:

Q  What is your name?  A John M. Smith.
Q  What is your age?  A Seventy-three.
Q  Your postoffice address?  A Tahlequah.
Q  You are an applicant for enrollment as a citizen by intermarriage of the Cherokee Nation?  A Yes sir.
Q  You have no Cherokee blood?  A No sir.
Q  You are only claiming the right to enrollment as a citizen of the Cherokee nation by virtue of your marriage to a Cherokee by blood?  A Yes sir.
Q  What is the name of the Cherokee citizen through whom you claim the right to enrollment?  A Narcissa E. Martin.
Q  Was she a recognized citizen of the Cherokee nation at the time you married her?
A  Yes sir.
Q  When did you marry her?  A December, 1869.
Q  Was she living in the Cherokee Nation at that time?
A  Yes sir.
Q  Was she your first wife?  A Yes sir.
Q  Were you her first husband?  A Yes sir.
Q  Since your marriage to her in 1869 have you and she continuously resided together in the Cherokee Nation as husband and wife?  A Yes sir.
Q  And you have always lived in the Cherokee nation have you?
A  Yes sir.

> The applicant John M. Smith is identified on the Cherokee authenticated tribal roll of 1880, Saline District, No. 20
> The name of his wife Narcissa E. Smith, is included in an approved partial list of citizens by blood of the Cherokee Nation opposite No. 14090.

Q  Have you any evidence of a documentary character showing your marriage to your wife, Narcissa?  A There was some. Tom Wolfe, his father gave me the license; he was here awhile ago. I believe we filed the marriage license with the commission, but I don't know. My wife couldn't find it. We got it years ago.

Q   You married your wife in accordance with the laws of the Cherokee nation?
A   Yes sir. These two men here, they signed my license.
Q   In what district?   A   Tahlequah District.
Q   In 1869?   A   Yes sir.

Witness excused.

Joseph B. Antoine, being first duly sworn by Frances R. Lane, A notary public for the Western District of Indian Territory, testified as follows:

Q   What is your name?   A   Joseph B. Antoine.
Q   What is your age?   A   Sixty-six.
Q   What is your postoffice address?   A   Tahlequah I. T.
Q   Do you know a peron[sic] in the Cherokee nation by the name of John M. Smith?
A   Yes sir.
Q   Do you know when he married his wife, Narcissa E. Smith:
A   I couldn't tell you exactly but I believe it was in the fall of 1868
Q   Did he marry her in accordance with the laws of the Cherokee Nation?   A   As far as I know he did. I fully believe he did. I remember when he got his license. I signed his petition.
Q   You were allowed to sign this petition although you were a white man?   A   Yes sir.
Q   Do you know whether or not a license was issued to John M. Smith?[sic] to marry his wife Narcissa E. Smith?   A   I couldn't say as to that
Q   You didn't see the license?   A   No sir.
Q   Is it generally understood that he married his wife in accordance with the laws of the Cherokee nation?   A   Yes sir.
Q   And they have lived together as husband and wife since their marriage have they?
A   Yes sir.
Q   And always lived in the Cherokee Nation?   A   Yes sir. I have known Mr. smith ever since that time, and been a neighbor to him.

The original marriage record, Tahlequah District, Cherokee Nation, Book B, now in the possession of the Commissioner, shows the following entry:
No. 19 "John M. Smith, issued Nov. 30th, 1867, to marry Miss E. Martin."

Witness excused.

John M. Smith Recalled:
The Commissioner?
Q   Who married you?     A   Steve Foreman, a Presbyterian minister.   He was a missionary.
Q   Did he give you a certificate of marriage?   A   Yes sir.
Q   And you think that is on file in this office?   A   A[sic] Yes, it was in the records of the Cherokee Nation. I don't know what has become of it.

Q    Are they any persons living who witnesses[sic] your marriage?
A    I think every one of them is dead.  My wife and I were talking about it the other day.  Everybody is dead but her and me.

----------

Frances R. Lane upon oath states that as stenographer to the Commission to the Five Civilized Tribes she reported the testimony in the above entitled cause and that the foregoing is an accurate transcript of her stenographic notes thereof.

Frances R Lane

Subscribed and sworn to before me this January 5, 1907.

Edward Merrick
Notary Public.

◇◇◇◇◇

E C M                                                                                                Cherokee 5855.

## DEPARTMENT OF THE INTERIOR,
## COMMISSIONER TO THE FIVE CIVILIZED TRIBES

In the matter of the application for the enrollment of JOHN M. SMITH as a citizen by intermarriage of the Cherokee Nation.

## D E C I S I O N

THE RECORDS OF THIS OFFICE SHOW:  That at Tahlequah, Indian Territory, November 30, 1900 application was received by the Commission to the Five Civilized Tribes for the enrollment of John M. Smith as a citizen by intermarriage of the Cherokee Nation.   Further proceedings in the matter of said application were had at Tahlequah, Indian Territory, October 1, 1902, May 13, 1903 and at Muskogee, Indian Territory, January 4, 1907.

THE EVIDENCE IN THIS CASE SHOWS:  That the applicant herein, John M. Smith, a white man, was married in accordance with Cherokee law about 1867 to his wife, Narcissa E. Smith, nee Martin, who was at the time of said marriage a recognized citizen by blood of the Cherokee Nation, who is identified on the Cherokee authenticated tribal roll of 1880, Saline District No. 1121 as a native Cherokee, and whose name is included on the approved partial roll of citizens by blood of the Cherokee Nation opposite No. 14090.  It is further shown that from the time of said marriage the said John M. Smith and Narcissa E. Smith resided together as husband and wife and continuously lived in the Cherokee Nation up to and including September 1, 1902.   Said applicant is identified on the Cherokee authenticated tribal roll of 1880 and the Cherokee census roll of 1896 as an intermarried citizen of the Cherokee Nation.

IT IS, THEREFORE, ORDERED AND ADJUDGED: That in accordance with the decision of the Supreme Court of the United States, dated November 5, 1906, in the cases of Daniel Red Bird, et al. vs. the United States, Nos. 125, 126, 127, and 128, the said applicant, John M. Smith, is entitled, under the provisions of Section Twenty-one of the Act of Congress approved June 28, 1898 (30 Stats. 495), to enrollment as a citizen by intermarriage of the Cherokee Nation, and his application for enrollment as such is accordingly granted.

Tams Bixby

Commissioner.

Dated at Muskogee, Indian Territory,
this    FEB 28 1907

## DEPARTMENT OF THE INTERIOR,
## COMMISSIONER TO THE FIVE CIVILIZED TRIBES.

In the matter of the application for the enrollment of John M. Smith as a citizen by intermarriage of the Cherokee Nation, Cherokee 5855.

### Protest of the Cherokee Nation.

The representative of the Cherokee Nation cannot consent to the enrollment of the applicant John M. Smith for the reasons more fully set out in the brief filed on behalf of the Cherokee Nation on December 22, 1902.

The record in this case shows that John M. Smith took an allotment out of the lands formerly a part of the Cherokee Strip, and so far as we know the Department has never enrolled any person applying as a citizen of the Cherokee Nation where they took an allotment from the Shawnee Reservation, the Quapaw Reservation of lands or lands from any other reservation, and inasmuch as the records show that John M. Smith took an allotment of Cherokee lands from the Cherokee Strip and paid no compensation therefor, we have always contended and still contend that he is not entitled to two allotments from the Cherokee lands, and is therefore not entitled to be enrolled as a citizen by intermarriage of the Cherokee Nation, and we still insist upon the protest heretofore filed in this case.

Respectfully submitted,

Attorney for the Cherokee Nation.

Cherokee
5885

Muskogee, Indian Territory, December 27, 1906.

John M. Smith,
    Tahlequah, Indian Territory.

Dear Sir:

November 6, 1906, the United States Supreme Court held that white persons who intermarried with Cherokee citizens according to Cherokee law prior to November 1, 1875, are entitled to enrollment and allotments of land as citizens of the Cherokee Nation.

You are advised that to properly determine your right to enrollment as a citizen by intermarriage of the Cherokee Nation, it will be necessary for you to appear before the Commissioner for the purpose of giving testimony as to the date of your marriage and whether or not your wife, by reason of your marriage to whom you claim the right to enrollment as a citizen of the Cherokee Nation, was a recognized citizen of the Cherokee Nation at the time of your marriage to her, and whether or not you were married to her in accordance with Cherokee laws

You are therefore directed to appear before the Commissioner at Muskogee, Indian Territory, at 9 o'clock A. M., on Saturday, January 5, 1907, and give testimony as above indicated.

Respectfully,

S.W.                                                                                 Acting Commissioner.

◇◇◇◇◇

Cherokee
5885

Muskogee, Indian Territory, February 28, 1907

W. W. Hastings,
    Attorney for the Cherokee Nation,
        Muskogee, Indian Territory.

Dear Sir:

There is enclosed herewith a copy of the decision of the Commissioner to the Five Civilized Tribes, dated February 28, 1907, granting the application for the enrollment of John M. Smith as a citizen by intermarriage of the Cherokee Nation.

The record of proceedings, together with the Commissioner's decision has been this day forwarded to the Secretary of the Interior for review. The action of the Secretary will be made known to you when this office is informed of the same.

Respectfully,

Encl. B-2                                    Commissioner.

<>><><><><>

Muskogee, Indian Territory, February 28, 1907.

The Honorable,
        The Secretary of the Interior.

Sir:

There is transmitted here with the record of proceedings had in the matter of the application of John M. Smith for enrollment as a citizen by intermarriage of the Cherokee Nation, together with the Commissioner's decision of this date granting his application.

The Attorney for the Cherokee Nation protests against the Commissioner's decision in this case, and his protest, filed this day, is also enclosed.

There is enclosed a schedule containing the name of said John M. Smith and in event the Department concurs in the Commissioner's decision therein, the approval of this schedule is recommended. It will be noted that no number has been given the name of this person on the schedule herewith transmitted. This action is taken in accordance with the procedure reported by me to the Department on January 28, 1907, and approved by the Department's telegram of February 9, 1907.

In case of the approval of this schedule, it is recommended that a number be placed thereon by Mr. McGarr, the employe[sic] of my office now in Washington.

Respectfully,

Commissioner.

Through
        The Commissioner of Indian Affairs.

Encl. W-1.
S.W.

<>><><><><>

Tahlequah, Ind, Terry. 3/1/07.

Hon. Tams Bixby
    Muskogee, Ind. terry.

Sir:

    The Indian Appropriation Bill approved March, 3rd, 1893, provides that those citizens of the Cherokee Nation, who had improvements on the Cherokee Strip, prior to making of the agreement between the Government and the Nation in the sale of the Strip, should have Eighty acres of land there by paying to the Cherokee Nation $112.00 out of their money, known as the Strip money, I am one among the Seventy citizens who took an allotment there, my being an adopted citizen by marriage. I received no part of the Strip money, Hence I have not paid the $112.00 to the Nation as have the citizens by blood who took the Eighty acres of land on the Strip under the provisions of the above named act of Congress, but I am willing to pay the $112.00 for the Eighty acres of land, I received on the Cherokee Strip as provided for in the Agreement and the act of Congress notifying the Agreement for the sale of the Cherokee Strip. That is, if you and the Honorable Secretary of the Interior are of the opinion that I should do so, and I here-with enclose a Bank draft for $112.00.

    If you do not think that I should pay the $112.00 please return same to me inasmuch as I received no part of the Strip money, I do not think that I should pay the $112.00 but if I am compelled to pay same to save my allotment, I am willing to do so, if so adjudged by you and the Honorable Secretary of the Interior. I have the Honor to be,

Yours very truly,

(Signed)  John M. Smith.

◇◇◇◇◇

Tahlequah, I. T.  March 2nd, 1907.

Hon. Tams Bixby.
    Commissioner to Five Civilized Tribes.
        Muskogee, I. T.

Sir:-

    I am in receipt of a protest filed by the attorneys for the Cherokee nation against my enrollment as a citizen by intermarriage of the Cherokee nation. The protest is based on the fact that I received lands in the Cherokee strip without paying for the same. I am unable to see what possible bearing this would have on my enrollment, but in order to protect my rights in the premises I am inclosing herewith payable to your order a draft of $112.00 which is the amount demanded of me on account of the strip lands. This draft is sent you upon the condition, that if it be determined that the payment of such sum is necessary and a condition precedent of my enrollment, the the[sic] draft is to be considered as in payment of said strip lands and a compliance with such condition precedent, and you are authorized to pay the same to the Cherokee nation; otherwise the draft is to be returned to me.

Respectfully,

(Signed) John M. Smith.

◇◇◇◇◇

COPY

Land
21729-1907.
21730-1907        DEPARTMENT OF THE INTERIOR,
                 OFFICE OF INDIAN AFFAIRS,
                 WASHINGTON.

March 2, 1907.

The Honorable,
     The Secretary of the Interior.

Sir:

     I have the honor to transmit herewith two communications from Commissioner Bixby, dated February 28, 1907, enclosing the record and schedule in the case of John M. Smith, applicant for enrollment as a citizen by intermarriage of the Cherokee Nation, and the case of Mary J. Catron, applicant for enrollment as a citizen by intermarriage of the Cherokee Nation.

     The record in these cases has been examined and the Office is of the opinion that the decision of the Commission granting the application in each of these cases is correct, and it is recommended that it be affirmed and the schedule containing the names of these applicants be approved.

     Attention is invited to the fact that the Commissioner desires Mr. McGarr, now in this city, to properly number the schedules in these cases.

Very respectfully,

C. F. Larrabee,

EWE-W                                         Acting Commissioner.

◇◇◇◇◇

# Cherokee Intermarried White 1906
## Volume X

D.C. 14852 SPECIAL Y.P.

DEPARTMENT OF THE INTERIOR, S.P.
WASHINGTON.

I.T.D. 7896-1907. March 4, 1907.

LRS

<u>DIRECT</u>.

Commissioner to the Five Civilized Tribes,
Muskogee, Indian Territory.

Sir:

In accordance with the recommendation of the Indian Office in letter of March 2, 1907, your decision in the case of Jacob (John) M. Smith, applicant for enrolment[sic] as a citizen by intermarriage of the Cherokee Nation and in the case of Mary J. Catron for her enrolment[sic] by intermarriage in the same Nation, are affirmed.

The schedule transmitted with your letter of February 28, 1907, bearing the name of these claimants, is approved and will be disposed in the usual manner.

A copy of Indian Office letter is inclosed.

Respectfully,
(Signed) E. A. Hitchcock.
Secretary.

5 inc. and
9 for Ind. Of.
with copy hereof.

A F Mc
3-5-07

◇◇◇◇◇

Cherokee
5885

Muskogee, Indian Territory, March 5, 1907

John M. Smith,
      Tahlequah, Indian Territory.

Dear Sir:

There is enclosed herewith a copy of the decision of the Commissioner to the Five Civilized Tribes, dated February 28, 1907, granting your application for enrollment as a citizen by intermarriage of the Cherokee Nation. The Cherokee Nation protests against your enrollment.

The record of proceedings had in your case, together with the Commissioner's decision, has been this day forwarded to the Secretary of the Interior for review. You will be advised of any further action taken in your case.

Respectfully,

Commissioner

Encl. B-1

◇◇◇◇◇

( C O P Y )

J F Jr

D.C. 16823-1907                                      S. P.
I.T.D. 7994-1907

DEPARTMENT OF THE INTERIOR
WASHINGTON.

L R S.                                              March 13, 1907.

Commissioner to the Five Civilized Tribes,
      Muskogee, Indian Territory.

Sir:

The receipt is acknowledged of your telegram of March 2, 1907, in the matter of the application of John M. Smith for enrollment as an intermarried citizen of the Cherokee Nation and the offer of payment by him of $112 said to be due the Cherokee Nation to secure the enrollment of said applicant.

You are advised that no action was taken upon this telegram prior to March 5, 1907.

Respectfully,

(Signed)  JESSE E. WILSON
Assistant Secretary

Through the Commissioner
of Indian affairs.

◇◇◇◇◇

Cherokee 5885

COPY
Muskogee, Indian Territory, March 22, 1907.

John M. Smith,
Tahlequah, Indian Territory.

Dear Sir:

You are hereby advised that the decision of the Commissioner to the Five Civilized Tribes, dated February 28, 1907, granting the application for your enrollment as a citizen by intermarriage of the Cherokee Nation, was affirmed by the Secretary of the Interior, March 4, 1907.

Respectfully,

SIGNED  *Tams Bixby*

RPI                                                    Commissioner.

◇◇◇◇◇

Cherokee 5885                              COPY

Muskogee, Indian Territory, March 22, 1907.

W. M. Cravens,
Attorney for John M. Smith,
Muskogee, Indian Territory.

Dear Sir:

You are hereby advised that the decision of the Commissioner to the Five Civilized Tribes, dated February 28, 1907, granting the application for the enrollment of John M. Smith as a citizen by intermarriage of the Cherokee Nation, was affirmed by the Secretary of the Interior, March 4, 1907.

For your information, there is enclosed herewith a copy of Departmental decision referred to.

# Cherokee Intermarried White 1906
## Volume X

Respectfully,

SIGNED *Jams Bixby*
Commissioner.

Enc I-639
RPI

◇◇◇◇◇

Cherokee 5885                    COPY
7622

Muskogee, Indian Territory, March 22, 1907.

W. W. Hastings,
    Attorney for the Cherokee Nation,
        Muskogee, Indian Territory.

Dear Sir:

You are hereby advised that the decision of the Commissioner to the Five Civilized Tribes, dated February 28, 1907, granting the applications for the enrollment of John M. Smith and Mary J. Catron, as citizens by intermarriage of the Cherokee Nation, was affirmed by the Secretary of the Interior, March 4, 1907.

For your information, there is enclosed herewith a copy of Departmental decision referred to.

Respectfully,

SIGNED *Jams Bixby*
Commissioner.

Enc I-638

RPI

◇◇◇◇◇

Muskogee, Indian Territory, April 15, 1907.

John M. Smith,
    Tahlequah, Indian Territory.

Dear Sit:

On March 2, 1907, you deposited with me a draft drawn by the First National Bank of Tahlequah upon the State National Bank of St. Louis, dated March 1, 1907, numbered 63,567, for $112.00 payable to my order. This draft was deposited with me upon the condition as stated in the letter which accompanied the draft "that if it be determined that the payment of such sum is necessary and a condition precedent of my (your) enrollment, then the draft is to be considered as in payment of" - certain strip lands

- "and a compliance with such condition precedent, and you are authorized to pay the same to the Cherokee Nation; otherwise the draft is to be returned to me."

On March 2, 1907, your application for enrollment as a citizen by intermarriage of the Cherokee Nation was pending before the Secretary of the Interior having been favorably recommended by this office. On that day this office telegraphed the Secretary of the Interior stating that you had deposited the said draft with me to be turned over to the Cherokee Nation in case it should be determined that the payment of said sum by you was necessary as a condition precedent to enrollment. On March 4, 1907, your enrollment as an intermarried citizen of the Cherokee Nation was approved by the Secretary of the Interior without any condition being attached thereto, and on March 13, 1907, the Department wrote this office that they had received my telegram of March 2, 1907, but that no action had been taken upon said telegram prior to March 5, 1907.

Under these circumstances I herewith return to you the said draft above described in accordance with the conditions upon which it was deposited with me. Please acknowledge receipt of this draft.

Respectfully,

FEL-15-1                                                      Commissioner.

◇◇◇◇◇

GAW

DEPARTMENT OF THE INTERIOR
OFFICE OF INDIAN AFFAIRS,
WASHINGTON.

I.T.                                                      May 11, 1907.
References in body
of letter.

Subject: Motions for
review in certain Chero-
kee citizenship cases.

The Honorable,
      The Secretary of the Interior.

Sir:

There are inclosed herewith motions filed by W. W. Hastings, National Attorney for the Cherokee Nation, praying for review and rehearing of Departmental decisions authorizing the enrollment as citizens by intermarriage of the Cherokee Nation of the following persons:

## Cherokee Intermarried White 1906
## Volume X

| | | |
|---|---|---|
| 42893-1907, | | Jacob A. Bartles, |
| 42895- | " | Osburn J. Byrd, |
| 42886- | " | Amanda Beck, |
| 42894- | " | Sarah F. Gage, |
| 42892- | " | Phirena Harris, |
| 42888- | " | Daniel Harmon, |
| 42891- | " | Emma L. Ironsides, |
| 42896- | " | Sarah A. Jordan |
| 42881- | " | Dovie Johnson, |
| 42882- | " | Andrew H. Norwood, |
| 42887- | " | Stacy E. Perry, |
| 42885- | " | Martha Randolph, now Kernan |
| 42893- | " | John W. Smith |
| 42884- | " | John J. Smith, |
| 42890- | " | Robert H. F. Thompson, |
| 42889- | " | Hattie Wright, |
| 42883- | " | Nancy Wolfe, |
| 42880- | " | E. A. Welch. |

In view of the provisions of section 2 of the act of April 26, 1906 (34 Stat. L., 137), providing that the rolls of the Five Civilized Tribes shall be fully completed on or before March 4, 1907, there appears to be no authority in law for the reconsideration of any enrollment cases at this time, and it is recommended that the office be authorized to advise Mr. Hastings that the motions for review herewith transmitted cannot be considered.

Very respectfully,

C. F. Larrabee

Acting Commissioner.

AJW-FHE.

May 13, 1907.

Approved.

Thos Ryan

First Assistant Secretary.

◇◇◇◇◇

14

I. T. references
in body of letter.

DEPARTMENT OF THE INTERIOR,
OFFICE OF INDIAN AFFAIRS,
WASHINGTON.                    GAW

May 15, 1907.

Commissioner to the Five Civilized Tribes,
Muskogee, Indian Territory.

Sir:

There is inclosed copy of Office letter of May 11, 1907, approved by the Department on May 13, 1907, recommending that motions filed by W. W. Hastings, National Attorney for the Cherokee Nation, praying for a review and rehearing of Departmental decisions authorizing the enrollment of the following persons as citizens by intermarriage of the Cherokee Nation, be denied, in view of the fact that there appears to be no authority in law at this time for the reconsideration of any enrollment case.

| | |
|---|---|
| 42893-1907 | Jacob A. Bartles |
| 42895- " | Osburn J. Byrd |
| 42886- " | Amanda Beck |
| 42894- " | Sarah F. Gage |
| 42892- " | Phirena Harris |
| 42888- " | Daniel Harmon |
| 42891- " | Emma L. Ironsides |
| 42896- " | Sarah A. Jordan |
| 42881- " | Dovie Johnson |
| 42882- " | Andrew H. Norwood |
| 42887- " | Stacy E. Perry |
| 42885- " | Martha Randolph, now Kernan |
| 42893- " | John W. Smith |
| 42884- " | John J. Smith |
| 42890- " | Robert H. F. Thompson |
| 42889- " | Hattie Wright |
| 42883- " | Nancy Wolfe |
| 42880- " | E. A. Welch |

You are requested to advise the interested parties, including Mr. Hastings, of the Department's action.

Very respectfully,
C. F. Larrabee
Acting Commissioner.

AJW-FHE.

◇◇◇◇◇◇

Cherokee
267

Muskogee, Indian Territory, May 25, 1907.

John M. Smith,
Tahlequah, Indian Territory.

Dear Sir:

You are hereby advised that on May 13, 1907, the Secretary of the Interior denied a motion filed by the Attorney for the Cherokee Nation, for a review of its decision authorizing your enrollment as a citizen by intermarriage of the Cherokee Nation.

For your information, there is enclosed herewith a copy of Departmental decision referred to.

Respectfully,

Commissioner.

Encl. C-14
LMC

◇◇◇◇◇◇

Cherokee
253 et al.

Muskogee, Indian Territory, May 25, 1907.

W. W. Hastings,
Attorney for the Cherokee Nation,
Muskogee, Indian Territory.

Dear Sir:

You are hereby advised that on May 13, 1907, the Secretary of the Interior denied the motion filed by you for a review of its decision authorizing the enrollment of Jacob A. Bartles, et al., as citizens by intermarriage of the Cherokee Nation.

For your information, there is enclosed herewith a copy of Departmental decision referred to.

Respectfully,

Commissioner.

Encl. C-20
LMC

◇◇◇◇◇

GAW

D.C. 28530-1907.

DEPARTMENT OF THE INTERIOR,
OFFICE OF INDIAN AFFAIRS,
WASHINGTON.

I.T.
47950-1907.

June 5, 1907.

The Commissioner
to the Five Civilized Tribes,
Muskogee, Ind. Ter.

Sir:

On May 17, 1907, the Department transmitted to this Office a communication from Herbert C. Smith, of Tahlequah, Ind. Ter., dated May 6, 1907, objecting to motion for review of Departmental decision of Mar. 4, 1907, in the matter of the application of John M. Smith for enrollment as a citizen by intermarriage of the Cherokee Nation. The Department says that the motion referred to has not been received. The records of this Office do not show that such motion was filed with it. You are requested to advise Mr. Smith of the status of the matter.

Very respectfully,

C. F. Larrabee,

Acting Commissioner.

GAW-GH.

**Cher IW 268**

◇◇◇◇◇

CHEROKEE-7622.

DEPARTMENT OF THE INTERIOR,
COMMISSIONER TO THE FIVE CIVILIZED TRIBES.
Muskogee, Indian Territory, January 5, 1907.

---------------------

In the matter of making proof of the marriage of Mary J. Catron to her Cherokee husband, prior to November 1, 1875.

------------------

Mary Jane Catron, after having first been duly sworn by B. P. Rasmus, a Notary Public, testified as follows:

COMMISSIONER:

Q. What is your name?   A. Mary Jane Catron.
Q. What is your age?   A. 56.
Q. What is your post office address?   A. Wauhillau.
Q. Do you claim to be a citizen by intermarriage of the Cherokee Nation?
A. Yes sir.
Q. Through whom do you claim that right?   A. Lafayette Catron.
Q. When were you married?   A. In 1874.
Q. Where were you living?   A. Right where we are now.
Q. Were you ever married before you married Lafayette Catron?   A. No sir.
Q. Was he married before he married you?   A. Yes sir, he was married before the war.
Q. What was the name of his first wife?   A. Martha Roach.
Q. Was she living when he married you?   A. Yes sir.
Q. Had he ever been divorced?   A. He never said whether he had been or not.
Q. Who married you?   A. Preacher Foreman.
Q. Did he give you a certificate?   A. No sir. I don't know whether there was one recorded in the office or not, but the office has been burned up.
Q. Have you always lived in the Cherokee Nation since your marriage[sic]
A. Yes sir.
Q. Was your husband a recognized citizen of the Cherokee Nation when you married him in '74?   A. Yes sir.
Q. How[sic] rights were never questioned?   A. No sir.
Q. Was your right as a citizen by adoption ever questioned in any manner?
A. No sir.

Witness excused.

Elijah Stevens, being duly sworn by B. P. Rasmus, a Notary Public, testified as follows:

COMMISSIONER:

Q. What is your name?  A. Elijah Stevens.
Q. What is your age?  A. 58.
Q. What is your post office address?  A. Park Hill.
Q. Are you acquainted with Mary J. Catron?  A. Yes sir.
Q. Do you know her husband?  A. Yes sir.
Q. Do you know when they were married?  A. Yes sir, I seen them married.
Q. You were present at their marriage?  A. Yes sir.
Q. When were they married?  A. In '74. I don't know the date.
Q. Where were they married?  A. Close to Wauhillau post office.
Q. Who married them?  A. Steven Foreman.
Q. Have they lived together continuously as husband and wife since their marriage?
   A.  I think so. I live within 12 miles of them, and I don't know that they have ever had any trouble.
Q. Do you know anything about Lafayette Catron's former wife?  A. No sir, I heard that he had been married.
Q. Do you know whether he was divorced or not?  A. No sir I dont[sic].

(Commissioner --  The applicant in this case is identified on the 1880 Roll, Tahlequah District, opposite No. 397. Her husband, through whom she claims the right to enrollment, is identified upon said roll in said District, opposite No. 396. He is also identified upon the final roll of citizens by blood of the Cherokee Nation, opposite No. 17982.)

Witness excused.

Mary J. Catron recalled.

It will be necessary for you to furnish proof to this office that your husband was lawfully divorced from his former wife before he married you?  A. There were no divorces in them days, under the Cherokee law. I guess the war and her conduct divorced them.

Witness excused.

Martin A. Wallace, being first duly sworn by B. P. Rasmus, a Notary Public, testified as follows:

 COMMISSIONER:

Q. What is your name?  A. Martin A. Wallace.
Q. What is your age?  A. 60.
Q. What is your post office address?  A. Tahlequah.

# Cherokee Intermarried White 1906
## Volume X

Q.  Are you acquainted with Mary J. Catron?  A.  Yes sir.

Q.  Do you know Lafayette Catron?  A.  Yes sir.

Q.  Did you know Lafayette Catron's first wife?  A.  Yes sir, I was acquainted with her.

Q.  Do you know whether or not Lafayette Catron was divorced from his first wife?  A. I do not, only this -- when I came to this country in '71, there was no divorce law among the Indians, nor no marriage law.  They just courted the woman and if she greed they lived together, and when they got tired they quit.

Q.  Had Lafayette Catron said he would quit when he married this woman?
A.  I guess so.

Q.  Do you know when they separated?  A.  I do not.  They were separated as long as I know.  They were separated when I came to this country.

Q.  You know that Lafayette Catron did not live with her after '69?
A.  He wasn't living with her when I came here -- or first knew him.

Q.  When did you first get acquainted with his first wife?  A.  I don't know as I could tell you.  She wasn't living in that immediate settlement when I got acquainted with her.

Q.  Is she living at this time?  A No sir.

Q.  When did she die?  A.  I couldn't tell you the date, but it has been several years.

Q.  About how many years?  A.  I couldn't hardly say about how many.  It must have been 6 or 7 or 8 years.

Q.  When she did was she married to someone else?  A.  She had been married, but wasn't living with the man when she died.  He had left her.

Q.  What was the name of her husband?  A.  I don't know whether she had had one between Catron and this man or not, but I can't think of his name.  Lewis Bowers lived with her.  I remember him coming to Henderson's and she and Bowers lived together.

Q.  When was that?  A.  I don't remember the date.  It was in the 70s or 80s, but before she died she was married to another man -- a white man.

Q.  Do you know how many men she lived with during her lifetime?
A.  No sir.  I wouldn't begin to try to tell.

Q.  Have Lafayette Catron and Mary J. Catron been recognized as husband and wife since 1874?  A.  According to my understanding they have.

Q.  Were you present when they were married?  A.  No sir.  But she was living at my house, and I know she left my house that morning to marry.

Q.  And they have lived together, and held themselves out as husband and wife since that time?  A.  Yes sir.

Witness excused.

Wilson Ryder, being sworn by B. P. Rasmus, testified as follows:

COMMISSIONER:

Q.  What is your name?  A.  Wilson Ryder.

Q.  Do you know Lafayette Catron?  A.  Yes sir, I know him.

Q.  How long have you known him?  A.  Ever since before the war.

Q. Did you know his first wife?   A. Yes sir.

Q. What was her name?   A. Nancy Roach before she married Catron.

Q. When was she married to Catron?   A. Before the war.

Q. How long did she and Catron live together?   A. About 4 years, and then the war broke out and they separated during the war, in the Choctaw Nation.

Q. Which one left the other?   A. The woman come back. She left her man in the Choctaw Nation. She brought the children back.

Q. What did Catron do?   A. He come home. He had a place over there.

Q. Did he come to his place?   A. Yes sir.

Q. Did he live with his wife anymore?   A. No sir.

Q. Did he get a divorce?   A. No sir, there was no divorce law then.

Q. What did his first wife do?   A. Got another man.

Q. When?   A. I think about 10 years after the war she took up with Ocie Sanders.

Q. How long did she live with Ocie Sanders?   A. 2 or 3 months.

Q. What did she do then?   A. She stayed around there for a while and then married a dutchman[sic] named Lewis.

Q. Did she get a divorce from Ocie Sanders?   A. No sir.

Q. Did she get a divorce from Lafayette Catron?   A. No sir.

Q. She married this dutchman[sic] without a divorce?   A. Yes sir.

Q. How long did she live with him?   A. A Few months, and then in a year or two she took up with a man by the name of Ka-la-ne-ske.

Q. How long did she live with Ka-la-ne-she[sic]?   A. About 2 years up there on the river.

Q. Then what did she do?   A. She would stay with her daughter every once in a while. She would stay there a while and the next time, as near as I can guess at it, she was living with this last man, named Joe Pyle -- I think she married him according to the law. She was living with Joe Pyle when she took sick and died.

Q. When did she die?   A. I don't know. It has been a good while[sic] About a year after the Strip Payment she died.

Q. Did she have any children by Lafayette Catron?   A. Yes sir she did.

Q. What became of those children?   A. They are living up there.

Q. Who do they live with?   A. The girl, she married one of the Stevens boys.

Q. Was there a boy?   A. Yes sir, he lives up there close to his father.

Q. Who raised them after Lafayette Catron and this woman parted?
A. Their granny -- Lafayette Catron's mother.

Q. This woman didn't raise them?   A. They never stayed with her. She throwed them away.

Q. They didn't stay with Lafayette Catron either?   A. Yes sir, Lafayette Catron and his mother kept house, and the children stayed there with their granny. Lafayette Catron and his mother together raised them, but Nancy Roach throwed the children away. We was living close together.

Witness excused.

--------------------------------------------------------------------------

# Cherokee Intermarried White 1906
## Volume X

Eula Jeanes Branson, being sworn, states that she correctly reported the proceedings had in the above and foregoing, on the 5th. day of January, 1907.

Eula Jeanes Branson

Subscribed and sworn to before me, this the 8th. day of January, 1907

Walter W. Chappell
Notary Public.

◇◇◇◇◇

E C M                                                                              Cherokee 7622.

DEPARTMENT OF THE INTERIOR,
COMMISSIONER TO THE FIVE CIVILIZED TRIBES.

In the matter of the application for the enrollment of MARY J. CATRON as a citizen by intermarriage of the Cherokee Nation.

D E C I S I O N

THE RECORDS OF THIS OFFICE SHOW: That at Tahlequah, Indian Territory, November 21, 1901 application was received by the Commission to the Five Civilized Tribes for the enrollment of Mary J. Catron as a citizen by intermarriage of the Cherokee Nation. Further proceedings in the matter of said application were had at Tahlequah, Indian Territory, October 8, 1902 and at Muskogee, Indian Territory, January 5, 1907.

THE EVIDENCE IN THIS CASE SHOWS: That the applicant herein, Mary J. Catron, a white woman, was married in 1874 to one Lafayette Catron, who was at the time of said marriage a recognized citizen by blood of the Cherokee Nation, who is identified on the Cherokee authenticated tribal roll of 1880, Tahlequah District No. 396, as a native Cherokee, and whose name is included on the approved partial roll of citizens by blood of the Cherokee Nation opposite No. 17892. It is further shown that from the time of said marriage the said Lafayette Catron and Mary J. Catron resided together as husband and wife and continuously lived in the Cherokee Nation up to and including September 1, 1902.

Evidence has been introduced in this case tending to show the said Lafayette Catron to have been married prior to his marriage to his marriage[sic] to the said Mary J. Catron, but the rule of law is that there must be strict proof of a former marriage and its validity. The law raises a presumption in favor of the validity of the second marriage as against a prior alleged marriage, which presumption has not been overcome after ample opportunity having been allowed for same. The applicant in this case, Mary J. Catron, is identified on the Cherokee authenticated tribal roll of 1880 and the Cherokee census roll of 1896 as an intermarried citizen of the Cherokee Nation.

22

IT IS, THEREFORE, ORDERED AND ADJUDGED: That in accordance with the decision of the Supreme Court of the United States, dated November 5, 1906, in the cases of Daniel Red Bird, et al. vs. the United States, Nos. 125, 126, 127, and 128, the said applicant, Mary J. Catron is entitled, under the provisions of Section Twenty-one of the Act of Congress approved June 28, 1898 (30 Stats. 495), to enrollment as a citizen by intermarriage of the Cherokee Nation, and her application for enrollment as such is accordingly granted.

Tams Bixby

Commissioner.

Dated at Muskogee, Indian Territory,
this    FEB 28 1907

◇◇◇◇◇

DEPARTMENT OF THE INTERIOR,
COMMISSIONER TO THE FIVE CIVILIZED TRIBES.

In the matter of the application for the enrollment of Mary J. Catron as a citizen by intermarriage of the Cherokee Nation, Cherokee 7622.

Protest of the Cherokee Nation.

The applicant Mary J. Catron claims her right to enrollment by virtue of her marriage to LaFayette Catron prior to November 1, 1875, but the testimony of the applicant herself shows that LaFayette Catron had been previously married and that his former wife was alive at the time of her alleged marriage to him, and there is no evidence whatever that a divorce had been procured by or against the said LaFayette Catron from his former wife and our contention is that the said LaFayette Catron was not free to contract the marital relation with Mary J. Catron at the time he attempted to enter into the same, and that therefore there was no lawful marriage and that the said Mary J. Catron is not entitled to be enrolled as a citizen by intermarriage of the Cherokee Nation.

We contend that the burden of proof is upon the applicant, and we cannot subscribe to the statement in the decision of the Commissioner that the burden is upon the Cherokee Nation "after ample opportunity having been allowed for same," but we contend that the burden is upon Mary J. Catron to show that LaFayette Catron was free to contract the marital relation at the time they were alleged to have been married.

Respectfully submitted,
W. W. Hastings
Attorney for the Cherokee Nation.

◇◇◇◇◇

Cherokee
7622

Muskogee, Indian Territory, February 28, 1907

W. W. Hastings,
        Attorney for the Cherokee Nation,
                Muskogee, Indian Territory.

Dear Sir:

There is enclosed a copy of the decision of the Commissioner to the Five Civilized Tribes, dated February 28, 1907, granting the application for the enrollment of Mary J. Catron as a citizen by intermarriage of the Cherokee Nation.

The record of proceedings had in the case, together with the Commissioner's decision, has been this day forwarded to the Department for review. You will be advised of any further action taken in the case.

Respectfully,

Encl. B-8                                        Commissioner

◇◇◇◇◇

Cherokee
7622

Muskogee, Indian Territory, March 5, 1907.

Mary J. Catron,
        Wauhillau, Indian Territory.

Dear Madam:

There is enclosed herewith a copy of the decision of the Commissioner to the Five Civilized Tribes, dated February 28, 1907, granting your application for enrollment as a citizen by intermarriage of the Cherokee Nation. You are advised that the Cherokee Nation protests against your enrollment, a copy of which protest, filed February 28, 1907, is enclosed for your information.

The record of proceedings had in your case, together with the Commissioner's decision and the Nation's protest, has been this day forwarded to the Department for review. You will be advised of any further action taken in your case.

Respectfully,

Encl. B- 7                                        Commissioner.

◇◇◇◇◇

Muskogee, Indian Territory, February 28, 1907

The Honorable,
> The Secretary of the Interior.

Sir:

There is enclosed herewith the record of proceedings had in the matter of the application for the enrollment of Mary J. Catron as a citizen by intermarriage of the Cherokee Nation, together with the decision of the Commissioner dated February 28, 1907, granting her application. You are advised the Attorney for the Cherokee Nation protests against her enrollment, and his protest, filed this day, is enclosed.

There is also enclosed a schedule containing the name of Mary J. Catron, and in the event of the approval of the Commissioner's decision in this case, the approval of the schedule is also recommended.

It will be noted that no roll number has been given the person whose name appears upon the schedule herewith transmitted. This action is taken in accordance with procedure reported by me to the Department on January 28, 1907, and approved by the Department on January 28, 1907, and approved by the Department's telegram of February 9, 1907. It is recommended that a number be placed upon this schedule by Mr. McGarr, the employe[sic] of my office now in Washington.

Respectfully,

Commissioner.

Through the Commissioner of
> Indian Affairs.

Encl. B-85

LMB

◇◇◇◇◇

# Cherokee Intermarried White 1906
## Volume X

Cherokee 7622

COPY

Muskogee, Indian Territory, March 22, 1907.

Mary J. Catron,
     Wauhillau, Indian Territory.

Dear Madam:

     You are hereby advised that the decision of the Commissioner to the Five Civilized Tribes, dated February 28, 1907, granting the application for your enrollment as a citizen by intermarriage of the Cherokee Nation, was affirmed by the Secretary of the Interior, March 4, 1907.

     For your information, there is enclosed herewith a copy of Departmental decision referred to.

Respectfully,

SIGNED Jams Bixby<br>Commissioner.

Enc I-640

RPI

◇◇◇◇◇

Cherokee 5885
   7622

COPY

Muskogee, Indian Territory, March 22, 1907.

W. W. Hastings,
     Attorney for the Cherokee Nation,
         Muskogee, Indian Territory.

Dear Sir:

     You are hereby advised that the decision of the Commissioner to the Five Civilized Tribes, dated February 28, 1907, granting the applications for the enrollment of John M. Smith and Mary J. Catron, as citizens by intermarriage of the Cherokee Nation, was affirmed by the Secretary of the Interior, March 4, 1907.

     For your information, there is enclosed herewith a copy of Departmental decision referred to.

Respectfully,

SIGNED Jams Bixby<br>Commissioner.

Enc I-638

RPI

DEPARTMENT OF THE INTERIOR,
COMMISSION TO THE FIVE CIVILIZED TRIBES,
VINITA, I.T., SEPTEMBER 21, 1900.

In the matter of the application of Dollie Perdue for enrollment as a citizen of the Cherokee Nation, said Perdue being sworn by Commissioner Needles, testified as follows:

Q    Your name?    A  Dollie Perdue.
Q    Your age?    A  73.
Q    Postoffice?    A  Vinita.
Q    What district do you live in?    A  Delaware.
Q    Are you a recognized citizen of the Cherokee Nation?    A  Yes.
Q    By blood?    A  No sir, intermarriage.
Q    For whom do you apply for enrollment?    A  Just myself.
Q    What was your husband's name?    A  James Perdue.
Q    Is he living?    A  No sir.
Q    When did you marry him?  Did you marry him before '80?    A  Yes, long before that.
Q    You lived with him until his death?    A  Yes.

   Applicant on '80 roll, page 302, number 2088, as Dorothy Perdee[sic].

   On '96 roll, page 585, number 430, as Dorothy Perdee.
Q    You have lived in the Cherokee Nation for how long?  More than 20 or 30 years?
A  Yes.
Q    Is your name Dorothy or Dollie?    A  They call me either.
Q    What do you call yourself?    A  Dollie.

The name of Dollie Perdue appears upon the authenticated roll of '80 as Dorothy Perdee as well as upon the census roll of '96, and she being fully identified as the applicant, Dollie Perdue, the testimony showing that she is an intermarried citizen, the said Dollie Perdue will be duly listed for enrollment by this Commission as a Cherokee citizen by intermarriage, having made satisfactory proof as to her residence.

The undersigned, being first duly sworn, states that as stenographer to the Commission to the Five Civilized Tribes, he correctly recorded the testimony and proceedings in this case, and that the foregoing is a true and complete transcript of his stenographic notes thereof.

B McDonald

Subscribed and sworn to before me this 24th day of September, 1900.

C R Breckinridge

Commissioner.

◇◇◇◇◇

Statement of Applicant Taken Under Oath.

## CHEROKEES BY BLOOD AND ADOPTION.

Date _____ SEP 21 1900 _____ 1900.

Name _____ Vinita ___ ___

District _____ Year _____ Page _____ No. _____

Citizen by blood _____ Mother's citizenship _____

Intermarried citizen _____

Married under what law _____ Date of marriage _____

License _____ Certificate _____

Wife's name _____ Dollie Perdue

District _____ DELAWARE. _____ Year 1880 _____ Page 302 No. 2088

Citizen by blood _____ Mother's citizenship _____

Intermarried citizen _____

Married under what law _____ Date of marriage _____

License _____ Certificate _____

Names of Children :

| | Dist. | Year | Page | No. | Age |
|---|---|---|---|---|---|
| | Dist. | Year | Page | No. | Age |
| | Dist. | Year | Page | No. | Age |
| | Dist. | Year | Page | No. | Age |
| | Dist. | Year | Page | No. | Age |
| | Dist. | Year | Page | No. | Age |
| | Dist. | Year | Page | No. | Age |
| | Dist. | Year | Page | No. | Age |
| | Dist. | Year | Page | No. | Age |
| | Dist. | Year | Page | No. | Age |

1 on 1880 roll as Dorothy Perdee

*(Copy of original document from case.)*

◇◇◇◇◇

28

Cher
Supp'l to # 3205

Department of the Interior,
Commission to the Five Civilized Tribes,
Muskogee, I. T., October 31, 1902.

In the matter of the application of DOLLIE PERDUE, for the enrollment of herself as a citizen by intermarriage of the Cherokee Nation:

DOLLIE PERDUE, being duly sworn and examined by the Commission, testified as follows:

Q   What is your name ?   A  Dollie Perdue.
Q   What is your post office address ?   A  Vinita.
Q   How old are you at this time ?   A  Seventy five years old.
Q   You are an applicant for enrollment as an intermarried Cherokee, aren't you ?
A   Yes sir.
Q   You are applying for enrollment as an intermarried citizen of the Cherokee Nation ?
A   Yes sir.
Q   Now what is your Cherokee husband's name ?   A  Jim Perdue.
Q   When were you married to him ?   A  I was married in 1851.
Q   Where ?   A  In Sequoyah District.
Q   Now, is Jim Perdue living or dead ?   A  He is dead.
Q   When did he die ?   A  He died in 1862, in the time of the war.
Q   You and he lived together from the time of your marriage up till the time he died ?
A   Yes sir.
Q   After his death did you marry again ?   A  No sir.
Q   You appear upon the 1880 roll do you ?   A  Yes sir.
Q   And you never have married since Mr. Perdue's death ?   A  No sir.
Q   You were still a single woman and a widow on the first day of September, 1902 ?
A   Yes sir.
Q   You have lived in the Cherokee Nation all the time since 1880 up to the present time?  A  Yes sir.

------------------------------

E. C. Bagwell, on oath states that, as stenographer to the Commission to the Five Civilized Tribes, he correctly recorded the testimony and proceedings had in the above entitled cause, and that the foregoing is an accurate transcript of his stenographic notes thereof.

E.C. Bagwell

Subscribed and sworn to before me this December 16, 1902.

B.C. Jones
Notary Public.

Cherokee Intermarried White 1906
Volume X

◇◇◇◇◇

## DEPARTMENT OF THE INTERIOR.
# COMMISSION TO THE FIVE CIVILIZED TRIBES.

---

In the matter of the death of **Dollie Perdue**
a citizen of the **Cherokee** Nation, who formerly resided at or near
**Vinita** , Ind. Ter., and died on the **14** day of **April** , **1903**

---

### AFFIDAVIT OF RELATIVE.

UNITED STATES OF AMERICA, INDIAN TERRITORY,⎫
**Second Record**     DISTRICT.⎭

I, **Ira Woodall** , on oath state that I am **26** years of age and a citizen
by **Blood** , of the **Cherokee** Nation; that my postoffice address is **Welch** , Ind. Ter.;
that I am **Grandson** of **Dollie Perdue** who was a citizen, by **adoption** , of
the **Cherokee** Nation and that said **Dollie Perdue** died on the **14** day of
**April** , **1903**

                                              **Ira Woodall**
Witnesses To Mark:
{

Subscribed and sworn to before me this **22** day of **Dec** , 1906

                                              **Omer Stroud**
My Commission expires Oct. 10, 1908                    Notary Public.

---

### AFFIDAVIT OF ACQUAINTANCE.

UNITED STATES OF AMERICA, INDIAN TERRITORY, ⎫
**Western**     DISTRICT. ⎭

I, **Joseph E Parker** , on oath state that I am **36** years of age, and a citizen
by **adoption** of the **Cherokee** Nation; that my postoffice address is **Welch** ,
Ind. Ter.; that I was personally acquainted with **Dollie Perdue** who was a citizen, by
**adoption** , of the **Cherokee** Nation; and that said **Dollie Perdue** died on the **14**
day of **April** , 1903

                                              **Joseph E. Parker**
Witnesses To Mark:
{

Subscribed and sworn to before me this **21** day of **December** , 1906

                                              **B.P. Rasmus**
                                              Notary Public.

◇◇◇◇◇

# Cherokee Intermarried White 1906
## Volume X

E.C.M.                                                          Cherokee 3205.

DEPARTMENT OF THE INTERIOR,
COMMISSIONER TO THE FIVE CIVILIZED TRIBES.
MUSKOGEE, I. T., FEBRUARY 15, 1907.

---

In the matter of the application for the enrollment of DOLLIE PERDUE as a citizen by intermarriage of the Cherokee Nation.

JOSEPH E. PARKER, being first duly sworn by Walter W. Chappell, Notary Public, testified as follows:

ON BEHALF OF THE COMMISSIONER:

Q   What is your name?   A Joseph E. Parker.
Q   What is your age?   A 36.
Q   What is your post office address?   A Welch, I.T.
Q   Do you appear here today for the purpose of giving testimony relative to the right to enrollment of Dollie Perdue as a citizen by intermarriage of the Cherokee Nation?   A Yes sir.
Q   What relation are you to Dollie Perdue?   A I married her grand-daughter.
Q   Is Dollie Perdue living?   A No sir.
Q   When did she die?   A About April 14, 1903.
Q   Do you represent the estate of Dollie Perdue?   A Yes sir.

The witness presents in evidence letters of administration granted to him in re the estate of Dollie Perdue.

Q   Is Dollie Perdue a white woman?   A Yes sir.
Q   Through whom does she claim the right to enrollment as a citizen by intermarriage of the Cherokee Nation?   A I suppose her husband, James Perdue.
Q   When was she married to him?   A I can't tell you.
Q   Is he dead?   A Yes sir.
Q   Do you know when he died?   A No sir.
Q   Since you can remember, did the applicant, Dollie Perdue, reside in the Cherokee Nation until her death in 1903?   A Yes sir.
Q   Did she remarry after the death of her husband?   A Not that I know of.

MARY WOODALL, being first duly sworn by Walter W. Chappell, Notary Public, testified as follows:

Q   What is your name?   A Mary Woodall.
Q   What is your age?   A 54.
Q   What is your post office address?   A Vinita.

# Cherokee Intermarried White 1906
## Volume X

Q   You appear here today, do you, to give testimony relative to the right to enrollment
    as a citizen by intermarriage of the Cherokee Nation of Dollie Perdue?
    A Yes sir.
Q   She is a white woman, is she?    A Yes sir.
Q   Through whom does she claim the right to enrollment?
    A Through her husband, James Perdue.
Q   Was James Perdue a Cherokee?    A Yes sir.
Q   When were Dollie and James Perdue married?    A I dont[sic] know, I never heard
    her say, but I guess it was in '51.
Q   When did you become acquainted with Dollie Perdue?
    A I am her daughter.
Q   You say you are the daughter of Dollie and James Perdue?
    A Yes sir.
Q   You can testify positively that they were married prior to November 1, 1875?
    A I was not born then.
Q   You were born before 1875, were you not?    A Yes, I guess so.
Q   When did James Perdue die?    A During the war.

Q   Did you mother remarry after the death of James Perdue?    A No sir.
Q   She has continuously resided in the Cherokee Nation from the time of her marriage,
    has she?    A Yes sir.
Q   Was your mother always regarded as a citizen of the Cherokee Nation after her
    marriage to James Perdue?    A Yes sir.
Q   Do you know whether or not James Perdue had been married prior to his marriage to
    your mother?    A No sir, he never was married before.

( Witness excused ).

JAMES M. BELL, being first duly sworn by Walter W. Chappell, Notary Public, testified
    as follows:

Q   What is your name?    A James M. Bell.
Q   What is your age?    A 74.
Q   What is your post office address?    A Needmore.
Q   Were you acquainted with the applicant in this case, Dollie Perdue?
    A No sir.
Q   Did you know her husband, James Perdue?    A Yes sir, I knew James Perdue when
    I was a boy.
Q   Was Dollie Perdue his wife?    A I couldn't say as to that.
Q   Was James Perdue a citizen by blood of the Cherokee Nation?    A Yes sir.
Q   When did he die?    A I never knew him after '47; he was a young boy, perhaps 18
    or 19; my father went to Texas, and I never saw him after that, but I was
    acquainted with his family?[sic]
Q   But you can testify positively that he was a recognized citizen by blood of the
    Cherokee Nation?    A Yes sir, a Cherokee by blood, there is no doubt about
    that.

Q   Did you know anything about his being married?   A  No sir.

( Witness excused ).

The undersigned, being first duly sworn, states that as stenographer to the Commission to the Five Civilized Tribes, she correctly reported the above and foregoing testimony, and that the same is a full, true and complete transcript of her stenographic notes thereof.

Sarah Waters

Subscribed and sworn to before me this 15th day of February, 1907.

Walter W. Chappell<br>Notary Public.

<><><><><>

E C M                                                          Cherokee 3205.

DEPARTMENT OF THE INTERIOR,<br>COMMISSIONER TO THE FIVE CIVILIZED TRIBES.

In the matter of the application for the enrollment of DOLLIE PERDUE as a citizen by intermarriage of the Cherokee Nation.

D E C I S I O N

THE RECORDS OF THIS OFFICE SHOW:   That at Vinita, Indian Territory, September 21, 1900 application was received by the Commission to the Five Civilized Tribes for the enrollment of Dollie Perdue as a citizen by intermarriage of the Cherokee Nation.   Further proceedings in the matter of said application were had at Muskogee, Indian Territory, October 31, 1902 and February 15, 1907.

THE EVIDENCE IN THIS CASE SHOWS:   That the applicant herein, Dollie Perdue, a white woman, married about 1851 one James Perdue, since deceased, who was at the time of said marriage a recognized citizen by blood of the Cherokee Nation.   It is further shown that from the time of said marriage until the death of said James Perdue, which occurred about 1862, the said James Perdue and Dollie Perdue resided together as husband and wife and continuously lived in the Cherokee Nation; that after the death of said James Perdue the said Dollie Perdue remained unmarried and continuously lived in the Cherokee Nation up to and including September 1, 1902.   Said applicant is identified on the Cherokee authenticated tribal roll of 1880 and the Cherokee census roll of 1896 as an intermarried citizen of the Cherokee Nation.

IT IS, THEREFORE, ORDERED AND ADJUDGED:   That in accordance with the decision of the Supreme Court of the United States, dated November 5, 1906, in the cases of Daniel Red Bird, et al. vs. the United States, Nos. 125, 126, 127, and 128, the said applicant, Dollie Perdue is entitled under the provisions of Section Twenty-one of the Act of Congress approved June 28, 1898 (30 Stats., 495), to enrollment as a citizen by intermarriage of the Cherokee Nation, and her application for enrollment as such is accordingly granted.

Tams Bixby

Commissioner.

Dated at Muskogee, Indian Territory,
this    FEB 28 1907

◇◇◇◇◇

| |
|---|
| REFER IN REPLY TO THE FOLLOWING: |
| Cherokee |
| 3205. |

**DEPARTMENT OF THE INTERIOR,**
**COMMISSIONER TO THE FIVE CIVILIZED TRIBES.**

Muskogee, Indian Territory, December 28, 1906.

Dollie Perdue,
     Vinita, Indian Territory.

Dear Madam:

     November 6, 1906, the United States Supreme Court held that white persons who intermarried with Cherokee citizens according to Cherokee law prior to November 1, 1875, are entitled to enrollment and allotments of land as citizens of the Cherokee Nation.

     You are advised that to properly determine your right to enrollment as a citizen by intermarriage of the Cherokee Nation, it will be necessary for you to appear before the Commissioner for the purpose of giving testimony as to the date of your marriage and whether or not your husband, by reason of your marriage to whom you claim the right to enrollment as a citizen by intermarriage of the Cherokee Nation, was a recognized Cherokee citizen at the time of your marriage to him.

     You are, therefore, directed to appear before the Commissioner at Muskogee, Indian Territory, at 9 o'clock A. M., on Friday, January 4, 1907, and give testimony as above indicated.

Respectfully,

Wm O. Beall

H.J.C.
Acting Commissioner.

◇◇◇◇◇

# Cherokee Intermarried White 1906
## Volume X

*(Copy of original document from case.)*

◇◇◇◇◇

REFER IN REPLY TO THE FOLLOWING:

Cherokee 3205.

**DEPARTMENT OF THE INTERIOR,**
**COMMISSIONER TO THE FIVE CIVILIZED TRIBES.**

ECM

Muskogee, Indian Territory, February 12, 1907

SPECIAL.

Ira Woodall,
        Welch, Indian Territory.

Sir:

The Commission sent you this day a telegram as follows:

"Intermarried case of Dollie Perdue incomplete. Have witnesses
appear immediately to establish date of marriage".

The Act of Congress approved April 26, 1906 provides that the Secretary
of the Interior shall have no jurisdiction to approve the enrollment of any person as
a citizen of the Cherokee Nation after March 4, 1907. This matter therefore
demands your immediate attention.

Respectfully,

GHC                                                  Commissioner

◇◇◇◇◇

Cherokee 3205

ECM                          Muskogee, Indian Territory, February 22, 1907

SPECIAL.

       Joseph E. Parker,
          Welch, Indian Territory.

Sir:

       The Commission sent you this day a telegram as follows:

       "Intermarried case of Dollie Perdue incomplete. Have witnesses
appear immediately to establish date of marriage".

       The Act of Congress approved April 26, 1906 provides that the Secretary
of the Interior shall have no jurisdiction to approve the enrollment of any person as
a citizen of the Cherokee Nation after March 4, 1907. This matter, therefore,
demands your immediate attention.

Respectfully,

GHC                                                  Commissioner

◇◇◇◇◇

Muskogee, Indian Territory, February 28, 1907

The Honorable,
       The Secretary of the Interior.

Sir:

       There is transmitted herewith a schedule of intermarried white citizens of the
Cherokee Nation, Numbers       to       inclusive, found to be entitled to
enrollment in accordance with the decision of the Supreme Court of the United States of
November 6, 1906, in the cases of Daniel Red Bird et al. vs. the United States, and who
were living September 1, 1902, as provided by the Act of Congress approved July 1,
1902 ( 32 Stat. 716).

# Cherokee Intermarried White 1906
## Volume X

A decision was rendered in the case of each person appearing on this schedule, a copy of which decision was furnished the Attorney for the Cherokee Nation, and said attorney advised by letter that he did not protest against the Commissioner's decision enrolling these persons.

The names of the persons appearing upon this schedule here follow in the same numerical order as on the schedule together with the tribal roll of the Cherokee Nation upon which their names are identified.

| No. | Name | Roll | District. |
|---|---|---|---|
| | Perdue, Dollie | 1880 | Delaware |
| | Jeffrey, Nancy | 1880 | Delaware |
| | McAlister, Louisa | 1880 | Delaware. |

After having considered such evidence as has been submitted affecting the right of these persons to enrollment as citizens by intermarriage of the Cherokee Nation, I am of the opinion that all should be enrolled as such, and it is so ordered.

It will be noted that no numbers have been given the names of the persons appearing upon this schedule. This action is taken in accordance with procedure reported by me to the Department January 28, 1907 and approved by Departmental telegram of February 9, 1907. In the event of the approval of this schedule it is recommended that numbers be given the names of the persons appearing thereon, in consecutive order, by Mr. McGarr, the employe[sic] of my office now in Washington.

Respectfully,

Commissioner.

Through the Commissioner of
      Indian Affairs.

Encl. B-96

L M B

Form No. 1511.    **NIGHT MESSAGE.**
**THE WESTERN UNION TELEGRAPH COMPANY.**
INCORPORATED
**24,000 OFFICES IN AMERICA.    CABLE SERVICE TO ALL THE WORLD.**
ROBERT C. CLOWRY, President and General Manager.

| Receiver's No. | Time Filed | Check |
|---|---|---|
| | | Cherokee No.3205,    ECM |

**SEND** the following night message subject to the
terms on back hereof, which are hereby agreed to.

February 22, 1907.

Joseph E. Parker,

Welch, Indian Territory.

Intermarried case of Dollie Perdue incomplete.

Produce witnesses immediately to establish marriage.

BIXBY,

Commissioner.

O.B.C.R.    Paid.

☞ READ THE NOTICE AND AGREEMENT ON BACK. ☜

*(Copy of original document from case.)*

◇◇◇◇◇

Cherokee 3205

ECM                                        Muskogee, Indian Territory, February 22, 1907

SPECIAL.

Joseph E. Parker,
    Welch, Indian Territory.

Sir:

    The Commission sent you this day a telegram as follows:

    "Intermarried case of Dollie Perdue incomplete.  Have witnesses
appear immediately to establish date of marriage".

    The Act of Congress approved April 26, 1906 provides that the Secretary
of the Interior shall have no jurisdiction to approve the enrollment of any person as
a citizen of the Cherokee Nation after March 4, 1907.  This matter, therefore,
demands your immediate attention.

Respectfully,

GHC                                                    Commissioner

◇◇◇◇◇

Cherokee 3205.

Muskogee, Indian Territory, February 28, 1907.

W. W. Hastings,
    Attorney for the Cherokee Nation,
        Muskogee, Indian Territory.

Dear Sir:

      There is enclosed herewith a copy of the decision of the Commissioner to the Five Civilized Tribes, dated February 28, 1907, granting the application for the enrollment of Dollie Perdue as a citizen by intermarriage of the Cherokee Nation.

Respectfully,

Enc I-402                                               Commissioner.

RPI

◇◇◇◇◇

Muskogee, Indian Territory, Feby. 28, 1907

The Commissioner to the Five Civilized Tribes,
    Muskogee, Indian Territory

Sir:

      I do not desire to protest against the enrollment of Dollie Perdue as a citizen by intermarriage of the Cherokee Nation, and I consent to her immediate enrollment as such.

Respectfully,

W.W. Hastings
Att'y for Cherokee Naio[sic]

◇◇◇◇◇

REFER IN REPLY TO THE FOLLOWING:

Cherokee 3205

**DEPARTMENT OF THE INTERIOR,**
**COMMISSIONER TO THE FIVE CIVILIZED TRIBES.**

Muskogee, Indian Territory, February 28, 1907.

Mary Woodall,
    Vinita, Indian Territory.

Dear Madam:

There is enclosed herewith a copy of the decision of the Commissioner to the Five Civilized Tribes, dated February 28, 1907, granting the application for the enrollment of your mother, Dollie Perdue, as a citizen by intermarriage of the Cherokee Nation.

You will be advised when the name of your mother has been placed upon a schedule of citizens of the Cherokee Nation and approved by the Secretary of the Interior.

Respectfully,
Tams Bixby

Enc I-403                               Commissioner.

RPI

◇◇◇◇◇

Cherokee
    3205

Muskogee, Indian Territory, March 15, 1907.

J. E. Parker,
    Welch, Indian Territory.

Dear Sir:

This office is in receipt of your letter of February 22, 1907, relative to the Cherokee intermarried case of Dollie Perdue.

In reply you are advised that on February 28, 1907, the Commissioner rendered his decision granting the application for the enrollment of Dollie Perdue as a citizen by intermarriage of the Cherokee Nation, and on the same date said decision was forwarded to the Secretary of the Interior for review. The parties interested will be advised of the Secretary's action as soon as this office is informed of the same.

Respectfully,

LMB                                      Commissioner

◇◇◇◇◇

Cherokee
3205

Muskogee, Indian Territory, March 26, 1907

W. I. Thornton,
    Southwest City, Missouri.

Dear Sir:

This office is in receipt, on March 4, 1907, of an affidavit executed by you with reference to the marriage of Dollie Perdue, an applicant for enrollment as a citizen by intermarriage of the Cherokee Nation.

In reply you are advised that your affidavit has been noted and filed. You are further advised that Dollie Perdue has been duly enrolled as a citizen by intermarriage of the Cherokee Nation, her name appearing opposite Number 269 on a schedule of such citizens approved by the Secretary of the Interior.

Respectfully,

L M B                              Acting Commissioner.

                 ◇◇◇◇◇

Cherokee
    I. W. 269

Muskogee, Indian Territory, May 27, 1907.

J. E. Parker,
    Administrator estate of Dollie Perdue,
        Welch, Indian Territory.

Dear Sir:

This office in in receipt of your letter of May 20, 1907, asking to be advised the status of the Cherokee Intermarried case of Dollie Perdue.

In reply you are advised that the application for the enrollment of Dollie Perdue as a citizen by intermarriage of the Cherokee Nation was granted February 28, 1907, and her name now appears upon a final roll of such citizens approved by the Secretary of the Interior.

Respectfully,

L M B                              Commissioner.

                 ◇◇◇◇◇

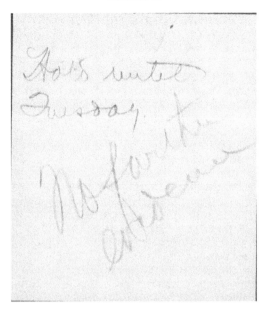

*(Copies of original documents from case.)*

Department of the Interior.
Commissioner to the Five Civilized Tribes,
MUSKOGEE, IND. TER.

Return to W
UNCLAIMED

...ary Woodall,

Vinita, Indian Territory.

**Cher IW 270**

◇◇◇◇◇

# Cherokee Intermarried White 1906
## Volume X

DEPARTMENT OF THE INTERIOR.
COMMISSION TO THE FIVE CIVILIZED TRIBES.
TAHLEQUAH, I.T., DECEMBER 18th, 1900/[sic]

IN THE MATTER OF THE APPLICATION OF Nancy Jeffrey for enrollment as a citizen of the Cherokee Nation, represented by her son, Daniel H. Jeffrey, who being sworn and examined by Commissioner T. B. Needles, testified as follows:

Q   What is your mother's name?   A  Nancy Jeffrey.
Q   How old is she?   A  She is about sixty years old.
Q   What is her Post office address?   A  Eureka.
Q   What district does she live in?   A  Tahlequah.
Q   Is she a recognized citizen of the Cherokee Nation?   A  No sir; she is a white woman.
Q   What is her husband's name?   A  John[sic] M. Jeffrey.
Q   Is he living?   A  No sir, he is dead.
Q   When were they married; a long time ago?
A   Yes sir, before the War.
Q   Has she ever married since the death of her husband?   A  No sir.
Q   Has she always lived in the Cherokee Nation?   A  Yes sir; she lives with me.
Q   Did she live with her husband, John M., until he died?   A  Yes sir.
Q   You say she is physically unable to get here?   A  Yes sir.
Q   How long has her husband been dead?   A  A year last August.

(1880 Roll, Page 772, #1119, Nancy Jeffries, Tahlequah D'st)
(1896 Roll, Page 1283, #134, Nancy J. Jeffrey, Tahlequah D'st)

Com'r. T. B. Needles: The name of Nancy Jeffrey appears upon the authenticated roll of 1880, as well as the census roll of 1896, as an intermarried white. She is duly identified and satisfactory proof of her residence is made: Satisfactory proof of her non appearance in person is given: Consequently, she will be duly listed for enrollment as a Cherokee citizen by intermarriage.

---

The undersigned, being sworn, states that as stenographer to the Commission to the Five Civilized Tribes, he correctly recorded the testimony and proceedings in this case, and the foregoing is a true and complete transcript of his stenographic notes thereof.

R R Cravens

Subscribed and sworn to before me this 12th day of January, 1902.

C R Breckinridge
COMMISSIONER.

◇◇◇◇◇

# Cherokee Intermarried White 1906
## Volume X

### CHEROKEES BY BLOOD AND ADOPTION.

Date _____ DEC 18 1900 _____ 1900.

*Ewira Into Bp*

Name _____

District _____ Year _____ Page _____ No. _____

Citizen by blood _____ Mother's citizenship _____

Intermarried citizen _____

Married under what law _____ Date of marriage _____

License *(to)* _____ Certificate _____

Wife's name _____ *Nancy Jeffrey* _____

District _____ TAHLEQUAH _____ Year *1882* Page *772* No. *"19*

Citizen by blood *No* Mother's citizenship _____

Intermarried citizen _____

Married under what law _____ Date of marriage _____

License _____ Certificate _____

Names of Children:

_____ Dist. _____ Year _____ Page _____ No. _____ Age _____
_____ Dist. _____ Year _____ Page _____ No. _____ Age _____
_____ Dist. _____ Year _____ Page _____ No. _____ Age _____
_____ Dist. _____ Year _____ Page _____ No. _____ Age _____
_____ Dist. _____ Year _____ Page _____ No. _____ Age _____
_____ Dist. _____ Year _____ Page _____ No. _____ Age _____
_____ Dist. _____ Year _____ Page _____ No. _____ Age _____
_____ Dist. _____ Year _____ Page _____ No. _____ Age _____
_____ Dist. _____ Year _____ Page _____ No. _____ Age _____
_____ Dist. _____ Year _____ Page _____ No. _____ Age _____
_____ Dist. _____ Year _____ Page _____ No. _____ Age _____

*1 on 1880 and as Nancy Jeffries*

*(Copy of original document from case.)*

◇◇◇◇◇

44

JOR.
Cher. 6902.

Department of the Interior.
Commission to the Five Civilized Tribes.
Tahlequah, I. T., October 18, 1902.

SUPPLEMENTAL TESTIMONY in the matter of the application for the enrollment of NANCY JEFFREY as a citizen by intermarriage of the Cherokee Nation.

NANCY JEFFREY, being first duly sworn, and being examined, testified as follows:

BY COMMISSION: What is your name?   A  Nancy Jeffrey.
Q  How old are you?   A  I could not tell you my age exactly.
Q  About how old are you?   A  They made me out fifty-six, that was two or three years ago.
Q  You are something near sixty?   A  Yes sir.
Q  What is your present post office address?   A  I guess I might just as well keep it here. This man is my agent, and I might just as well keep it here.
Q  Mail addressed to you at Tahlequah will reach you?   A  Yes sir, put it in the care of him and I will get it. Put it Melvin, Indian Territory then.
Q  Melvin is your post office?   A  Yes sir.
Q  That is your right post office, is it?   A  Yes sir.
Q  You are a white woman, are you?   A  Yes sir.
Q  Have you heretofore made application to the Commission for enrollment as a citizen by intermarriage of the Cherokee Nation?   A  Yes sir
Q  What is the name of the husband through whom you claim your citizenship?
A  Jehu[sic] Jeffrey.
Q  Is he living?   A  No sir, he is dead.
Q  Was he a Cherokee by blood?   A  Yes sir.
Q  When were you and he married?   A  We were married the year the war came up.
Q  Did you and he live together continuously until the time of his death?  A  Yes sir.
Q  You were living together when he died?   A  Yes sir, I was.
Q  Have you married since he died?   A  No sir.
Q  Were you ever married before you married him?   A  Ni[sic] sir.
Q  Was he ever married before he married you?   A  Yes sir, I think he was, but I never saw his first wife, and don't know anything about it.
Q  Was she living at the time he married you?   A  No sir.
Q  That was the only time he married before he married you?   A  Yes sir.
Q  Have you resided in the Cherokee Nation continuously since your marriage?
A  Ever since peace was made.
Q  Did he reside in the Cherokee Nation until his death after peace was made?
A  Yes sir.
Q  You have no minor children, have you?   A  No sir.

This testimony will be filed with and made a part of the record in the matter of the application for the enrollment of Nancy Jeffrey as a citizen by intermarriage of the Cherokee Nation, Cherokee straight card field No. 6902.

--------------------

Wm. Hutchinson, being first duly sworn, states that as stenographer to the Commission to the Five Civilized Tribes he correctly recorded the testimony and proceedings in this case, and that the foregoing is a true and complete transcript of the stenographic notes thereof.

Wm Hutchinson

Subscribed and sworn to before me this 28th day of October, 1902.

John O Rosson<br>NP

◇◇◇◇◇

E C M                                                            Cherokee 6904.

DEPARTMENT OF THE INTERIOR,

COMMISSIONER TO THE FIVE CIVILIZED TRIBES.

---

In the matter of the application for the enrollment of NANCY JEFFRIES[sic] as a citizen by intermarriage of the Cherokee Nation.

O R D E R

An examination of the Cherokee authenticated tribal roll of 1880 shows that said applicant and her family appear on said roll, their names and ages being as follows:

1880 Roll, Page 772,  No. 1118,  Jayhu Jeffries, Native Cherokee marked "Dead".
1880 Roll, Page 772,  No. 1119,  Nancy Jeffries, Adopted white.
1880 Roll, Page 772,  No. 1120,  Maggie Jeffries, Native Cherokee,
fifteen years old.

IT IS ORDERED: That this statement be filed with and made a part of the record in the matter of the application for the enrollment of Nancy Jeffries as a citizen by intermarriage of the Cherokee Nation.

Tams Bixby
Commissioner.

Dated at Muskogee, Indian Territory,
this    FEB 28 1907

◇◇◇◇◇

46

E.C.M.                                                    Cherokee 6904.

### DEPARTMENT OF THE INTERIOR,

### COMMISSIONER TO THE FIVE CIVILIZED TRIBES.

-------------------------------

In the matter of the application for the enrollment of Nancy Jeffrey as a citizen by intermarriage of the Cherokee Nation.

## D E C I S I O N

THE RECORDS OF THIS OFFICE SHOW: That at Tahlequah, Indian Territory, December 18, 1900, application was received by the Commission to the Five Civilized Tribes for the enrollment of Nancy Jeffrey as a citizen by intermarriage of the Cherokee Nation. Further proceedings in the matter of said application were had at Tahlequah, Indian Territory, October 18, 1902.

THE EVIDENCE IN THIS CASE SHOWS: That the applicant herein, Nancy Jeffrey, a white woman, married about 1861, one Jehu Jeffrey, who was, at the time of said marriage, a recognized citizen by blood of the Cherokee Nation, who is identified on the Cherokee authenticated tribal roll of 1880, Tahlequah District, opposite No. 1118 as a native Cherokee "Dead"; that from the time of said marriage until the death of said Jehu Jeffrey, the said Nancy Jeffrey and Jehu Jeffrey resided together as husband and wife and continuously lived in the Cherokee Nation since 1865; that since the death of said Jehu Jeffrey the said Nancy Jeffrey has remained unmarried and continuously lived in the Cherokee Nation. Said applicant is identified on the Cherokee authenticated tribal roll of 1880, and the Cherokee census roll of 1896 as an intermarried citizen of the Cherokee Nation.

IT IS, THEREFORE, ORDERED AND ADJUDGED: That in accordance with the decision of the Supreme Court of the United States, dated November 5, 1906, in the cases of Daniel Red Bird, et al., vs. the United States, Nos. 125, 126, 127, and 128, the said applicant, Nancy Jeffrey, is entitled, under the provisions of Section twenty-one of the Act of Congress approved June 28, 1898 (30 Stats. 495), to enrollment as a citizen by intermarriage of the Cherokee Nation, and her application for enrollment as such is accordingly granted.

Tams Bixby

Commissioner.

Dated at Muskogee, Indian Territory,
this     FEB 28 1907

◇◇◇◇◇

<table>
<tr><td>

REFER IN REPLY TO THE FOLLOWING:

_____ Cherokee

6904

</td><td>

**DEPARTMENT OF THE INTERIOR,**
**COMMISSIONER TO THE FIVE CIVILIZED TRIBES.**

</td></tr>
</table>

Muskogee, Indian Territory, December 26, 1906.

Nancy Jeffrey,
    Eureka, Indian Territory.

Dear Madam:

    November 6, 1906, the United States Supreme Court held that white persons who intermarried with Cherokee citizens according to Cherokee law prior to November 1, 1875, are entitled to enrollment and allotments of land as citizens of the Cherokee Nation.

    You are advised that to properly determine your right to enrollment as a citizen by intermarriage of the Cherokee Nation, it will be necessary for you to appear before the Commissioner for the purpose of giving testimony as to the date of your marriage and whether or not your husband, by reason of your marriage to whom you claim the right to enrollment as a citizen by intermarriage of the Cherokee Nation, was a recognized Cherokee citizen at the time of your marriage to him.

    You are therefore directed to appear before the Commissioner at Muskogee, Indian Territory, at 9 o'clock A. M., on Saturday, January 5, 1907, and give testimony as above indicated.

                  Respectfully,
                  Wm O. Beall

GHL                      Acting Commissioner.

◇◇◇◇◇

Form No. 1811.  **NIGHT MESSAGE.**
**THE WESTERN UNION TELEGRAPH COMPANY.**
INCORPORATED
**24,000 OFFICES IN AMERICA.  CABLE SERVICE TO ALL THE WORLD.**
ROBERT C. CLOWRY, President and General Manager.

Receiver's No.    Time Filed    Check

Cherokee 6904.  BOX

**SEND** the following night message subject to the terms on back hereof, which are hereby agreed to.

February 20, 1907.

Nancy Jeffrey,

    Tahlequah, Indian Territory.

Intermarried case incomplete. Appear immediately with witnesses to establish marriage.

            Bixby,

               Commissioner.

O.N.O.R. Paid.

☞ READ THE NOTICE AND AGREEMENT ON BACK. ☜

*(Copy of original document from case.)*

REFER IN REPLY TO THE FOLLOWING:

Cherokee 6904.

DEPARTMENT OF THE INTERIOR,
COMMISSIONER TO THE FIVE CIVILIZED TRIBES.


ECM                                    Muskogee, Indian Territory, February 20, 1907


SPECIAL.

    Nancy Jeffrey,
        Tahlequah, Indian Territory.

    Dear Madam:

        The Commission sent you this day a telegram as follows:

        "Intermarried case incomplete.
        Appear immediately with witnesses
        to establish marriage.

        The Act of Congress approved April 26, 1906 provides that the Secretary
of the Interior shall have no jurisdiction to approve the enrollment of any person as
a citizen of the Cherokee Nation after March 4, 1907. This matter, therefore,
demands your immediate attention.

                            Respectfully,

GHC                                    Tams Bixby    Commissioner


◇◇◇◇◇

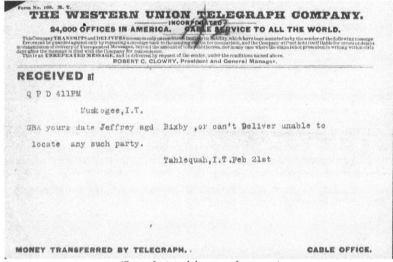

Form No. 108. 35. T.

## THE WESTERN UNION TELEGRAPH COMPANY.
INCORPORATED

### 24,000 OFFICES IN AMERICA.  CABLE SERVICE TO ALL THE WORLD.

This Company TRANSMITS and DELIVERS messages only on conditions limiting its liability, which have been assented to by the sender of the following message.
Errors can be guarded against only by repeating a message back to the sending station for comparison, and the Company will not hold itself liable for errors or delays
in transmission or delivery of Unrepeated Messages, beyond the amount of tolls paid thereon, nor in any case where the claim is not presented in writing within sixty
days after the message is filed with the Company for transmission.
This is an UNREPEATED MESSAGE, and is delivered by request of the sender, under the conditions named above.
ROBERT C. CLOWRY, President and General Manager.

### RECEIVED at

Q P D 411PM

Muskogee,I.T.

GBA yours date Jeffrey sgd  Bixby ,or can't Deliver unable to

locate any such party.

Tahlequah,I.T.Feb 21st

**MONEY TRANSFERRED BY TELEGRAPH.**          **CABLE OFFICE.**

*(Copy of original document from case.)*

◇◇◇◇◇

Muskogee, Indian Territory, February 28, 1907

The Honorable,
     The Secretary of the Interior.

Sir:

      There is transmitted herewith a schedule of intermarried white citizens of the Cherokee Nation, Numbers          to          inclusive, found to be entitled to enrollment in accordance with the decision of the Supreme Court of the United States of November 6, 1906, in the cases of Daniel Red Bird et al. vs. the United States, and who were living September 1, 1902, as provided by the Act of Congress approved July 1, 1902 ( 32 Stat. 716).

      A decision was rendered in the case of each person appearing on this schedule, a copy of which decision was furnished the Attorney for the Cherokee Nation, and said attorney advised by letter that he did not protest against the Commissioner's decision enrolling these persons.

      The names of the persons appearing upon this schedule here follow in the same numerical order as on the schedule together with the tribal roll of the Cherokee Nation upon which their names are identified.

| No. | Name | Roll | District. |
|-----|------|------|-----------|
| | Perdue, Dollie | 1880 | Delaware |
| | Jeffrey, Nancy | 1880 | Delaware |
| | McAlister, Louisa | 1880 | Delaware. |

After having considered such evidence as has been submitted affecting the right of these persons to enrollment as citizens by intermarriage of the Cherokee Nation, I am of the opinion that all should be enrolled as such, and it is so ordered.

It will be noted that no numbers have been given the names of the persons appearing upon this schedule. This action is taken in accordance with procedure reported by me to the Department January 28, 1907 and approved by Departmental telegram of February 9, 1907. In the event of the approval of this schedule it is recommended that numbers be given the names of the persons appearing thereon, in consecutive order, by Mr. McGarr, the employe[sic] of my office now in Washington.

Respectfully,

Commissioner.

Through the Commissioner of
　　　Indian Affairs.

Encl. B-96

L M B

◇◇◇◇◇

Cherokee 6904

Muskogee, Indian Territory, February 28, 1907.

W. W. Hastings,
　　　Attorney for the Cherokee Nation,
　　　　　　Muskogee, Indian Territory.

Dear Sir:

There is enclosed herewith a copy of the decision of the Commissioner to the Five Civilized Tribes, dated February 28, 1907, granting the application for the enrollment of Nancy Jeffrey as a citizen by intermarriage of the Cherokee Nation.

Respectfully,

Enc I-400　　　　　　　　　　　　　　　　　　　Commissioner.

RPI

◇◇◇◇◇

Muskogee, Indian Territory, Feby 28, 1907.

The Commissioner to the Five Civilized Tribes,
Muskogee, Indian Territory.

Sir:

I do not desire to protest against the enrollment of Nancy Jeffrey as a citizen by intermarriage of the Cherokee Nation and I consent to her immediate enrollment as such.

Respectfully,

W. W. Hastings
Att'y for Cherokee Nai[sic]

◇◇◇◇◇

Cherokee 6904.

Muskogee, Indian Territory, February 28, 1907.

Nancy Jeffrey,
Eureka, Indian Territory.

Dear Madam:

There is enclosed herewith a copy of the decision of the Commissioner to the Five Civilized Tribes, dated February 28, 1907, granting the application for your enrollment as a citizen by intermarriage of the Cherokee Nation.

You will be advised when your name has been placed upon a schedule of citizens of the Cherokee Nation and approved by the Secretary of the Interior.

Respectfully,

Enc I-401                                         Commissioner.

RPI

◇◇◇◇◇

*(Copy of original document from case.)*

---

**Cher IW 271**

◇◇◇◇◇

R
Cher   **D 1642**

Department of the Interior,
Commission to the Five Civilized Tribes,
Muskogee, I. T., June 30, 1902.

In the matter of the application of JAMES BULLETT, ET AL., for enrollment as citizens of the Cherokee Nation.

EMMET STARR, being duly sworn and examined by the Commission, testified as follows:

Q    What is your name  ?    A    Emmet Starr.
Q    What is your age  ?      A    Thirty one years.
Q    What is your post office address  ?      A Claremore, I. T.
Q    You are a citizen by blood of the Cherokee Nation  ?
A    Yes sir, I am.
Q    For whom do you desire to make application for enrollment  ?
A    For the following names persons on the 1896 Cherokee roll, their families and descendants:

Q   Are there any other persons for whom you desire to make application for enrollment?

A   I desire to apply for the following named persons on the 1880 Cherokee roll, their families and their descendants:


**Louisa McAlister, page 292, # 1864, Delaware District;**


--------------------------------

E. C. Bagwell, on oath states that, as stenographer to the Commission to the Five Civilized Tribes, he correctly recorded the testimony and proceedings had in the above entitled cause, and that the foregoing is an accurate transcript of his stenographic notes thereof.

E.C. Bagwell

Subscribed and sworn to before me this 19 day of July, 1902.

PG Reuter<br>Notary Public.

◇◇◇◇◇

Cherokee D 1642

DEPARTMENT OF THE INTERIOR,
COMMISSIONER TO THE FIVE CIVILIZED TRIBES.
MUSKOGEE, IND. TER. DECEMBER 18, 1906.

In the matter of the application for the enrollment of LOUISA MC ALISTER as a citizen by intermarriage of the Cherokee Nation.

LOUISA MC ALISTER being first duly sworn testified as follows:

ON BEHALF OF COMMISSIONER:

Q.   What is your name?   [sic] Louvica[sic] McAlister. I don't know what way it is down here, he always said Louisa, he might have sent it in that way.
Q.   How old are you?   A. I couldn't tell exactly, our names all got burned.
Q.   Well, about how old do you think? About when were you born?
A.   Born in '69.
Q.   No, you are older than that?   A. Well, I know my mother said I was married when I was thirteen years old.
Q.   When were you married?   A. '71.
Q.   What is your postoffice address?   A. Oklahoma; keeping a boarding house there.

# Cherokee Intermarried White 1906
## Volume X

Q. Give your full address, please?     A. 900 South Walker Street, Oklahoma City, Oklahoma.

Q. You are a white woman are you?     A. Yes sir; well not all white, but I am supposed to be a white woman

Q. You appear here to-day in connection with your right to enrollment as an intermarried citizen of the Cherokee Nation?     A. Yes sir.

Q. What is the name of the husband through whom you claim the right to enrollment?

A. James H. McAlester.

Q. Is he living?     A. No sir.

Q. How long has he been dead?     A. About seven or eight years

Q. Was he a Cherokee by blood?     A. Yes sir.

Q. Did you and he have some children?     A. Yes sir.

Q. Give their names?     A. Charles M. McAlester and Ellen McAndrews.

Q. Is Charles dead?     A. Yes sir.

Q. He has been dead a number of years?     A. He has been dead 11 years in March.

Q. Is Ellen married?     A. Yes sir

Q. What is her name now?     A. McAndrews.

Q. What is the name of her husband?     A. Mike McAndrews.

The applicant is duly identified with the members of her family on the 1880 authenticated roll of citizens of the Cherokee Nation, page 292, No. 1864, as Louisa McAlister. She has been listed for enrollment under the name of Louisa McAlister on Cherokee card Number D 1642, and the application for her enrollment was dismissed, without prejudice under a general order of the Commissioner on December 27, 1905, no information having been received that she was living and entitled to enrollment on September 1, 1902.

Q. When did you state you and your husband were married?

A. We was married in '71, the last of '69 or '71. I just can't give the date.

Q. You do not remember the exact correct date?     A. No sir, I do not.

Q. Was he a recognized Cherokee citizen at the time of your marriage to him?

A. Yes sir.

Q. Were you married by a Minister ?     A. Yes sir.

Q. What was his name?     A. Tom Pustell, we was married on Horse Creek.

Q. Did he give you a certificate of marriage?     A. No sir

Q. Have you any documentary evidence showing your marriage to your husband?

A. No sir, none only his brother; I don't know where he lives. Them days they didn't give us anything you know.

Q. You were married in the Cherokee Nation were you?     A. Yes sir.

Q. Now, after the time of your marriage up to the present time, state the different places you have lived?

A. I have lived-- when we were first married we lived on Grand River, eighteen miles from Vinita, on Ben Landrum's place.

Q. How long did you live there?     A. A couple of years; then we moved down on White Oak on Jack Cookston's place; his mother died and he sold out, and he went to Kansas; went to Joplin to work in the mines.

Q. When was it you went to Kansas?     A. Not to Kansas--to Joplin.

Q. When was it you went to Joplin?     A. In '79.

Q. On 1879; that is right is it? A. Yes sir.
Q. How long did you live there? A. About four months; he got blowed up and then we came back.
Q. You stayed there four months and then you came back to the Cherokee Nation?
A. Yes sir.
Q. Whereabouts in the Cherokee Nation did you return?
A. Over here on Grand River; do you know where Joe Bowlen's Prairie is?
A. How long did you stay there? A. One summer.
Q. Then where did you go? A. Down near Jack Coosstons[sic] place on White Oak.
Q. Still in the Cherokee Nation? A. Yes sir.
Q. How long did you live there that time? A. I couldn't tell you hardly. Well, I guess we stayed there about two years and then we went back up to Webb City and lived there a while.
Q. Missouri? A. Yes sir. He was a miner you know.
Q. How long did you stay at Webb City that time? A. I couldn't tell you just exactly; we was there a year or about and then we moved back to Vinita and stayed awhile.
Q. How long did you live there? A. I am about that like the other; I never kept no account and I can't tell, two or three years. I could not say, I guess, something like that.
Q. Then where did you go? A. Well, then we visited my mother in Texas and stayed awhile.
Q. How long? A. Just a month or two, about two months.
Q. Well, where did you go then? A. We came back down here south of Tahlequah, Indian Territory near old man Turner's place and settled.
Q. How long did you live there? A. We stayed there pretty near two years, something like two years.
Q. Then where did you move?
A. Then we moved to Muldrow, there's where he died.
Q. Cherokee Nation? A. Yes sir.
Q. In what year did your husband die? A. Well, I cannot tell that until I get back home.
Q. Did you live there at Muldrow until he died? A. Yes sir; he was traveling from place to place after he went blind, but I stayed right there.
Q. How long did you live up there near Muldrow after he died; I mean you yourself lived there? A. I just could not tell you until I go home; I have got it set down when he died and all.
Q. Well, about how long did you, yourself, live there at Muldrow, before he died, about how long do you think?
A. Two or three years, about three years I guess. Two or three years.
Q. You say you do not remember the date of his death?
A. No I don't remember it; I have it down.
Q. After he died where did you go? A. I went to Texas and stayed with my mother awhile.
Q. How long after his death? A. About three months
Q. How long did you stay with your mother in Texas?

A. I stayed with mother just a month and then I went on the railroad to board railroad hands, and I have been just here and there and everywhere every[sic] since.

Q. Where did you first go?  A. To Corsicanna[sic] Texas with a bridge gang.

Q. Then, if I understand it about three months after the death of your husband you went to Texas to your mother's.

A. Yes sir, I went to my mother's in Texas.

Q. Now, since you went to your mothers[sic] after your husband's death, have you lived in the Cherokee Nation at all, since that time?  A. Yes, I stayed in Texas just a year and then I came up and boarded Section hands

Q. Whereabouts was that?  A. At Sapulpa; but that's in the Creek Nation. I lived there five years, and I boarded an extra gang through the Cherokee Nation, last summer.

Q. Last summer?  A. Yes sir.

Q. Where were you when you boarded the extra gang through the Cherokee Nation?

A. It was Extra gangs, not Section hands, I took the gang at the station north of Vinita that is the last place.

Q. On the Frisco?  A  Yes sir; that is the the[sic] station north of Vinita, Indian Territory or east; I don't know harly[sic] which it is

Q. That was the first station north of Vinita, Indian Territory on the Frisco.

A. Yes sir; that is its[sic] the other side of Vinita.

Q. Is that in the Cherokee Nation?  A. Yes sir.

Q. How long did you stay there?  A. Well, sir, you know these extra gangs, it was just an extra gang I was with.

Q. But how long did you stay there?  A. Just two weeks. You know they move about that way, and they was sent up of Missouri.

Q. Now, after the death of your husband you say you lived in Texas about a year?

A. Yes sir, about a year.

Q. And then you came to Sapulpa and you said you lived there about five years?

A. Yes sir, something near five years, I wouldn't say exactly, but about.

Q. How long has it been since you left Sapulpa?  A. It was a year, something about a year.

Q. Now, since thinking about it, are there any other places you have lived besides those you have told me?

A. Yes, we lived at Claremore a while.

Q. About how long?

A. We wasn't there but a little time, we stayed there about four months.

Q. Do you know when that was?  A. Let me see; my boy died there, the 22nd day of March it will be eleven years since he died. And it was just a month before that.

Q. Have you ever had, owned, any property in the Cherokee Nation in the way of improvements on the Public Domain?

A. Yes sir, we owned a place on Grand River where we lived but he sold it.

Q. Since you husband's death have you owned any property.

A. No, they have always told me I couldn't hold it. I had my son's place up at Claremore and wanted to improve it, but the people said I could not hold it.

Q. Then you have had no property, no farm or improvements?

A. Not since my husband died, before he died we owned that place on Grand River.

Q. Were you ever married before you married your husband, James H. McAlester?
A. No sir.
Q. Was he ever married before he married you?    A. No sir, not that I know of.
Q. Did you and he live together continuously until the time of his death?    A. Yes sir; you know he did stay at home all the time after he went blind, but he was always my husband.
Q. You never separated?    A. Oh, no.
Q. Have you narried[sic] since he died?    A. No sir.
Q. Your memory is not good as to dates?    A. No, since my son died I can't remember; If I want to remember anything just exactly I have to set it down.
Q. Have you kept a record as to the date of the death of your husband?    A. Yes sir, I have, if I have not lost it in my traveling around.
Q. Do you think you can advise us as to the date of his death?
A. Yes sir, when I go home I will look it up.
Q. Is the man who married you living?    A. I can't tell you that; I haven't saw him since; my husband's brother knew;  If I could find Lewis Ralston I could prove it.

)))))))))))))

The undersigned being first duly sworn, states that as stenographer to the Commission to the Five Civilized Tribes she correctly recorded the testimony taken in this case and that the foregoing is a full, true and correct transcript of her stenographic notes thereof.

Lucy M. Bowman

Subscribed and sworn to before me this 10th day of January, 1907.

B.P. Rasmus
Notary Public.

◇◇◇◇◇

Cherokee D 1642

Muskogee, Indian Territory, January 22, 1907.

Mrs. Louisa McAllister,
Oklahoma City, Oklahoma.

Dear Madam:

In the matter of your application for enrollment as a citizen by intermarriage of the Cherokee Nation, you are informed that it will be necessary that you furnish this office with the testimony of witnesses who know of your marriage to your husband, James H. McAllister, prior to November 1, 1875.

As this matter is important, you are requested to give it your immediate attention.

Respectfully,

MMP                                    Commissioner.

◇◇◇◇◇

**Cherokee D 1642**
DEPARTMENT OF THE INTERIOR,
COMMISSIONER TO THE FIVE CIVILIZED TRIBES.

In the matter of the application for the enrollment of **Louisa McAlister** as a citizen of the Cherokee Nation.

--o--

ORDER.

--o--

THE RECORDS OF THIS OFFICE SHOW: That ON June 30, 1902, Emmet Starr appeared before the Commission to the Five Civilized Tribes and made application for the enrollment of **Louisa Mc Alister** as a citizen of the Cherokee Nation.

THE EVIDENCE IN THIS CASE SHOWS: That said **Louisa Mc Alister** is identified on the Cherokee **authenticated** roll of **1880** as **a Cherokee by blood.**

The application made on June 30, 1902, in behalf of the above named applicant, included all persons whose names were found upon the Cherokee rolls of 1880 and 1896, not theretofore accounted for. Since these applications were made the Commission, and the Commissioner, to the Five Civilized Tribes, have diligently sought information that would enable them to identify the persons whose names are included therein.

During the months of August, September and October, 1902 the Commission to the Five Civilized Tribes maintained an office at Tahlequah, the Capital of the Cherokee Nation, during which time the National Council of said Nation was in session, each and every member of which, upon request, appeared before said office and gave such information as he possessed relative to the identity of the persons whose name are included in said applications; a special enrolling party, traveling overland, has covered the Cherokee Nation seeking information as to these persons; at the Cherokee Land office opened on January 1, 1903, at Vinita, and afterward removed to Tahlequah, Indian Territory, such information has been constantly sought; and since the filing of said

59

applications the General Office of the Commission and the Commissioner, located at Muskogee, Indian Territory, has used all available means to secure evidence as to whether or not the persons whose names are included in said applications were living on September 1, 1902, and if so, whether or not they were entitled to Cherokee citizenship on that date.

On July 31, 1905, a published list containing the names of all persons included in these applications, who had not theretofore been accounted for, was issued in the form of a supplement to several newspapers in general circulation in the Cherokee and Creek Nations, and notice was given that the applications for the enrollment of the persons named in said list concerning whom no information could be secured prior to December 1, 1905, would be dismissed. No information has been obtained tending to show the status of      Louisa Mc Alister      on September 1, 1903.

IT IS THEREFORE ORDERED: That the application for the enrollment of Louisa Mc Alister      as a citizen of the Cherokee Nation be, and the same is, hereby dismissed, without prejudice.

Tams Bixby
Commissioner.

Dated at Muskogee, Indian Territory,
this      DEC 27 1905

◇◇◇◇◇

E.C.M.

## DEPARTMENT OF THE INTERIOR,

## COMMISSIONER TO THE FIVE CIVILIZED TRIBES.

Supplemental in the matter of the application for the enrollment of Louisa McAlister as a citizen by intermarriage of the Cherokee Nation.

## O R D E R

The 1880 roll examined, Delaware District, page 292 opposite number 1863, J. A. McAlister, dead, nationality not given.      1880 roll opposite No. 1864, Louisa McAlister nationality not given.

Tams Bixby
Commissioner.

Dated at Muskogee, Indian Territory,
this      FEB 28 1907

◇◇◇◇◇

E.C.M.                                                              Cherokee D. 1642.

### DEPARTMENT OF THE INTERIOR,
### COMMISSIONER TO THE FIVE CIVILIZED TRIBES.

In the matter of the application for the enrollment of LOUISA McALISTER as a citizen by intermarriage of the Cherokee Nation.

### D E C I S I O N

THE RECORDS OF THIS OFFICE SHOW: That at Muskogee, Indian Territory June 30, 1902 application was received by the Commission to the Five Civilized Tribes for the enrollment of Louisa McAlister as a citizen by intermarriage of the Cherokee Nation. Further proceedings in the matter of said application were had at Muskogee, Indian Territory, December 18, 1906.

THE EVIDENCE IN THIS CASE SHOWS: That the applicant herein, Louisa McAlister, a white woman, married in 1871 one James A. McAlister, since deceased, whose[sic] was at the time of said married a recognized citizen by blood of the Cherokee Nation, who is identified on the Cherokee authenticated tribal roll of 1880, Delaware District No. 1863 as a citizen of the Cherokee Nation, nationality not given. It is further shown that from the time of said marriage until the death of the said James A. McAlister, which occurred about 1898, the said James A. McAlister and Louisa McAlister resided together as husband and wife and continuously retained their citizenship in the Cherokee Nation; that after the death of the said James A. McAlister the said Louisa McAlister remained unmarried and continuously retained her citizenship in the Cherokee Nation up to and including September 1, 1902. Said applicant is identified on the Cherokee authenticated tribal roll of 1880 as the wife of one James A. McAlister, nationality not given.

IT IS, THEREFORE, ORDERED AND ADJUDGED: That in accordance with the decision of the Supreme Court of the United States, dated November 5, 1906, in the cases of Daniel Red Bird, et al. vs. the United States, Nos. 125, 126, 127, and 128, the said applicant, Louisa McAlister, is entitled, under the provisions of Section Twenty-one of the Act of Congress approved June 28, 1898 (30 Stats. 495), to enrollment as a citizen by intermarriage of the Cherokee Nation, and her application for enrollment as such is accordingly granted.

Tams Bixby

Commissioner.

Dated at Muskogee, Indian Territory,
this     FEB 28 1907

◇◇◇◇◇

Cherokee
D. 1642

Muskogee, Indian Territory, January 21, 1907

W. W. Hastings,
    Attorney for the Cherokee Nation,
        Muskogee, Indian Territory.

Dear Sir:

There is enclosed herewith copy of the testimony of December 18, 1906, taken in the matter of the application for the enrollment of Louisa McAlister as a citizen of the Cherokee Nation.

Respectfully,

Enc I-22                                                  Commissioner.

RPI

◇◇◇◇◇

| REFER IN REPLY TO THE FOLLOWING: |
| --- |
| Cherokee D 1642 |

**DEPARTMENT OF THE INTERIOR,
COMMISSIONER TO THE FIVE CIVILIZED TRIBES.**

Muskogee, Indian Territory, January 22, 1907.

Mrs. Louisa McAllister,
    Oklahoma City, Oklahoma.

Dear Madam:

In the matter of your application for enrollment as a citizen by intermarriage of the Cherokee Nation, you are informed that it will be necessary that you furnish this office with the testimony of witnesses who know of your marriage to your husband, James H. McAllister, prior to November 1, 1875.

As this matter is important, you are requested to give it your immediate attention.

Respectfully,
    Tams Bixby
        Commissioner.

MMP

◇◇◇◇◇

62

# Cherokee Intermarried White 1906
## Volume X

REFER IN REPLY TO THE FOLLOWING:

Cherokee D 1642

DEPARTMENT OF THE INTERIOR,
COMMISSIONER TO THE FIVE CIVILIZED TRIBES.

Muskogee, Indian Territory, February 28, 1907.

Louisa McAllister,
   Oklahoma City, Oklahoma.

Madam:

   There is enclosed herewith a copy of the decision of the Commissioner to the Five Civilized Tribes, dated February 28, 1907, granting the application for your enrollment as a citizen by intermarriage of the Cherokee Nation.

   You will be advised when your name has been placed upon a schedule of citizens of the Cherokee Nation and approved by the Secretary of the Interior.

Respectfully,

Tams Bixby

Encl. E-53
BLE

Commissioner.

◇◇◇◇◇

Muskogee, Indian Territory, February 28, 1907

The Honorable,
   The Secretary of the Interior.

Sir:

   There is transmitted herewith a schedule of intermarried white citizens of the Cherokee Nation, Numbers            to            inclusive, found to be entitled to enrollment in accordance with the decision of the Supreme Court of the United States of November 6, 1906, in the cases of Daniel Red Bird et al. vs. the United States, and who were living September 1, 1902, as provided by the Act of Congress approved July 1, 1902 ( 32 Stat. 716).

   A decision was rendered in the case of each person appearing on this schedule, a copy of which decision was furnished the Attorney for the Cherokee Nation, and said attorney advised by letter that he did not protest against the Commissioner's decision enrolling these persons.

   The names of the persons appearing upon this schedule here follow in the same numerical order as on the schedule together with the tribal roll of the Cherokee Nation upon which their names are identified.

# Cherokee Intermarried White 1906
## Volume X

| No. | Name | Roll | District. |
|-----|------|------|-----------|
| | Perdue, Dollie | 1880 | Delaware |
| | Jeffrey, Nancy | 1880 | Delaware |
| | McAlister, Louisa | 1880 | Delaware. |

After having considered such evidence as has been submitted affecting the right of these persons to enrollment as citizens by intermarriage of the Cherokee Nation, I am of the opinion that all should be enrolled as such, and it is so ordered.

It will be noted that no numbers have been given the names of the persons appearing upon this schedule. This action is taken in accordance with procedure reported by me to the Department January 28, 1907 and approved by Departmental telegram of February 9, 1907. In the event of the approval of this schedule it is recommended that numbers be given the names of the persons appearing thereon, in consecutive order, by Mr. McGarr, the employe[sic] of my office now in Washington.

Respectfully,

Commissioner.

Through the Commissioner of
Indian Affairs.

Encl. B-96

L M B

◇◇◇◇◇

Cherokee D. 1642                    COPY

Muskogee, Indian Territory, February 28, 1907.

W. W. Hastings,
Attorney for the Cherokee Nation,
Muskogee, Indian Territory.

Dear Sir:

There is enclosed herewith a copy of the decision of the Commissioner to the Five Civilized Tribes, dated February 28, 1907, granting the application for the enrollment of Louisa McAlister as a citizen by intermarriage of the Cherokee Nation.

Respectfully,

SIGNED *Tams Bixby*

Encl. E-54                          Commissioner.
BLE

◇◇◇◇◇

*(The letter below typed as given.)*

Muskogee, Indint Territory, 2;28, 1907/

The Commissi-ner to the Five Civili ed Tribes,
    Muskogee, Indian Territory.

Sir:

I do not desire to protest against the enrollment of Louisa McAlister as a citizen by inte4marriage of the Cherokee Nation,and I consent to her immediate enrollment as such.

Respectfully,

W. W. Hastings
Att'y for Cherokee Nation.

◇◇◇◇◇

COPY

Cherokee D. 1642

Secretary of the Interior Indian Territory,
February 28, 1907.

Louisa McAlister,
    Oklahoma City, Oklahoma.

Madam:

Secretary of the Interior copy of the decision of the Secretary of the Interior Five Civilized Tribes, dated February 28, 1907, granting the application for your enrollment as a citizen by intermarriage of the Cherokee Nation.

Secretary of the Interior your name has been placed upon a schedule of citizens of the Cherokee Nation and approved by the Secretary of the Interior the Interior.

Respectfully,

SIGNED *Jams Bixby*

Encl. E-53                                   Commissioner.
BLE

◇◇◇◇◇

*(Copy of original document from case.)*

**Cher IW 272**

◇◇◇◇◇

F.R.                                                                 Cherokee D-1074

## DEPARTMENT OF THE INTERIOR,

### COMMISSIONER TO THE FIVE CIVILIZED TRIBES.

In the matter of the application for the enrollment of Martha A. Reaves as a citizen by intermarriage of the Cherokee Nation.

### D E C I S I O N

THE RECORDS OF THIS OFFICE SHOW: That at Muskogee, Indian Territory, January 29, 1901, application was received by the Commission to the Five Civilized Tribes for the enrollment of Martha A. Reaves as a citizen by intermarriage of the Cherokee Nation. Further proceedings in the matter of said application were had at Muskogee, Indian Territory, March 15, 1902, June 12, 1902, June 23, 1902, October 28, 1902, and January 3, 1907.

THE EVIDENCE IN THIS CASE SHOWS: That the applicant herein, Martha A. Reaves is a white woman who is identified on the Cherokee census roll of 1896, Canadian District, Page 92, No. 240, as an intermarried citizen of the Cherokee Nation, and was lawfully married in the State of Texas in the year 1869, to her husband, John A. Reaves, who was, at the time of said marriage, a recognized citizen by blood of the Cherokee Nation who is identified on the Cherokee census roll of 1896, Canadian District, Page 62, No. 1694, as a native Cherokee, and whose name in[sic] included on the approved partial roll of citizens by blood of the Cherokee Nation opposite No. 29420.

66

The evidence further shows that John A. Reaves is a Cherokee Indian and is identified on the roll of "Old Settler Cherokees" taken in 1851, and also on the Cherokee pay rolls of 1890 and 1894.

It is further shown that said John A. Reaves left the Cherokee Nation in 1854, being, at that time, twelve years old. He returned to said nation in 1888, and has resided continuously therein since that time.

On September 11, 1903, the Commission to the Five Civilized Tribes rendered its decision in this case wherein it was held that the said John A. Reaves did not forfeit or adjure his Cherokee citizenship during his absence from the Cherokee Nation and that he was entitled to be enrolled as a citizen by blood of the Cherokee Nation in accordance with the provisions of Section 21 of the Act of Congress approved June 28, 1898 (30 Stats., 495).

It further appears that the said John A. Reaves and his wife Martha A. Reaves have been residing together as husband and wife from the time of their said marriage in 1869, and have continuously lived in the Cherokee Nation from the time of their removal to said Nation in 1888, up to and including September 1, 1902.

In view of the foregoing, it is considered that the applicant, Martha A. Reaves, was married to a recognized citizen by blood of the Cherokee Nation prior to November 1, 1875.

IT IS, THEREFORE, ORDERED AND ADJUDGED: That in accordance with the decision of the Supreme Court of the United States, dated November 5, 1906, in the cases of Daniel Red Bird, et al., vs. the United States, Nos. 125, 126, 127, and 128, the said applicant, Martha A. Reaves, is entitled under the provisions of Section 21 of the Act of Congress approved June 28, 1898, (30 Stats., 495), to enrollment as a citizen by intermarriage of the Cherokee Nation and her application for enrollment as such is accordingly granted.

Tams Bixby

Commissioner.

Dated at Muskogee, Indian Territory,
this     FEB  23 1907

◇◇◇◇◇

DEPARTMENT OF THE INTERIOR,
COMMISSIONER TO THE FIVE CIVILIZED TRIBES.

In the matter of the application for the enrollment of MARTHA A. REAVES as a citizen by intermarriage of the Cherokee Nation.

Protest of the Cherokee Nation.

The record in this case shows that John A. Reaves went to the State of Texas prior to the Civil War; that he married Martha A. Reaves in Texas in the year of 1869, where they continued to live as husband and wife until about the year 1888, and we cannot agree with the Commissioner to the Five Civilized Tribes that John A. Reaves was a citizen of the Cherokee Nation in 1869 at the time Martha A. Reaves married him, nor was he a citizen of the Cherokee Nation for the 19 years that followed his marriage. In other works, it is contended on behalf of the Cherokee Nation that he never became a citizen of the Cherokee Nation after his marriage prior to 1888, and it is contended on behalf of the Cherokee Nation that he, not being a citizen of the Cherokee Nation on November 1, 1875, could not confer rights by intermarriage upon his wife, Martha A. Reaves. But it is contended that the name of John A. Reaves appears upon the final roll of citizens of the Cherokee Nation, but his name appears upon that roll because of the fact that he was enrolled by the Cherokee Council upon the 1890 Pay Roll, the 1894 Pay Roll and the Cherokee census roll of 1896, and Section 21 of the Act of June 28, 1898 (30 Stat., L 495), after confirming the authenticated roll of 1880, provides:

*****and (The Commission to the Five Civilized Tribes) shall investigate the right of all other persons whose names are found on any other rolls and omit such as may have been placed thereon by fraud or without authority of law, enrolling only such as may have legal right thereto,***

While the Commission to the Five Civilized Tribes may have been justified under the law in the enrollment of John A. Reaves as a citizen by blood of the Cherokee Nation from his enrollment in 1890, yet certainly prior to 1888, while he was a citizen and resident of the State of Texas, where he married his wife, and where practically all of his children were born, he was not a citizen of the Cherokee Nation and the marriage of Martha A. Reaves to the said John A. Reaves conferred no rights of citizenship by intermarriage upon her, and the said John A. Reaves not being a recognized citizen of the Cherokee Nation after his marriage to her prior to November 1, 1875, it is contended on behalf of the Cherokee Nation that the applicant is not entitled to be enrolled as a citizen by intermarriage of the Cherokee Nation, but that her citizenship in the Cherokee Nation if she acquired any dated from the recognition or enrollment of her husband upon the 1890 Pay Roll and this was too late under the decision of the Supreme Court of the United States, dated November 5, 1906, in the case of Daniel Redbird, et al., vs the United States to entitle Martha A. Reaves to be enrolled as an intermarried citizen of the Cherokee Nation.

Respectfully submitted,
W. W. Hastings
Attorney for the Cherokee Nation.

Muskogee, I. T., Feb. 25, 1907.

◇◇◇◇◇

DEPARTMENT OF THE INTERIOR.
COMMISSIONER TO THE FIVE CIVILIZED TRIBES.

CHIEF CLERK,                                          CFB
CHEROKEE LAND OFFICE.

DEAR SIR:

The records of this office show     **Martha A. Reaves**

listed on Cherokee card No.  **D 1074**
to be prima facie entitled to enrollment as   **Citizen by Intermarriage**   of the Cherokee
Nation for the following reason, viz:     **On schedule affirmed by Dept**
**March 4, 1907**

Respectfully,

Commissioner.

Dated      **March 29 1907**

◇◇◇◇◇

Cherokee
D 1074

Muskogee, Indian Territory, February 26, 1907

Martha A. Reaves,
Muskogee, Indian Territory.

Dear Madam:

There is herewith enclosed a copy of the decision of the Commissioner to the
Five Civilized Tribes, dated February 23, 1907, granting your application for enrollment
as a citizen by intermarriage of the Cherokee Nation. A copy of said decision is also
forwarded your attorney of record, Thomas Owen, Muskogee, Indian Territory, and he
has heretofore been furnished a copy of the record of proceedings had in your case. The
Attorney for the Cherokee Nation protests against your enrollment.

The decision, together with the record of proceedings had, and the Nation's
protest, has this day been forwarded to the Secretary of the Interior for review. You will
be advised of the Secretary's action as soon as this office is informed of the same.

Respectfully,

Encl. B 52                                          Commissioner

◇◇◇◇◇

Cherokee
D 1074

Muskogee, Indian Territory, February 28, 1907

Thomas Owen,
    Attorney for Martha A. Reaves,
    Muskogee, Indian Territory.

Dear Sir:

    There is enclosed a copy of the decision of the Commissioner to the Five Civilized Tribes, dated February 23, 1907, granting the application for the enrollment of Martha A. Reaves as a citizen by intermarriage of the Cherokee Nation. You have heretofore been furnished a copy of the record of proceedings had in the case. The Attorney for the Cherokee Nation protests against the action of the Commissioner in granting said application.

    Said decision, together with the record of proceedings had in the case, and the Nation's protest, has this day been forwarded to the Secretary of the Interior for review. The action of the Secretary will be made known to you as soon as the Commission is informed of the same.

Respectfully,

Encl. B-53                                    Commissioner

◇◇◇◇◇

Muskogee, Indian Territory, February 26, 1907

The Honorable,
    The Secretary of the Interior.

Sir:

    There is transmitted herewith the record of proceedings had in the matter of the application of Martha A. Reaves for the enrollment as a citizen by intermarriage of the Cherokee Nation, together with the Commissioner's decision dated February 23, 1907, granting said application.

    The Attorney for the Cherokee Nation protests against the action of the Commission in this case, a copy of which protest is enclosed. the enrollment of this applicant as a citizen by intermarriage of the Cherokee Nation and his protest filed February 23, 1907, is enclosed.

There is also enclosed a schedule containing the name of this applicant, and in the event of the approval of the Commissioner's decision favorable to her, the approval of this schedule is recommended. It will be noted that no roll number has been given this person upon this schedule. This action is taken in accordance with procedure reported by me to the Department on January 28, 1907, and approved by the Department in its telegram of February 9, 1907. If the Department approves my decision in this case, I recommend that a number be placed upon this schedule, in consecutive order, by Mr. McGarr, the employe[sic] of my office now in Washington.

Respectfully,

Commissioner.

Through the Commissioner of
    Indian Affairs.

Encl. B-50

DEPARTMENT OF THE INTERIOR,

Land.               OFFICE OF INDIAN AFFAIRS,
21253-1907

WASHINGTON.

March 2, 1907.

The Honorable,
    The Secretary of the Interior.

Sir:

    I have the honor to transmit herewith a communication from the Commissioner Bixby, dated February 26, 1907, enclosing record of proceedings in the matter of the application for the enrollment of Martha A. Reaves as a citizen by intermarriage of the Cherokee Nation, together with the Commissioner's decision.

    There is also enclosed with the case a schedule in quintuplicate, containing the name of this applicant, and in the event of the approval of the Commissioner's decision favorable to her, the Commissioner recommends the approval of the schedule.

    Attention is invited to the fact that the Commissioner requests that Mr. McGarr, now of this city, places the proper number on this schedule, in the event of its approval.

    The Office has examined the record and decision, and it is recommended that the decision of the Commissioner, admitting the applicant to enrollment, be affirmed, and the schedule containing her name, be approved.

Very respectfully,

C. F. Larrabee,

EWE-SD                                              Acting Commissioner.

D.C. 14853-1907.                                                          J.P.

FHE

DEPARTMENT OF THE INTERIOR,
WASHINGTON.

I.T.D. 7892-1907.                                              March 4, 1907.
DIRECT.

LRS

Commissioner to the Five Civilized Tribes,
    Muskogee, Indian Territory.

Sir:

February 26, 1907, you submitted the papers in the matter of the application of Martha A. Reaves for enrollment as a citizen by intermarriage of the Cherokee Nation, having decided in her favor; also a protest by the attorney for the Cherokee Nation against her enrollment.

In accordance with your recommendation and that of the Indian Office in letter of March 2, 1907 (Land 21253-07), copy inclosed, your decision is affirmed.

The schedule bearing her name, submitted with your letter, has also been approved and will be disposed of in the usual manner, with the papers in the case.

Respectfully,
(Signed) E. A. Hitchcock,
3 inc. and                                              Secretary.
5 for Ind. Of. with
copy hereof.

WCF 3-5-07

Cherokee
D 1074.

COPY

Muskogee, Indian Territory, March 22, 1907.

Martha A. Reaves,
    Muskogee, Indian Territory.

Dear Madam:

    You are hereby advised that the decision of the Commissioner to the Five Civilized Tribes, dated February 25, 1907, granting your application for enrollment as a citizen by intermarriage of the Cherokee Nation, was affirmed by the Department March 4, 1907.

Respectfully,

SIGNED *James Bixby*

HJC
                                        Commissioner.

◇◇◇◇◇

Cherokee
D 1074.

COPY

Muskogee, Indian Territory, March 22, 1907.

Thos. Owen,
    Attorney for Martha A. Reaves,
        Muskogee, Indian Territory.

Dear Sir:

    You are hereby advised that the decision of the Commissioner to the Five Civilized Tribes, dated February 25, 1907, granting the application for the enrollment of Martha A. Reaves as a citizen by intermarriage of the Cherokee Nation was affirmed by the Department March 4, 1907.

    For your information there is enclosed herewith a copy of Departmental decision referred to.

Respectfully,

SIGNED *James Bixby*

Encl. HJ-80.
                                        Commissioner.
  HJC

◇◇◇◇◇

Cherokee
D 1074.                          ʎdOƆ

Muskogee, Indian Territory, March 22, 1907.

W. W. Hastings,
> Attorney for the Cherokee Nation,
>> Muskogee, Indian Territory.

Dear Sir:

You are hereby advised that the decision of the Commissioner to the Five Civilized Tribes, dated February 25, 1907, granting the application for the enrollment of Martha A. Reaves as a citizen by intermarriage of the Cherokee Nation was affirmed by the Department March 4, 1907.

For your information there is enclosed herewith a copy of Departmental decision referred to.

> Respectfully,

> SIGNED  *Jams Bixby*
> Commissioner.

Encl. HJ-81.
HJC

---

**Cher IW 273**

◇◇◇◇◇

### DEPARTMENT OF THE INTERIOR,
### COMMISSION TO THE FIVE CIVILIZED TRIBES,
### WESTVILLE, I.T.  JULY 19, 1900.

Isaac J. Vanmatre makes application for Joel Kelly and his wife, Nellie Kelly, for enrollment as Cherokee citizens, said Vanmatre being sworn, testified.

Q  Why aren't they here?    A  He is crippled and she is too old to appear.
Q  Are their names upon the roll of '80?    A  Yes, I think so-- upon all the rolls.
> Joel Kelly on '80 roll, page 447, number 987.
> Nellie Kelly on '80 roll, page 447, number 988.
> Joel Kelly on '96 roll, page 824, number 105.
> Nellie Kelly on '96 roll, page 700, number 1168.
Q  Are they living?    A  Yes.
Q  Living at your house?    A  Yes.
Q  How long have they been living in the Cherokee Nation?    A  They have been living here ever since I have known them about 18 years.
Q  Is Joel a white man or Indian?    A  White man.

74

# Cherokee Intermarried White 1906
## Volume X

The name of Joel Kelly being found upon the authenticated rolls of '80, and testimony showing that he is an interrmarried[sic] citizen of the Cherokee Nation; and his wife, Nellie, appearing upon the '80 roll and also upon the roll of '96, and satisfactory evidence being given as to their residence, she is ordered enrolled as a Cherokee by blood.

Brown McDonald, being sworn by Commissioner Needles, says as Stenographer to the Commission to the Five Civilized Tribes, he reported in full the testimony of the above named witness and that the foregoing is a full, true and correct transcript of his stenographic notes.

Brown McDonald

Sworn to and subscribed before me this 20th of July 1900 at Westville I.T.

TB Needles
Commissioner.

◇◇◇◇◇

Commissioner Breckinridge: In Cherokee Straight Case 392, the same being entitled Joel Kelly et al, it is found upon consulting the roll of 1880, that Joel Kelly was then sixty-one years of age. That would make his age at the time of the application for him eighty-one, and he is on the 1880 roll as an intermarried white citizen.

On the 1880 roll Nellie Kelly is identified as fifty-three years of age. That would make her age at the time of her application seventy-three years, and she is identified on said roll as a native Cherokee.

It is ordered that a copy of this statement be attached to each copy of the testimony in this case.

Arthur G. Croninger, being duly sworn, states that as stenographer to the Commission to the Five Civilized Tribes he took in full the proceding[sic] statement and order, and that the foregoing is a true and complete transcript of his stenographic notes thereof.

Arthur G. Croninger

Subscribed and sworn to before me this 18th day of October, 1901.

C. R. Breckinridge
Commissioner.

◇◇◇◇◇

JOR.
Cher. 392.

Department of the Interior.
Commission to the Five Civilized Tribes.
Tahlequah, I. T., October 16, 1902.

SUPPLEMENTAL TESTIMONY AND PROCEEDINGS in the matter of the application for the enrollment of JOEL KELLY as a citizen by intermarriage of the Cherokee Nation.

ISAAC J. VANMATRE, being first duly sworn, and being examined, testified as follows:

BY COMMISSION: What is your name?    A  Isaac Jefferson Vanmatre.
Q  How old are you?    A  Fifty-one.
Q  What is your post office address?    A  Westville.
Q  Are you a white man?    A  Yes sir.
Q  Do you know Joel Kelly?    A  I do.
Q  Do you desire to give testimony in regard to his status as a citizen by intermarriage of the Cherokee Nation?    A  Yes sir.
Q  What is her[sic] reason he is not here in person before the Commission[sic]
A  His age would not admit of it.  Besides he is a cripple.  They have to dress him and undress him, and lift him about in a chair.
Q  How old a man is he?    A  He is about eighty-five years old.
Q  He is unable to get around without help?    A  Has been for over two years.
A  Are you related to him[sic]  A  By marriage I am.. Son-in-law.
Q  How far do you live from him?    A  I am in the house with him.

S. J. RENEKER, being first duly sworn, and being examined, testified as follows:

BY COMMISSION: What is your name?    A  S. J. Reneker.
Q  How old are you?    A  Thirty-eight.
Q  What is your post office address?    A  Chance.
Q  Do you know Joel Kelly?    A  Yes sir.
Q  About how old a man is he now?    A  I don't know, could not say, but he is getting up in years.
Q  Very old man?    A  Yes sir.
Q  Do you know the name of his wife?    A  Nellie.
Q  What is the present physical condition of Joel Kelly?    A  Why, he is unable to move himself without help.  Even when he lies down in bed, and when they take him to bed, they have to catch hold and help him, and he can't help himself a particle without assistance.  He could not walk or anything like that.  He has been right in by the fireplace for over a year.  I don't know just exactly how long, but around that.

# Cherokee Intermarried White 1906
## Volume X

Isaac J. Vanmatre recalled.

BY COMMISSION:   Q  Is Joel Kelly a white man?   A  Yes sir.
Q  What is the name of his wife?   A  Nellie.
Q  Is she living?   A  Yes sir.
Q  Is she a Cherokee by blood?   A  Yes sir.
Q  Application has been made for Joel Kelly's enrollment as a citizen by intermarriage of the Cherokee Nation, has it?   A  Yes sir.
Q  Where was he enrolled?   A  At Westville.
Q  Does he claim his right to enrollment by reason of his marriage to his present wife Nellie?   A  Yes sir, never was married before.
Q  When was he married to her?   A  Could not tell you that.  They have got children sixty years old, if they were living.
Q  How long have you known Joel Kelly?   A  Eighteen years, I expect, not over that, nor under it, I don't think.
Q  Were they living together as husband and wife when you first knew them?
A  Yes sir.
Q  Do you know whether or not Joel Kelly's name appears upon the roll of 1880?
A  No sir.
Q  Where was he residing about twenty years ago?   A  Right close to Westville, I guess.
Q  What are the names of some of the children of Joel and Nellie Kelly?   A  Levi and Thomas and John, and a girl named Nancy Jane and one named Martha living.  There is a child dead, I don't know---

It is shown upon examination of the copy of the Cherokee authenticated roll of citizens of the Cherokee Nation of 1880 that Joel Kelly is duly identified thereon as an adopted white, 61 years of age, appearing with nelly Kelly, native Cherokee, 53 years of age, Goingsnake District.

Q  Do you know whether Joel Kelly was ever married before he married his present wife?
A  He says he was not.
Q  Was his wife Nellie ever married before she married him?   A  No sir
Q  Have they lived together continuously since they were married?
A  I guess they have.  They have ever since I knew them.
Q  Were they living together on the 1st day of September, 1902?
A  Yes sir.
Q  They have never been separated while you have known them?
A  No sir.
Q  Your wife is their daughter?   A  Yes sir.
Q  Has Joel Kelly lived in the Cherokee Nation continuously since you have known him?
A  Yes sir.
Q  How long have you lived in the house with them?   A  Ten years the 6th of this coming January.
Q  They have been living together all the time, have they?
A  Yes sir.

This testimony will be filed with and made a part of the record in the matter of the application for the enrollment of Joel Kelly as a citizen by intermarriage of the Cherokee Nation, Cherokee straight card field No. 392.

---------------------

Wm. Hutchinson, being first duly sworn, states that as stenographer to the Commission to the Five Civilized Tribes he correctly recorded the testimony and proceedings in this case, and that the foregoing is a true and complete transcript of the stenographic notes thereof.

Wm Hutchinson

Subscribed and sworn to before me this 25th day of October, 1902.

John O Rosson<br>Notary Public.

◇◇◇◇◇

*(The Affidavit below was originally handwritten on the microfilm, and is typed as given.)*

United States of America  ⟨ ss
Northern District of Ind Ter  ⟨

Nellie Kelly being first duly sworn deposes & says she was married to Joel Kelly a white man about 1840 in Goingsnake Dist Cherokee Nation Indian Territory and lived with him continuously till his death Sept 26th 1904  the witnesses to said marriage are all dead  herself on account of infirmities is unable to go before the Commission at Muskogee  She has raised a family with Joel Kelly 6 of whom are still living in Cherokee Nation

|  |  |
|---|---|
| | her |
| Witness to Mark | Nellie x Kelly |
| Martha Vanmatre | mark |
| R.L. Sellers | |

Subscribed & sworn to before
me this 24th day of Jany 1907

P J Dore<br>Notary Public

My commission ex June 4 1908

◇◇◇◇◇

# Cherokee Intermarried White 1906
## Volume X

*(The Affidavit below typed as given.)*

(COPY)

United States of America   |

                               |   ss

Northern Dist. Ind. Ter.   |

To the Hon Commissioner

To the 5 Civilized Tribes

I hereby certify that I am a Regularly Liscensed & Practing physician in Northern Dist Ind Terrory  that I this day examined Mrs. Nellie Kelly at Her Residence 5 miles North west of Westville I.T. & Find her Physically unable to appear before your body at this time.

                           (Signed)  R. L. Sellers M.D.

Subscribed & Sworn to before me this

24th day of January 1907.

(SEAL)                          (Signed)  P. J. Dore

My Com ex June 4th 1908.              Notary Public.


Homer J. Councilor being first duly sworn states that as stenographer to the Commissioner to the Five Civilized Tribes he made the above and foregoing copy from the original thereof and tht the same is true and correct.

                           Homer J Councilor

Subscribed and sworn to before me this 1st day of February 1907.

                           Chas E Webster
                           Notary Public.

# Cherokee Intermarried White 1906
## Volume X

DEPARTMENT OF THE INTERIOR,
COMMISSIONER TO THE FIVE CIVILIZED TRIBES.
WESTVILLE, I. T., FEBRUARY 8, 1907.

———————

In the matter of the application for the enrollment of JOEL KELLEY[sic] as a citizen by intermarriage of the Cherokee Nation.

◇◇◇◇◇

*(The questionnaire below was originally handwritten on the microfilm and is typed as given.)*

George Crittenden being first duly sworn by P. J. Dore a Notary Public testified as follows

What is your name?   A- George Crittenden
How old are you?   A- Sixty two years
Do you know Joel Kelly?   A- Yes sir
Do you know his wife Nellie?   A- Yes sir.
How long have you know them?   A- I have known them since 1863 sometime during the war.   Were they married at that time?   A- I know that they were living together and lived together up to the time of his death about four or five years ago   I was not present at their marriage but they were always considered husband and wife in the neighborhood
How many children were born to them?   A- I dont remember.
How long have they lived together in this Territory?   A- Since about the year 1868
Is Nellie Kelley a Cherokee by blood?   A- Yes sir.   Was Joel Kelly a white man?
A- Yes sir.
   Charles B. Wilson, being first duly sworn, doth depose and say that the above and foregoing at the original questions propounded by him to, and the answers returned thereto by  George Crittenden  the above anmed[sic] witness.

Charles B. Wilson

Subscribed and sworn to before me this 11th day of February, 1907.

Walter W. Chappell
Notary Public.

◇◇◇◇◇

80

# Cherokee Intermarried White 1906
## Volume X

*(The questionnaire below was originally handwritten on the microfilm and is typed as given.)*

Nellie Kelley, being first duly sworn by P.J. Dore a Notary Public, testified as follows
What is your name? A- Nellie Kelley How old are you? A- About 86 or 87 years of age What is your husband's name? A- Joel Kelly. Is he alive? A- No. When did he die? A- Sept 6th 1904. Are you a Cherokee by blood? A- Yes sir. Was Joel Kelley your husband a white man? A- Yes sir. About what year was your married to Joel Kelley? A- About year 1840. When were your married to him? A- In the Cherokee Nation, Indian Territory and according to Cherokee law Were you married by a minister of the Gospel? Yes sir What was his name? A- I think his name was Duncan but I have forgotten his given name.
Did he give you a certificate of marriage at that time? A- He might have done so but I can not now remember
Was Joel Kelly, your husband, ever married to or lived with any other woman as his wife other than yourself? A- He never did
From the time you were married to Joel Kelley in 1840 did you and he live together as husband and wife until his death? Yes sir
How many children were born to you and Joel Kelly? A- Thirteen
What is the age of your oldest child and what is her name? Her name was Nancy and she was born in the winter of 1841 & 1842. Have you any record bible or otherwise showing the births of your children? A- I did have but they were destroyed by fire at the home of my son in law William Kirk about twelve years ago


Charles B. Wilson, being first duly sworn, doth depose and say that the above and foregoing at the original questions propounded by him to, and the answers returned thereto by __Nellie Kelley__ the above anmed[sic] witness.

Charles B. Wilson


Subscribed and sworn to before me this 11th day of February, 1907.

Walter W. Chappell<br>Notary Public.

*(The questionnaire below was originally handwritten on the microfilm and is typed as given.)*

Martha Van Matre, being first duly sworn by P. J. Dore a Notary Public testified as follows

What is your name?   A-   Martha Van Matre.   What relation are you to Nellie Kelly?   A- I am a daughter.   Was Joel Kelly your father?   A- Yes sir.   When were you born?   A-   In the year 1868.   How many brothers and sisters have you? A- Twelve.
How many older than you?   A- Twelve.   Did your father and mother live together as husband and wife from the time that you remember until his death?   A- Yes sir.


Charles B. Wilson, being first duly sworn, doth depose and say that the above and foregoing at the original questions propounded by him to, and the answers returned thereto by __Martha Van Matre__ the above named witness.

Charles B. Wilson

Subscribed and sworn to before me this 11th day of February, 1907.

Walter W. Chappell<br>Notary Public.

◇◇◇◇◇

E C M                                                        Cherokee 392.

DEPARTMENT OF THE INTERIOR,
COMMISSIONER TO THE FIVE CIVILIZED TRIBES.

---

In the matter of the application for the enrollment of JOEL KELLY as a citizen by intermarriage of the Cherokee Nation.

D E C I S I O N

THE RECORDS OF THIS OFFICE SHOW:   That at Westville, Indian Territory, July 19, 1900 application was received by the Commission to the Five Civilized Tribes for the enrollment of Joel Kelly as a citizen by intermarriage of the Cherokee Nation.   Further proceedings in the matter of said application were had at Tahlequah, Indian Territory, October 16, 1902 and Westville, Indian Territory, February 8, 1907.

# Cherokee Intermarried White 1906
## Volume X

THE EVIDENCE IN THIS CASE SHOWS: That the applicant herein, Joel Kelly, a white man, was married in accordance with Cherokee law in the year 1840 to one Nellie Kelly, nee Quinton, who was at the time of said marriage a recognized citizen by blood of the Cherokee Nation, who is identified on the Cherokee authenticated tribal roll of 1880, Going Snake District, No. 988, as a native Cherokee and whose name is included on the approved partial roll of citizens by blood of the Cherokee Nation opposite No. 1204. It is further shown that since said marriage the said Joel Kelly and Nellie Kelly resided together as husband and wife and continuously lived in the Cherokee Nation up to and including September 1, 1902. Said applicant is identified on the Cherokee authenticated tribal roll of 1880 and the Cherokee census roll of 1896 as an intermarried citizen of the Cherokee Nation.

IT IS, THEREFORE, ORDERED AND ADJUDGED: That in accordance with the decision of the Supreme Court of the United States, dated November 5, 1906, in the cases of Daniel Red Bird, et al. vs. the United States, Nos. 125, 126, 127, and 128, the said applicant, Joel Kelly is entitled, under the provisions of Section Twenty-one of the Act of Congress approved June 28, 1898, (30 Stats. 495), to enrollment as a citizen by intermarriage of the Cherokee Nation and his application for enrollment as such is accordingly granted.

Tams Bixby

Commissioner.

Dated at Muskogee, Indian Territory,
this    FEB 27 1907

◇◇◇◇◇

(COPY)

Westville, Ind. Ter. Jan. 25, 1907.

Hon. Bixby Commission

I am submitting you evidence in Joe Kelly case. This man Joel Kelly & his Cherokee wife Nellie Kelly lived together as man & wife 63 years til his death.

Kindly let me know if any thing further is needed.

Yours Respy

P.J. Dore

◇◇◇◇◇

Cherokee
392.

COPY

Muskogee, Indian Territory, February 27, 1907.

W. W. Hastings,
      Attorney for the Cherokee Nation,
         Muskogee, Indian Territory.

Dear Sir:

      There is enclosed herewith a copy of the decision of the Commissioner to the Five Civilized Tribes, dated February 27, 1907, granting the application for the enrollment of Joel Kelly as a citizen by intermarriage of the Cherokee Nation.

Respectfully,

SIGNED *Jams Bixby*

Encl. HJ-139.
HJC

Commissioner.

◇◇◇◇◇

Cherokee
392.

Muskogee, Indian Territory, February 27, 1907.

The Commissioner to the Five Civilized Tribes,
      Muskogee, Indian Territory.

Sir:

      Receipt is acknowledged of the testimony and of your decision enrolling Joel Kelly as a citizen by intermarriage of the Cherokee Nation. Time for protesting said decision is waived and I consent that said person may be placed upon the schedule immediately.

Respectfully,

W. W. Hastings
Attorney for Cherokee Nation.

◇◇◇◇◇

Cherokee
392.                                              COPY

Muskogee, Indian Territory, February 27, 1907.

Nellie Kelly,
      Chance, Indian Territory.

Dear Madam:

      There is enclosed herewith a copy of the decision of the Commissioner to the Five Civilized Tribes, dated February 27, 1907, granting the application for the enrollment of Joel Kelly as a citizen by intermarriage of the Cherokee Nation.

      You will be advised when the name of said applicant has been placed upon a schedule of citizens of the Cherokee Nation and approved by the Secretary of the Interior.

                    Respectfully,

                        SIGNED *Tams Bixby*

Encl. HJ-138.
   HJC                                         Commissioner.

---

**Cher IW 274**

          ◇◇◇◇◇

Department of the Interior,
Commission to the Five Civilized Tribes,
Bunch, I. T., August 1st, 1900.

      In the matter of the application of Gaines C. Smith et al for enrollment as Cherokee citizens; being sworn and examined by Commissioner Needles he testifies as follows:

Q    What is your name?. A Gaines C. Smith.
Q    What is your age? A Fifty-six.
Q    What is your post-office address? A Bunch.
Q    Have you ever been recognized by the Tribal authorities of the Cherokee Nation as a citizen? A Yes sir.
Q    Does your name appear upon the Tribal rolls? A Yes sir.
Q    In what district do you live? A Sequoyah.
Q    How long have you lived there? A Twenty-eight years.
Q    Continuously all the time, never lived outside the Cherokee Nation Indian Territory for the last twenty-eight years? A No sir.
Q    What is the name of your father? A John Smith.
Q    Is he living? A No sir.

Q   Was he a Cherokee?   A  No sir.
Q   Does his name appear upon the roll of 1880?   A  No sir.
Q   How long has he been dead?   A  He never lived in the Cherokee Nation.
Q   What is the name of your mother?   A  Her name was Charlotte White.
Q   Is she living?   A  No sir.
Q   Is her name on any of the rolls of the Cherokee Nation?   A  No sir.
Q   Does your name appear upon the 1880 authenticated roll of the Cherokee Nation?
A   Yes sir.
    Note:   1880 roll examined, page 719 #1143 as Gains C. Smith Sequoyah
District  1896 roll page 1113 #165 as Gaines C. Smith Sequoyah District.
Q   You don't claim any Cherokee blood yourself?   A  No sir.
Q   Under what law were you married?   A  A Cherokee law.
Q   Have you a marriage license or certificate?   A  No sir.
Q   For whom do you apply here for enrollment, anybody but yourself?   A  My wife
and my son.
Q   Where were you living at the time of your marriage?   A  I was living in this
District,- Flint.
Q   What was the name of your wife before she was married?   A  Esther Sanders.
Q   Is she now living?   A  Yes sir.
Q   Is she a citizen by blood of the Cherokee Nation?   A  Yes sir.
    Note:  1880 roll examined for wife:  page 719 #1144 as Ester Smith, Sequoyah
Dist.  1896 roll page 1100 #1354 as Ester Smith Sequoyah Dist:  1894 roll page 995
#1281 as Esther Smith Sequoyah District.
Q   What is the name of her father?   A  Robert Sanders.
Q   Was he a Cherokee?   A  Yes sir.
Q   Is he now living?   A  No sir.
Q   How long has he been dead?   A  I don't know; he died time of the War.
Q   What is the name of your wife's mother?   A  Polly Sanders.
Q   Is she living?   A  No sir.
Q   Did she die before 1880?   A  She has been dead about fifteen years, she died before
eighty.
Q   Have you any children under twenty-one years of age and unmarried for whom you
desire to make application?   A  Yes sir, I have one.
Q   What is its name?   A  John, fifteen.
    (On 1896 roll page 1100 #1360 as John Smith, Sequoyah Dist.)
(On 1894 roll page 995 #1287 as John Smith Sequoyah District.)
Q   Is this boy alive and living with you?   A  Yes sir.

   Com'r Needles: The name of Gaines C. Smith appearing upon the authenticated roll of
1880 as well as upon the census roll of 1896, and the name of Esther, his wife, also
appearing upon the authenticated roll of 1880 as well as the pay roll of 1894 and the
census roll of 1896, they being fully identified according to page and number is said rolls
as indicated in the record, they are duly listed for enrollment by this Commission as
Cherokee citizens, he as a Cherokee citizen by intermarriage and she as a Cherokee
citizen by blood; and the name of John, their son, being found upon the census roll of
1896 and the pay roll of 1894, and he being fully identified according to page and

number as indicated, he is duly listed for enrollment by this Commission as a Cherokee citizen by blood.

M.D. Green, being first duly sworn, states that as stenographer to the Commission to the Five Civilized Tribes he reported the foregoing case and that the above and foregoing is a full true and complete transcript of his stenographic notes in said case.

MD Green

Subscribed and sworn to before me this 2nd day of August 1900.

TB Needles
Commissioner.

◇◇◇◇◇

Cher
Supp'l to # 907

Department of the Interior,
Commission to the Five Civilized Tribes,
Muskogee, I. T., October 21, 1902.

In the matter of the application of GAINES C. SMITH, for the enrollment of himself as a citizen by intermarriage, and his wife, ESTHER SMITH, and his son, JOHN SMITH, as citizens by blood, of the Cherokee Nation.

GAINES C. SMITH, being duly sworn and examined by the Commission, testified as follows:

Q   What is your name ?   A  Gaines C. Smith.
Q   What is your post office ?   A  Bunch.
Q   How old are you at this time ?   A  I am fifty nine.
Q   Are you the same Gaines C. Smith that applied to the Commission for enrollment as an intermarried citizen in August, 1900 ?   A  Yes sir.
Q   You applied two years ago last August ?   A  Yes sir.
Q   What was your wife's name ?   A  Esther Smith.
Q   Was she a Cherokee by blood ?   A  Yes sir.
Q   Is she living ?   A  Yes sir.
Q   When were you married to your wife Esther ?
A   I was married in 1870, I think.
Q   Were you and your wife Esther living together in 1880, and enrolled together on the 1880 roll ?   A  Yes sir.
Q   Have you and she lived together all the time as husband and wife since 1880 up to the present time ?   A  Yes sir.
Q   Never been separated ?   A  No sir.

Q   Were you living together as husband and wife on the first day of September, 1902 ?
A   Yes sir.
Q   Have you and your wife lived in the Cherokee Nation all the time since 1880 up to the present time ?   A  Yes sir.
Q   Never been out since then ?   A  No sir.
Q   This child John is your son by your wife Esther ?   A  Yes sir.
Q   Is he living at this time ?   A  Yes sir.
Q   Has he lived all his life in the Cherokee Nation ?   A  Yes sir.

------------------------------

E. C. Bagwell, on oath states that, as stenographer to the Commission to the Five Civilized Tribes, he correctly recorded the testimony and proceedings had in the above entitled cause, and that the foregoing is an accurate transcript of his stenographic notes thereof.

f.

E.C. Bagwell

Subscribed and sworn to before me this November 28, 1902.

BC Jones
Notary Public.

◇◇◇◇◇

C.F.B.                                                    Cherokee 907

### DEPARTMENT OF THE INTERIOR,
### COMMISSIONER TO THE FIVE CIVILIZED TRIBES.
### MUSKOGEE, IND. TER., JANUARY 3, 1907.

In the matter of the application for the enrollment of GAINES C. SMITH as a citizen by intermarriage of the Cherokee Nation.

--:--

Applicant appears in person:
APPEARANCES:  Cherokee Nation represented by H. M. Vance, on behalf of W.W. Hastings, attorney.

GAINES C. SMITH  being first duly sworn by B. P. Rasmus, a Notary Public, testified as follows:

Q.   What is your name please?   A.  Gaines C. Smith.
Q.   What is your age?   A.  Sixty-three.

Q. What is your postoffice address?    A. Sallisaw is now. Bunch was my postoffice, and I was notified at Bunch but Sallisaw is my postoffice address.

Q. Do you claim the right to enrollment as a citizen by intermarriage of the Cherokee Nation?    A. Yes sir.

Q. You have no Cherokee blood?    A. No sir.

Q. You claim that right solely by reason of your marriage to a Cherokee by blood, do you?    A. Yes sir.

Q. What was the name of your wife through whom you claim the right to enrollment as a citizen by intermarriage of the Cherokee Nation?    A. Esther Sanders.

Q. Is she living at this time?    A. Yes sir.

Q. Where were you married to her?    A. I was married in Flint District.

Q. In the Cherokee Nation?    A. Yes sir.

Q. When were you married?    A. In '69 or '70, I do not remember the exact date.

Q. Were you married according to Cherokee law?    A. Yes sir.

Q. Since your marriage to your wife have you and she continuously lived together as husband and wife, and in the Cherokee Nation?    A. We have.

Q. Been in the Cherokee Nation all the time, have you?

A. Yes sir; Never have been out.

Q. Were you ever married prior to your marriage to her?    A. No sir.

Q. Was she ever married prior to her marriage to you?    A. No sir.

> The applicant, Gaines C. Smith, is identified upon the Cherokee authenticated tribal roll of 1880, Sequoyah District, No. 1143. His wife Esther Smith is included in an approved partial roll of citizens by blood of the Cherokee Nation, opposite No. 2460.

Q. Did you secure a license at the time you were married?

A. Yes sir.

Q. Have you a copy of that marriage license with you?

A. No sir, I have not; I have no copy.

Q. Who married you?    A. Judge Christy.

Q. Did you ever make any attempt to secure your marriage license after it was sent to the Clerk to be recorded?    A. I did; I tried to find out whether or not they was on record; whether they had a record of it, and I couldn't fine it.

Q. You could not find any record of it?    A. No sir, I went to the Clerk-- that was when they were taking the Census to pay out the Strip Payment-- they said we had to produce out license- and I went to the Clerk and he said part of the records had been destroyed; he had a part of the records, and part he could not find; and I went and got Judge Christy, the Judge who married us, and he went before the Clerk and testified that he married us, and that I had a license according to Cherokee Law, and that he sent the license to the Clerk.

Q. Did he give you a written statement to that effect?

A. He gave me a copy of it.

Q. Have you the copy?    A. No, after I got on the Roll I never paid any attention to it. I could bring the Clerk that he testified before; he can swear that the Judge went before him and testified that he married me and that I had a license. Judge Christy is dead, but I can prove it by the Clerk, and by the Census takers; they are living.

------------------------------------------------------------

The undersigned, being first duly sworn, states that as stenographer to the Commissioner to the Five Civilized Tribes she correctly recorded the testimony in this case, and that the above and foregoing is a full, true and correct transcript of her stenographic notes thereof.

Lucy M. Bowman

Subscribed and sworn to before me this 4th day of February, 1907

John E. Tidwell<br>Notary Public.

◇◇◇◇◇

*(Copies of original documents from case.)*

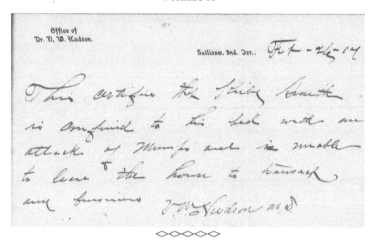

◇◇◇◇◇

E.C.M.                                                    Cherokee 907.

### DEPARTMENT OF THE INTERIOR,
### COMMISSIONER TO THE FIVE CIVILIZED TRIBES.
#### Muskogee, I. T., February 28, 1907.

In the matter of the application for the enrollment of Gaines C. Smith as a citizen by intermarriage of the Cherokee Nation.

W. W. Hastings, appearing on behalf of the Cherokee Nation.

John B. Adair, being first duly sworn by W. W. Chappell, a Notary Public for the Western District of Indian Territory, testified as follows:

By the Commissioner:
Q What is your name?   A John B. Adair.
Q Your age?   A Sixty-three.
Q What is your postoffice address?   A Sallisaw, I. T.
Q You appear here today for the purpose of giving testimony relation[sic] to the right of Gaines C. Smith to enrollment as a citizen by intermarriage of the Cherokee Nation?
A Yes sir.
Q How long have you been acquainted with Gaines C. Smith?
A Along in the '70's I think I first got acquainted with him.
Q Were you also acquainted with his wife, Esther?   A Yes, I was raised right with her.
Q Is she a Cherokee by blood?   A Yes sir.
Q And Gaines C. Smith is a white man?   A Yes sir.
Q When were they married?   A In '70; I don't know just when it was. It was in '70's a little while after I got acquainted with them.
Q Where were they married?   A Flint District.
Q Were they married under a license issued by the authorities of the Cherokee nation?
A That was my understanding.

Q  Did you see the license?    A  No, I didn't.

Q  Was Gaines C. Smith ever married prior to his marriage to Esther Smith?    A  I don't know that he was.

Q  Since their marriage have they continuously lived together as husband and wife and lived continuously in the Cherokee nation during this time?    A.  All the time, right close to me. Live there now.

-------------------

By Mr. Hastings:

Q  Did you ever hear of either of them ever having been married before their marriage in the '70's?    A  No sir.

Q  Have you any reason to believe that either of them ever were married before?    A  No, I don't; I know his wife was never married before, but he was a new man in there--

Q  So far as you know, and so far as you have heard or have had reason to believe, you don't think that he was ever married before?    A  No sir, I don't think he was.

Witness excused.

--------

Mitchell Ellis, being first duly sworn by W. W. Chappell, testified as follows:

By the Commissioner:

Q  What is your name?    A  Mitchell Ellis.

Q  What is your age?    A  Fifty-two years.

Q  What is your postoffice address?    A  Tahlequah, I. T.

Q  You appear here today for the purpose of giving testimony relative to the right of Gaines C. Smith to enrollment as a citizen by intermarriage of the Cherokee Nation?
A  Yes sir.

Q  How long have you been acquainted with Gaines C. Smith?

A  Its[sic] been about 30 or 35 years.

Q  Is he a white man?    A  yes, said to be.

Q  How long have you been acquainted with Gaines C. Smith's wife?

A  Ever since she was a child.

Q  Is she a Cherokee by blood?    A  Yes sir.

Q  When were they married?    A  I can't tell about that; I don't know; its[sic] been too long awhile.

Q  They were married when you first became acquainted with Smith?

A  Yes sir, they were said to be married, but I don't know anything about the marriage.

Q  Do you know whether they were married under a license issued by the Cherokee Nation?    A  No sir, but they were living together as husband and wife and are yet.

Witness excused.

-------------

G. W. Ellis, being first duly sworn by W. W. Chappell, testified as follows:

Q  What is your name?    A  G. W. Ellis.

Q  What is your age?    A  Forty-six.

Q  What is your postoffice address?    A  Muskogee, I. T.

Q  You appear here today for the purpose of giving testimony relative to the right of Gaines C. Smith to enrollment as a citizen by intermarriage of the Cherokee Nation.
A  Yes sir.

# Cherokee Intermarried White 1906
## Volume X

Q  Is Gaines C. Smith a white man?   A  That is my understanding.
Q  His wife, Esther, is a Cherokee by blood?   A  Yes sir.
Q  How long have you been acquainted with them?   A  I never was much acquainted with them.  I have known them and known where they lived for 20 to 25 years.
Q  Since you have known them they have resided together as husband and wife and continuously lived in the Cherokee Nation?   A  Yes sir.
Q  Do you know whether they were married under Cherokee license[sic]  A  No sir.
Q  Did you ever hear that either of them were married prior to their marriage to each other?   A  No sir.

-----------

Frances R. Lane upon oath states that as stenographer to the Commission to the Five Civilized Tribes she reported the testimony in the above entitled cause and that the foregoing is an accurate transcript of her stenographic notes thereof.

Frances R. Lane

Subscribed and sworn to before me this February 28, 1907.

Walter W. Chappell
Notary Public.

◇◇◇◇◇

E.C.M.                                                                                    Cherokee 907.

### DEPARTMENT OF THE INTERIOR,
### COMMISSIONER TO THE FIVE CIVILIZED TRIBES.

----------------------

In the matter of the application for the enrollment of Gaines C. Smith as a citizen by intermarriage of the Cherokee Nation.

### D E C I S I O N .

THE RECORDS OF THIS OFFICE SHOW: That at Bunch, Indian Territory, August 1, 1900, application was received by the Commission to the Five Civilized Tribes for the enrollment of Gaines C. Smith as a citizen by intermarriage of the Cherokee Nation.  Further proceedings in the matter of said application were had at Muskogee, Indian Territory, October 21, 1902, January 3 and February 28, 1907.

THE EVIDENCE IN THIS CASE SHOWS: That the applicant herein, Gaines C. Smith, a white man, was married in accordance with the Cherokee law about the year 1869, to his wife, Esther Smith, who was at the time of said marriage a recognized citizen by blood of the Cherokee Nation, who is identified on the Cherokee authenticated tribal roll of 1880, Sequoyah District, No. 1144, as a native Cherokee, and whose name is included on the approved partial roll of citizens by blood of the Cherokee Nation opposite

No. 2460. It is further shown that from the time of said marriage said Gaines C. Smith and Esther Smith resided together as husband and wife, and continuously lived in the Cherokee Nation up to and including September 1, 1902. Said applicant is identified on the Cherokee authenticated tribal roll of 1880, and Cherokee census roll of 1896, as an intermarried citizen of the Cherokee Nation.

IT IS, THEREFORE, ORDERED AND ADJUDGED: That in accordance with the decision of the Supreme Court of the United States, dated November 5, 1906, in the cases of Daniel Red Bird, et al., vs. the United States, Nos. 125, 126, 127, and 128, the said applicant, Gaines C. Smith, is entitled, under the provisions of Section 21 of the Act of Congress approved June 28, 1898 (30 Stats. 495), to enrollment as a citizen by intermarriage of the Cherokee Nation, and his application for enrollment as such is accordingly granted.

Tams Bixby
Commissioner.

Dated at Muskogee, Indian Territory,
this     FEB 28 1907

◇◇◇◇◇◇

*(The below typed as given.)*

POWER OF ATTORNEY.

J AMES C. SMITH.
TO
TILDEN SMITH.

### -DEPARTMENT OF THE INTERIOR-
### COMMISSIONER TO THE FIVE CIVILIZED TRIBES

#### P-O-W-E-R-O-F-A-T-T-R-N-E-Y-

Known all me by these presents. That I Gaines C. Smith of Sallisaw, Indian Territory, has made constituted and appointed, and by these presents do make constitute and appoint Tilden Smith of Sallisaw, Indian Territory, my true and lawful Attorney, for me and in my name place and stead, to act and prosecute my claim, before the Commissioner To the Five Civilized Tribes, for Citizenship as an Adopted Citizen of the Cherokee Nation, for the reason, that I am sick and unable to be present myself, as shown by Certificate of a regular practiceing Phycian hereto attached. Hereby ratifying and confirming all that my Attorney may lawfully do, in prosecuteing my Claim, hereby giveing and granting his full power to act in my place and stead. In witness wherof I have hereunto set my hand and seal this 20th day of February A.D.1907.

Gaines C. Smith

United States of America, )
                       )
Northern District,Indian )ss.
                       )
      Territory. )

          Personally appeared before me a Notary Public,duly commissioned and acting within and for the Northern Judicial District of the Indian Territory Gaines C. Smith,personally well known,to be the person mentioned in the foregoing Power Of Attorney,and being by me duly sworn,stated and acklnowledged,that he had executed the same,of his own free will and accord,and for the purposes,therein mentioned and set forth. And I do so hereby CERTIFY.
  This 26th day of February A.D.1907.

                                John Hannah
                                Notary Public.
My Commission Expires  Oct 3  1909.

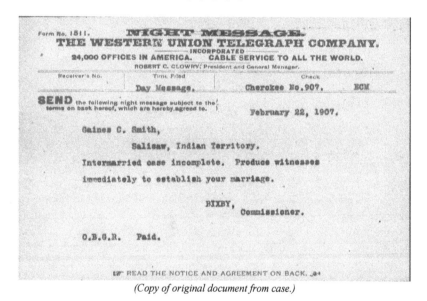

*(Copy of original document from case.)*

REFER IN REPLY TO THE FOLLOWING:

Cherokee No. 907.

**DEPARTMENT OF THE INTERIOR,**
**COMMISSIONER TO THE FIVE CIVILIZED TRIBES.**

95

ECM                 Muskogee, Indian Territory, February 22, 1907.

SPECIAL.

    Gaines C. Smith,
        Salisaw[sic], Indian Territory.

   Sir:

          The Commission sent you this day a telegram as follows:

          "Intermarried case incomplete. Produce witnesses
immediately to establish you marriage."

          The Act of Congress approved April 26, 1906 provides that the
Secretary of the Interior shall have no jurisdiction to approve the enrollment of
any person as a citizen of the Cherokee Nation after March 4, 1907.
This matter, therefore, demands your immediate attention.

               Respectfully,
                 Tams Bixby
GHC                     Commissioner.

◇◇◇◇◇

Form No. 2.

## THE WESTERN UNION TELEGRAPH COMPANY.
### INCORPORATED
**24,000 OFFICES IN AMERICA.  CABLE SERVICE TO ALL THE WORLD.**
ROBERT C. CLOWRY, President and General Manager.

| Receiver's No. | Time Filed | Check |
|---|---|---|
| | | Cherokee 997. |

**SEND** the following message subject to the terms Muskogee, Ind. Ter. January 28, 1907
on back hereof, which are hereby agreed to.          190

To Gaines C. Smith,

        Salisaw, Indian Territory.

        Documentary evidence or testimony of witnesses having actual

knowledge of your marriage necessary to complete your intermarriage

case.

                  Bixby

O. ?. G. R.    PAID.            Commissioner.

☞ READ THE NOTICE AND AGREEMENT ON BACK. ☜

*(Copies of original documents from case.)*

# Cherokee Intermarried White 1906
## Volume X

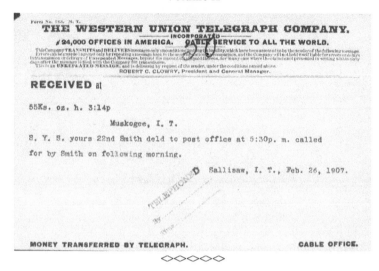

<>  <>  <>  <>  <>

Cherokee 907.

Muskogee, Indian Territory, February 28, 1907.

W. W. Hastings, Attorney for Cherokee Nation,
    Muskogee, Indian Territory.

Sir:

      There is inclosed herewith a copy of the decision of the Commissioner to the Five Civilized Tribes, dated February 28, 1907, granting the application for the enrollment of Gaines C. Smith as a citizen by intermarriage of the Cherokee Nation.

      The decision, together with the record of proceedings had in the case, has this day been transmitted to the Secretary of the Interior for his review and decision. You will be advised of the Secretary's action as soon as this office is informed of same.

Respectfully,

Commissioner.

Encl. C-1 1/2
  GHC

<>  <>  <>  <>  <>

Cherokee 907.

Muskogee, Indian Territory, February 28, 1907.

The Commissioner to the Five Civilized Tribes,
    Muskogee, Indian Territory.

Sir:

    I am in receipt of your decision of February 28, 1907, granting the application of Gaines C. Smith for enrollment as a citizen by intermarriage of the Cherokee Nation.

    I do not desire to protest against his enrollment and I consent that his name shall be placed upon the schedule of citizens by intermarriage of the Cherokee Nation and forwarded to the Secretary of the Interior for approval immediately.

                      Respectfully,
                      W. W. Hastings
                      Attorney for Cherokee Nation.

◇◇◇◇◇

Cherokee 907.

COPY

                Muskogee, Indian Territory, February 28, 1907.

Gaines C. Smith,
    Salisaw[sic], Indian Territory.

Sir:

    There is inclosed herewith a copy of the Commissioner's decision, dated February 28, 1907, granting your application for enrollment as a citizen by intermarriage of the Cherokee Nation.

    You will be advised when your name has been placed upon a schedule of citizens by intermarriage of the Cherokee Nation and approved by the Secretary of the Interior.

                    Respectfully,
                      SIGNED *Tams Bixby*
                      Commissioner.

Encl. C-1
  GHC

◇◇◇◇◇

Cherokee
~~N B~~ 274
I.W.

                Muskogee, Indian Territory, June 11, 1907

Gaines C. Smith,
    Sallisaw, Indian Territory.

Dear Sir:

In reply to your letter of June 3, 1907, asking information as to the status of your Cherokee intermarried case, you are advised that the records of this office show that your application for enrollment as a citizen by intermarriage of the Cherokee Nation was granted on February 28, 1907, and your name appears upon a roll of such citizens approved by the Secretary of the Interior.

Respectfully,

L M B                                                    Commissioner

---

**Cher IW 275**

◇◇◇◇◇◇

Department of the Interior,
Commission to the Five Civilized Tribes,
Sallisaw, I. T., August 9, 1900.

In the matter of the application of James W. Wilson for the enrollment of himself, wife and children as Cherokee citizens; being sworn and examined by Commissioner Breckinridge he testified as follows:

Q    What is your full name?    A James W. Wilson.
Q    What is your age?    A Forty-five.
Q    What is your post-office?    A Vian.
Q    And your district?    A Illinois District.
Q    For whom do you apply now for enrollment?    A Myself and family.
Q    Your wife and children?    A Yes sir.
Q    Do you apply for yourself as a Cherokee by blood?    A Yes sir.
Q    Do you apply for your wife as a Cherokee by blood?    A She is a white woman.
Q    Are you on any of the rolls of the Cherokee Nation?    A Yes sir, I am on all of them, I guess.
Q    How long have you lived in Illinois District?    A I was born in Illinois District, and I was raised in Cooweescoowee and moved back to Illinois District about fifteen years ago.
Q    You have lived now about fifteen years in Illinois?    A Yes sir.
Q    What proportion of Cherokee blood do you claim?    A A Quarter.
Q    What's your wife's name?    A Minta Wilson.
Q    How old is she?    A She is forty-one.
Q    What was her name before you married her?    A Harris.

Q    That her maiden name?    A  Yes sir.

Q    When were you married to her?    A  We have been married about twenty-five years.

Q    You and she have lived together ever since you were married, and are living together at this time?    A  Yes sir.

Q    Give me now the names of your children and their ages, those who are under twenty-one years old, and unmarried?    A  Albert M., eighteen; Sallie B., fourteen; Ida F., twelve; Robert, eight years old; Sue, four.

Q    These children are all living now are they?    A  Yes sir.

1880 roll examined for applicant; page 204, #3339 James Wilson, Cooweescoowee District

1880 roll, for wife, page 204 #3340, Minty Wilson, Cooweescoowee Dist.

1894 roll, page 852, #2222 James W. Wilson, Illinois District.

1894 roll, for children, page 853 #2225 Albert M. Wilson, Illinois.

1894 roll, page 853 #2226 Sallie B. Wilson, Illinois District.

1894 roll, page 853 #2227 Ida F. Wilson, Illinois District.

1894 roll, page 853 #2226[sic] Robert Wilson, Illinois District.

1896 roll, for applicant, page 916 #2135 James Wilson, Illinois.

1896 roll, for wife, page 937 #213[sic] Minta Wilson, Illinois District.

1896 roll, for children, page 916 #2137 Albert Wilson, Illinois.

1896 roll, page 916 #2138 Belle Wilson, Illinois District.

1896 roll, page 916 #2139 Ida Wilson, Illinois District.

1896 roll, page 916 #2140 Hobert[sic] Wilson, Illinois District.

1896 roll, page 916 #2142 Susie Wilson, Illinois District.

Com'r Breckinridge:  The applicant, James W. Wilson is duly identified on the rolls of 1880, 1894 and 1896, and he will be enrolled as a Cherokee by blood.  His wife, Minta Wilson, is duly identified on the rolls of 1880 and 1896, and she will be enrolled as a Cherokee by adoption; their five children as enumerated in the testimony, are all identified on the rolls of 1894 and 1896, and all of said children are now living and will be enrolled as Cherokees by blood.

M.D. Green, being first duly sworn, states that as stenographer to the Commission to the Five Civilized Tribes he reported the foregoing case and that the above and foregoing is a full true and complete transcript of his stenographic notes.

MD Green

Subscribed an sworn 15th day of August 1900.

C R Breckinridge
Commissioner.

◇◇◇◇◇

# Cherokee Intermarried White 1906
## Volume X

DEPARTMENT OF THE INTERIOR.
Commission to the Five Civilized Tribes.
Muskogee, Indian Territory, October 27th, 1902.

---

In the matter of the application of James W. Wilson for the enrollment of himself as a citizen by blood; his wife, Minta Wilson, as a citizen by intermarriage; his children, Albert M., Ida R., Robert and Sue Wilson and Sallie B. Burnes, as citizens by blood, and his grand-daughter, Viola Burnes, as a citizen by blood of the Cherokee Nation.

---

Supplemental to #1151.

---

JAMES W. WILSON, being duly sworn, testified as follows:
Examination by the Commission.

Q. What is your name?　A. James Wilson.

Q. What is your age?　A. 48.

Q. What is your post office address?　A. Vian.

Q. You are a citizen by blood of the Cherokee Nation?　A. Yes, sir.

Q. What is your wife's name?　A. Minta.

Q. How old is your wife Minta?　A. She is 44.

Q. Is she a white woman?　A. Yes sir.

Q. Is she an applicant for enrollment as an intermarried citizen?　A. Yes, sir.

Q. When were you married to your wife?　A. I don't know what date it was. We have been married 27 or 8 years.

Q. She is on the 1880 roll with you?　A. Yes, sir.

Q. Have you and your wife lived together all the time since 1880 up to the present time?　A. Yes, sir.

Q. Never have been separated?　A. No, sir.

Q. Were you living together on the first of September, 1902?　A. Yes, sir.

Q. Have you and your wife lived in the Cherokee Nation all the time since 1880 up to the present time?　A. Yes, sir.

Q. Are these children, Albert M., Sallie B., Ida F., Robert and Sue, your children by your wife Minta?　A. Yes, sir.

Q. Sallie B. and Ida F. are both married now, are they?

A. Sallie B. is married.

Q. Ida isn't married?　A. Ida isn't.

Q. Who is this child Viola Brown?　A. That is Bell's child.

Q. Sallie Bell?　A. Yes, sir.

Q. Your grand-daughter?　A. Yes, sir.

Q. Are all these children living?　A. Yes, sir.

Q. Have they lived all their lives in the Cherokee Nation?

A. Yes, sir.

::::::::::::::::::::::::::::::::::::::

Jesse O. Carr, being first duly sworn, states that as stenographer to the Commission to the Five Civilized Tribes he reported the above entitled case and that the foregoing is a true and complete transcript of his stenographic notes thereof.

Jesse O. Carr

Subscribed and sworn to before me this 7th day of February, 1903.

Samuel Foreman
Notary Public.

C. F. B.                                                                            Cherokee 1151.

DEPARTMENT OF THE INTERIOR,
COMMISSION TO THE FIVE CIVILIZED TRIBES.
Muskogee, Indian Territory, January 14, 1907.

In the matter of the application for the enrollment of Minta Wilson as a citizen by intermarriage of the Cherokee Nation.

Minta Wilson being first duly sworn by B. P. Rasmus, Notary Public, testified as follows:

Q   What is your name?                        A   Minta Wilson.
Q   What is your age?                         A   48.
Q   What is your post office address?
A   Turley.
Q   You are an applicant for enrollment as a citizen by intermarriage of the Cherokee Nation?
A   Yes sir.
Q   You have no Cherokee blood?
A   No sir.
Q   Your only claim to the right to enrollment as a citizen of the Cherokee Nation is by virtue of your marriage to a citizen by blood?
A   Yes sir.
Q   What is the name of that citizen?
A   J. W. Wilson.
Q   Is he living?                             A   Yes sir.
Q   When did you marry him?                   A   In 1875.
Q   Where was your husband living at the time you married him?
A   Cherokee Nation.
Q   He was a citizen by blood of the Nation?
A   Yes sir.

Q   And lived all the time in the Nation?
A   We lived out in the States a while?[sic]
Q   When did you live in the States?
A   We were married in the States.
Q   What state?                                                    A    Missouri.
Q   Did you come to the Nation immediately after your marriage?
A   Yes sir.
Q   The same year?                                          A    Yes sir.
Q   Since your marriage have you always considered the Cherokee Nation your home?
A   Yes sir.
Q   Any absence that you may have had from the Cherokee Nation has been of a temporary character?
A   Yes sir.


Q   Was James W. Wilson your first husband?
A   Yes sir.
Q   You were his first wife?
A   Yes sir.


The applicant, Minta Wilson, is identified on the Cherokee authenticated tribal roll of 1880, Cooweescoowee District, Number 3340. Her husband, James W. Wilson, is identified on said roll at Number 3339, and his name is included in the approved partial roll of citizens by blood of the Cherokee Nation, opposite Number 3167.

James W. Wilson being first duly sworn by B. P. Rasmus, Notary Public, testified as follows:

Q   What is your name?                                  A    James W. Wilson.
Q   What is your age?                                     A    52.
Q   What is your post office address?
A   Turley.
Q   Are you a citizen by blood of the Cherokee Nation?
A   Yes sir.
Q   What is your wife's name?                        A    Minta Wilson.
Q   She is an applicant for enrollment as a citizen by intermarriage of the Cherokee Nation?
A   Yes sir.
Q   When were you and she married?
A   In 1875.
Q   Where were you married?                         A    In Joplin, Missouri.
Q   Were you living in Missouri at that time or were you just temporarily absent from the Cherokee Nation?
A   I had just gone there on a visit.
Q   How soon after your marriage did you and she remove to the Cherokee Nation?

A   It wasn't but a month or so; I don't know just exactly how long.

Q   By whom were you married up there?

A   I have forgotten the preacher's name.

Q   Did he give you a certificate?

A   No sir; we have no papers or record of anything at all.

Q   You were a recognized citizen of the Cherokee Nation at that time?

A   Yes sir.

Q   You haven't been readmitted to citizenship in the Cherokee Nation since then?

A   No sir.

Q   You were a recognized citizen when you married Minta Wilson?

A   Yes sir.

Q   Since your marriage to her have you and she continuously lived together as husband and wife?

A   Yes sir.

Q   And have resided in the Cherokee Nation?

A   Yes sir.

Q   Was she your first wife?       A   Yes sir.

Q   Were you her first husband?     A   Yes sir.

        Belle Rush being first duly sworn by John E. Tidwell, Notary Public, testified as follows:

Q   What is your name?          A   Belle Rush.

Q   What is your age?            A   58.

Q   What is your post office address?

A   Muskogee.

Q   Do you know a person by the name of Minta Wilson?

A   Yes sir.

Q   What is her husband's name?    A   James W. Wilson.

Q   He is a Cherokee by blood?      A   Yes sir.

Q   She is a white woman?         A   Yes sir.

Q   When were they married?

A   Along about the spring of '75.

Q   Where were they living at the time they were married?

A   They were married in Missouri. He was living with me on Grand River. He is my brother.

Q   What time in the year 1875 were they married?

A   Along about February sometime.

Q   Was he a recognized citizen of the Cherokee Nation at that time?

A   Yes sir.

Q   Had he ever been married previous to that time?

A   No sir.

Q   Was he her first husband?       A   Yes sir.

Q   Did they return to the Cherokee Nation after their marriage?

A   Yes sir.

Q   What time in the year?

A    I don't remember but it wasn't more than a month or two after they were married. They came right back home.

Q    You know of your own personal knowledge that since that time they have lived together as husband and wife?

A    Yes sir.

Q    And lived continuously in the Cherokee Nation?

A    Yes sir.

Q    James W. Wilson you say is your brother and was living with you at the time of his marriage?

A    Yes sir.

Q    You didn't witness the marriage?

A    No sir.

Q    But you have every reason to believe they were married and you are certain that it was in the early part of the year 1875?

A    Yes sir.

Q    You are also positive that James W. Wilson was a citizen by blood of the Cherokee Nation at the time he married her?

A    Yes sir.

---

The undersigned being first duly sworn states that as stenographer to the Commission to the Five Civilized Tribes, she recorded the testimony taken in this case and that the foregoing is a full, true and correct transcript of her stenographic notes thereof.

Myrtle Hill

Subscribed and sworn to before me this the 19th day of January, 1907.

John E. Tidwell<br/>Notary Public.

C. F. B.                                                   Cherokee 1151.

DEPARTMENT OF THE INTERIOR,<br/>COMMISSIONER TO THE FIVE CIVILIZED TRIBES.<br/>Muskogee, Indian Territory, February 15, 1907.

In the matter of the application for the enrollment of Minta Wilson as a citizen by intermarriage of the Cherokee Nation.

SUPPLEMENTAL.

Minta Wilson being first duly sworn by Walter W. Chappell, Notary Public, testified as follows:

# Cherokee Intermarried White 1906
## Volume X

| Q | What is your name? | A | Minta Wilson. |
| Q | What is your age? | A | 48. |

Q What is your post office address?
A Turley.
Q When were you married to your husband, James W. Wilson?
A 16th of February, 1875.

| Q | Where were you married? | A | In Joplin, Missouri. |
| Q | In what year? | A | In 1875. |

Q What time of the year?
A I don't know what time,-- 16th of February.
Q You were married then in February, 1875?
A Yes sir.
Q How soon after your marriage did you come to the Cherokee Nation?
A Why, we wasn't married very long until we come there; about a year I guess; I can't remember; it was about a month I guess after we was married before we moved away from there.
Q And you came to the Cherokee Nation?
A Yes sir.
Q Since your arrival in the Cherokee Nation, have you continuously resided in the Nation?
A Yes sir.
Q And have live continuously with James W. Wilson as his wife?
A Yes sir.
Q Your husband was a recognized citizen by blood of the Cherokee Nation when you married him?
A Yes sir.
Q You have no certificate to show your marriage?
A No sir; there wasn't none issued them days at all.
Q By whom were you married?
A I've forgot the man's name that married us; it has been so long.
Q Was he a Minister of the Gospel?
A Yes sir.

(Witness excused)

James W. Wilson being first duly sworn by Walter W. Chappell, Notary Public, testified as follows:

| Q | What is your name? | A | James W. Wilson. |
| Q | What is your age? | A | 53. |

Q What is your post office address?
A Turley.
Q You are the husband of Minta Wilson?
A Yes sir.
Q Where were you born?
A I was born here in the territory.

Q Were you born to the allegiance of the Cherokee Nation?
A Yes sir.
Q You have then, continuously since birth, been recognized as a citizen by blood of the Cherokee Nation?
A Yes sir.
Q When were you married to your wife, Minta Wilson?
A It was 1875.
Q What time of the year 1875?          A 16th of February.
Q Where [sic] you and she married?          A Joplin, Missouri.
Q Were you living in Joplin when you married her?
A No sir.
Q Your home was in the Cherokee Nation at that time, was it?
A Yes sir.
Q By whom were you married?
A Why, I can't tell you; it has been quite a long time ago; I as just simply married by a preacher but I don't remember his name.
Q Did he give you a certificate?
A No sir.
Q How long after your marriage before you and your wife removed to the Cherokee Nation?
A It was inside a month.
Q You came then, to the Cherokee Nation, right away after you were married?
A Yes sir.
Q And since that time you have continuously lived in the Cherokee Nation, have you?
A Yes sir.
Q And lived with your wife, Minta Wilson, as her husband?
A Yes sir.
Q How long had you been in Joplin, Missouri, just prior to your marriage to your wife, Minta Wilson?
A Not more than two or three weeks; just a short time.

BY MR. HASTINGS.

Q Where did you get acquainted with your wife?
A In Cooweescoowee District.
Q Did she live up at Joplin?
A No sir, she lived here and went from here there.
Q And you just went up there and married her?
A Yes sir; and came back.

Q   How long had she been up in Joplin when you went up to marry her?
A   Not more than a month, I don't suppose.
Q   And you were living her and just went up there to get married and stayed up there two or three weeks and came back?
A   Yes sir.
Q   And that is all you ever lived in Joplin, Missouri?
A   Yes sir.

ON BEHALF OF COMMISSIONER.

Q   You are absolutely positive, are you, Mr. Wilson, that your marriage occurred in February, 1875?
A   Yes sir.

(Witness Excused)

--------------------------

The undersigned being first duly sworn states that as stenographer to the Commission to the Five Civilized Tribes, she recorded the testimony taken in this case and that the foregoing is a true and correct transcript of her stenographic notes thereof.

Myrtle Hill

Subscribed and sworn to before me this the 16th day of February, 1907.

Walter W. Chappell<br>Notary Public.

◇◇◇◇◇

E.C.M.                                                Cherokee 1151.

DEPARTMENT OF THE INTERIOR,

COMMISSIONER TO THE FIVE CIVILIZED TRIBES.
MUSKOGEE, I. T., FEBRUARY 26, 1907.

SUPPLEMENTAL:
      In the matter of the application for the enrollment of MINTA WILSON as a citizen by intermarriage of the Cherokee Nation.

BELLE RUSH, being first duly sworn by Walter W. Chappell, a Notary Public, testified as follows:

ON BEHALF OF THE COMMISSIONER:

Q   What is your name?   A  Belle Rush.
Q   What is your age?   A  58.
Q   What is your post office address?   A  Muskogee, I. T.
Q   Do you appear here today for the purpose of giving testimony relative to the right of Minta Wilson to enrollment as a citizen by intermarriage of the Cherokee Nation?   A  Yes sir.
Q   Did she receive a telegram requesting her to appear here today with witnesses?   A  Yes sir.
Q   Why did she not appear here?   A  She told me to come and see what was needed; I am the only witness.
Q   There is no one else living now who knew of their marriage?   A  No sir.
Q   It would be impossible for Minta Wilson to secure witnesses who could testify as to the date of her marriage?   A  Yes sir.
Q   She attempted to find some one, did she?   A  Yes sir, but there is no one living.
Q   She was married in Missouri?   A  Yes sir.
Q   They didn't get a certificate of marriage?   A  No sir.
Q   Were you present at their marriage?   A  No sir.
Q   But you knew when they were married?   A  Yes sir.
Q   When was it?   A  About the 16th of February, 1875.
Q   You can swear that they were married in February, or 1875?   A  Yes sir, they came right back home when they were married.
Q   When did you receive this telegram?   A  This morning.
Q   Didn't get it until this morning?   A  She sent it up here from Turley, and I got it this morning.
Q   Before coming, you made all effort to get some witnesses?   A  Yes sir, I studied up, but there is no one.

( Witness excused ).

-------------------------------------------------------------------------------

The undersigned, after being first duly sworn, states that as stenographer to the Commission to the Five Civilized Tribes, she correctly reported the above and foregoing testimony, and that the same is a full, true and complete transcript of her stenographic notes thereof.

Sarah Waters

Subscribed and sworn to before me this 26th day of February, 1907.

Frances R Lane
Notary Public.

◇◇◇◇◇

E C M                                                   Cherokee 1151.

## DEPARTMENT OF THE INTERIOR,

## COMMISSIONER TO THE FIVE CIVILIZED TRIBES.

---

In the matter of the application for the enrollment of MINTA WILSON as a citizen by intermarriage of the Cherokee Nation.

## D E C I S I O N

THE RECORDS OF THIS OFFICE SHOW:   That at Salisaw, Indian Territory, August 9, 1900 application was received by the Commission to the Five Civilized Tribes for the enrollment of Minta Wilson as a citizen by intermarriage of the Cherokee Nation. Further proceedings in the matter of said application were had at Muskogee, Indian Territory, October 27, 1902, January 14, 1907 and February 15, 1907.

THE EVIDENCE IN THIS CASE SHOWS:   That the applicant herein, Minta Wilson, a white woman, was married February 16, 1875 to her husband, James W. Wilson, who was at the time of said marriage a recognized citizen by blood of the Cherokee Nation, who is identified on the Cherokee authenticated tribal roll of 1880, Cooweescoowee District No. 3339 as a native Cherokee, and whose name is included on the approved partial roll of citizens by blood of the Cherokee Nation opposite No. 3167. It is further shown that from the time of said marriage the said James W. Wilson and Minta Wilson resided together as husband and wife and continuously lived in the Cherokee Nation up to and including September 1, 1902.  Said applicant is identified in the Cherokee authenticated tribal roll of 1880 and the Cherokee census roll of 1896 as an intermarried citizen of the Cherokee Nation.

IT IS, THEREFORE, ORDERED AND ADJUDGED:   That in accordance with the decision of the Supreme Court of the United States, dated November 5, 1906, in the cases of Daniel Red Bird, et al. vs. the United States, Nos. 125, 126, 127, and 128, the said applicant, Minta Wilson is entitled, under the provisions of Section Twenty-one of the Act of Congress approved June 28, 1898 (30 Stats. 495), to enrollment as a citizen by intermarriage of the Cherokee Nation and her application for enrollment as such is accordingly granted.

Tams Bixby
Commissioner.

Dated at Muskogee, Indian Territory,
this     FEB 27 1907

◇◇◇◇◇

Cherokee 1151.

E C M                                    Muskogee, Indian Territory, February 22, 1907.

SPECIAL.

     Minta Wilson,
          Turley, Indian Territory.

     Dear Madam:

        The Commission sent you this day a telegram as follows:

        "Intermarried case incomplete.  Produce witnesses to
establish your marriage".

        The Act of Congress approved April 26, 1906 provides that the Secretary of the Interior shall have no jurisdiction to approve the enrollment of any person as a citizen of the Cherokee Nation after March 4, 1907.  This matter, therefore, demands your immediate attention.

                Respectfully,

                     Commissioner.

GHC

◇◇◇◇◇

Cherokee                                    COPY
  1151.

             Muskogee, Indian Territory, February 27, 1907.

W. W. Hastings,
     Attorney for the Cherokee Nation,
          Muskogee, Indian Territory.

Dear Sir:

        There is enclosed herewith a copy of the decision of the Commissioner to the Five Civilized Tribes, dated February 27, 1907, granting the application for the enrollment of Minta Wilson, as a citizen by intermarriage of the Cherokee Nation.

                Respectfully,

                SIGNED *Tams Bixby*
                     Commissioner.

Encl. C-39
  LMC

◇◇◇◇◇

Cherokee
1151.

Muskogee, Indian Territory, February 27, 1907.

The Commissioner to the Five Civilized Tribes,
Muskogee, Indian Territory.

Sir:

Receipt is acknowledged of the testimony and of your decision enrolling Minta Wilson, as an intermarried citizen of the Cherokee Nation. Time for protesting said decision is waived, and I consent that said person may be placed upon the schedule immediately.

Respectfully,

W. W. Hastings
Attorney for Cherokee Nation.

◇◇◇◇◇

Cherokee
1151.

COPY

Muskogee, Indian Territory, February 27, 1907.

Minta Wilson,
Turley, Indian Territory.

Dear Madam:

There is enclosed herewith a copy of the decision of the Commissioner to the Five Civilized Tribes, dated February 27, 1907, granting your application for enrollment as an intermarried citizen of the Cherokee Nation.

You will be advised when your name has been placed upon a schedule of citizens of the Cherokee Nation and approved by the Secretary of the Interior.

Respectfully,

SIGNED *Tams Bixby*
Commissioner.

Encl. C-38
LMC

◇◇◇◇◇

Form No. 1.

## THE WESTERN UNION TELEGRAPH COMPANY.
### INCORPORATED
### 23,000 OFFICES IN AMERICA.    CABLE SERVICE TO ALL THE WORLD.

This Company TRANSMITS and DELIVERS messages only on conditions limiting its liability, which have been assented to by the sender of the following message. Errors can be guarded against only by repeating a message back to the sending station for comparison, and the Company will not hold itself liable for errors or delays in transmission or delivery of Unrepeated Messages, beyond the amount of tolls paid thereon, nor in any case where the claim is not presented in writing within sixty days after the message is filed with the Company for transmission.
This is an UNREPEATED MESSAGE, and is delivered by request of the sender, under the conditions named above.
ROBERT C. CLOWRY, President and General Manager.

| NUMBER | SENT BY | REC'D BY | | CHECK |
|--------|---------|----------|--|-------|

RECEIVED at _____                    190

Dated _____

To _____

*(Copy of original document from case.)*

◇◇◇◇◇

Form No. 2.

## THE WESTERN UNION TELEGRAPH COMPANY.
### INCORPORATED
### 24,000 OFFICES IN AMERICA.    CABLE SERVICE TO ALL THE WORLD.
ROBERT C. CLOWRY, President and General Manager.

| Receiver's No. | Time Filed | Check |
|----------------|------------|-------|

**SEND** the following message subject to the terms on back hereof, which are hereby agreed to.    Muskogee, I.T., January 23, 190 7

To    Minta Wilson,

Turley, Indian Territory.

You are directed to appear before the Commissioner immediately with witnesses to establish the date of your marriage.

BIXBY

O.B.G R.                                    Commissioner.

☞ READ THE NOTICE AND AGREEMENT ON BACK. ☜

*(Copies of original documents from case.)*

Form No. 168. 31. T.

# THE WESTERN UNION TELEGRAPH COMPANY.
### — INCORPORATED —
### 24,000 OFFICES IN AMERICA. CABLE SERVICE TO ALL THE WORLD.

This Company TRANSMITS and DELIVERS messages only on conditions limiting its liability, which have been assented to by the sender of the following message. Errors can be guarded against only by repeating a message back to the sending station for comparison, and the Company will not hold itself liable for errors or delays in transmission or delivery of Unrepeated Messages, beyond the amount of tolls paid thereon, nor in any case where the claim is not presented in writing within sixty days after the message is filed with the Company for transmission. This is an UNREPEATED MESSAGE, and is delivered by request of the sender, under the conditions named above.
ROBERT C. CLOWRY, President and General Manager.

**RECEIVED at**
48 KS CY E 315 p m,

Muskogee, I.T.

Yours 23rd 26 paid  Minta Wilson signed Bixby Commissioner undelivered

Party lives four miles in country  from Turley have mailed copy.

Owasso,  I.T. Jan. 24

**MONEY TRANSFERRED BY TELEGRAPH.**                    **CABLE OFFICE.**

◇◇◇◇◇

Form No. 1511.        # NIGHT MESSAGE.
# THE WESTERN UNION TELEGRAPH COMPANY.
### — INCORPORATED —
### 24,000 OFFICES IN AMERICA.    CABLE SERVICE TO ALL THE WORLD.
ROBERT C. CLOWRY, President and General Manager.

| Receiver's No. | Time Filed | Check |
|---|---|---|
| | | Cherokee No.1151.     ECM |

**SEND** the following night message subject to the terms on back hereof, which are hereby agreed to.

February 22, 1907.

Minta Wilson,

Turley, Indian Territory.

Intermarried case incomplete.  Produce witnesses to

establish your marriage.

BIXBY,

Commissioner.

O.B.G.R.  Paid.

☞ READ THE NOTICE AND AGREEMENT ON BACK. ☜

*(Copy of original document from case.)*

**Cher IW 276**

◇◇◇◇◇

(jacket missing)

---

**Cher IW 277**

◇◇◇◇◇

C.E.W.

## DEPARTMENT OF THE INTERIOR,
## COMMISSIONER TO THE FIVE CIVILIZED TRIBES.

---

In the matter of the application for the enrollment of

### CHARLES BRAY

as a citizen by intermarriage of the Cherokee Nation.

---

Cherokee 1907.

◇◇◇◇◇

## DEPARTMENT OF THE INTERIOR.
## COMMISSION TO THE FIVE CIVILIZED TRIBES.
## FT. GIBSON, I. T., AUGUST 24th, 1900.

IN THE MATTER OF THE APPLICATION OF Charles Bray and son, for enrollment as citizens of the Cherokee Nation, and he being sworn by Commissioner, C. R. Breckinridge, testified as follows:

Q What is your full name?   A  Charles Bray.
Q What is your age?   A  Sixty eight.
Q What is your Postoffice?   A  Bennett.
Q What is your District?   A  Canadian.
Q For whom do you apply for enrollment?   A  Myself and son, George.
Q Have you a wife?   A  She is dead.
Q How old is he?   A  Twenty one.
  He will have to apply for himself.
Q Do you apply as a Cherokee by blood?   A  No sir.
Q Intermarried?   A  Yes sir.
Q When were you married?   A  1869.
Q When did your wife die?   A  In 1888.

115

# Cherokee Intermarried White 1906
## Volume X

Q  What was your wifes[sic] name?    A  Jane C. Bray; her maiden name was Jane C. Berthold.
Q  Have you ever married since your wife die[sic]?    A  No sir.
Q  What is the name of your father[sic]    A  Enoch Bray.
Q  He was a white man?    A  Yes sir.
Q  Is he dead?    A  Yes sir.
Q  Has he been dead over twenty years?    A  He has been dead forty eight years.
Q  What is the name of your mother?    A  Susan Bray.
Q  White woman?    A  Yes sir.
Q  Dead?    A  Yes sir.
Q  Been dead over twenty years?    A  Been dead fifty years.
Q  Have you lived in the Cherokee Nation since 1880?    A  Yes sir.
Q  You are on the roll of 1880, are you?    A  Yes sir.
Q  What District were you enrolled in then?    A  Canadian District)[sic]
Q  In Canadian District in 1896?    A  Yes sir.
(Applicant identified on the roll of 1880, Page 5, #137, Chas. Bray, Canadian District)
(1896 Roll, Page 85, #22, Charles Bray, Canadian District)

The applicant is duly identified on the rolls of 1880, and 1896, as a Cherokee by adoption; he has lived in the Cherokee Nation ever since his enrollment in 1880; he has never remarried since his wifes[sic] death in 1888; and he will now be listed for enrollment as a Cherokee by ~~blood~~ adoption.

The undersigned, being sworn, states that as stenographer to the Commission to the Five Civilized Tribes, he correctly recorded the testimony and proceedings in this case, and that the foregoing is a true and complete transcript of his stenographic notes thereof.

R R Cravens

Subscribed and sworn to before
me this 5th day of September, 1900.

T B Needles

C O M M I S S I O N E R .

◇◇◇◇◇

ILLINOIS
Statement of Applicant Taken Under Oath.

## CHEROKEES BY BLOOD AND ADOPTION.

GP.

Name *Charles Bray, Senr, &c*     Date *August 24th* 1900.

District    CANADIAN.    Year *1882*   Page *5*   No. *137*

Citizen by blood *No*    Mother's citizenship *Sally M. Church Bray - White d*

Intermarried citizen *Yes*    Parents *person*   

Married under what law    Date of marriage *1889*

License    Certificate

Wife's name

District    Year   Page   No.

Citizen by blood    Mother's citizenship

Intermarried citizen

Married under what law    Date of marriage

License    Certificate

Names of Children:

| | Dist. | Year | Page | No. | Age |
|---|---|---|---|---|---|
| | Dist. | Year | Page | No. | Age |
| | Dist. | Year | Page | No. | Age |
| | Dist. | Year | Page | No. | Age |
| | Dist. | Year | Page | No. | Age |
| | Dist. | Year | Page | No. | Age |
| | Dist. | Year | Page | No. | Age |
| | Dist. | Year | Page | No. | Age |
| | Dist. | Year | Page | No. | Age |
| | Dist. | Year | Page | No. | Age |

* On 1882 Roll as Chas, Bray

*(Copy of original document from case.)*

◇◇◇◇◇

Cherokee 1907.

Department of the Interior.
Commission to the Five Civilized Tribes.
Muskogee, I. T., October 7, 1902.

In the matter of the application of Charles Bray for the enrollment of himself as a citizen by intermarriage of the Cherokee Nation: he being sworn and examined by the Commission, testified as follows:

Q   What is your name?   A   Charles Bray.

Q   What is your age at this time?   A   Seventy years old.

Q   What is your postoffice?   A   Bennett.

Q   Are you the same Charles Bray that made application to this Commission?   A   Yes sir, at Fort Gibson.

Q   For enrollment as an intermarried citizen of the Cherokee Nation on August 24, 1900?   A   Yes sir, I am the man.

Q   What is your wife's name?   A   Jane C.

Q   Was she a Cherokee by blood?   A   Yes sir.

Q   Is she living or dead?   A   She is dead.

Q   When did she die?   A   She died in '88 I believe.

Q   When were you and she married?   A   In '69.

Q   Married under a Cherokee license in '69?   A   Yes sir.

Q   Were you ever married prior to your marriage to that wife?   A   No sir.

Q   Was she ever married before she married you?   A   No sir.

Q   You her first husband and she your first wife?   A   Yes sir.

Q   Have you ever married any other woman since her death?   A   No sir.

Q   Did you live with her from the time of your marriage until the time she died?   A   Yes sir.

Q   You are still a widower and were a widower on the first day of September, 1902?   A   Yes sir.

Q   You never married any other woman except your wife, Jane C.?   A   That is all.

Q   Have you lived in the Cherokee Nation ever since 1880?   A   Yes sir.

Q   Never lived out of the nation since 1880?   A   No sir.

----------------------------------

The undersigned, being duly sworn, states that as stenographer to the Commission to the Five Civilized Tribes he correctly recorded the testimony and proceedings in this case, and that the foregoing is a true and correct transcript of his stenographic notes thereof.

E.G. Rothenberger

Subscribed and sworn to before me this 1st day of November, 1902.

B C Jones
Notary Public.

◇◇◇◇◇

DEPARTMENT OF THE INTERIOR.
## COMMISSION TO THE FIVE CIVILIZED TRIBES.

———

In the matter of the death of **Charles Bray**
a citizen of the **Cherokee (Intermarried)** Nation, who formerly resided at or near
**Bennett** , Ind. Ter., and died on the **20** day of **June** , **1904**

———

### AFFIDAVIT OF RELATIVE.

UNITED STATES OF AMERICA, INDIAN TERRITORY,
**Western** DISTRICT.

I, **George R Bray** , on oath state that I am **27** years of age and
a citizen by **Blood** , of the **Cherokee** Nation; that my postoffice address is **Warner** ,
Ind. Ter.; that I am **Son** of **Charles Bray** who was a citizen, by **Intermarriage** ,
of the **Cherokee** Nation and that said **Charles Bray** died on the **20th** day of
**June** , **1904**

**George R Bray**

Witnesses To Mark:

Subscribed and sworn to before me this **1** day of **October** , 1906

**B.P. Rasmus**
Notary Public.

———

### AFFIDAVIT OF ACQUAINTANCE.

UNITED STATES OF AMERICA, INDIAN TERRITORY,
**Western** DISTRICT.

I, **Bird Doublehead** , on oath state that I am **60** years of age, and a citizen
by **Blood** of the **Cherokee** Nation; that my postoffice address is **Warner** , Ind. Ter.;
that I was personally acquainted with **Charles Bray** who was a citizen, by
**Intermarriage** , of the **Cherokee** Nation; and that said **Charles Bray** died on the
**20** day of **June** , 1904
his
**Bird x Doublehead**
mark

Witnesses To Mark:
**Chas. R. Fillmore**
**I. N. Ury**

Subscribed and sworn to before me this  **1**  day of  **October**  , 1906

**B.P. Rasmus**
Notary Public.

L.G.D.                                                                 Cherokee 1907

## DEPARTMENT OF THE INTERIOR,
## COMMISSIONER TO THE FIVE CIVILIZED TRIBES.
## MUSKOGEE, IND. TER. JANUARY 3, 1907.

In the matter of the application of CHARLES BRAY for enrollment as a citizen by intermarriage of the Cherokee Nation.

Applicant represented by George R. Bray:

APPEARANCES:

Cherokee Nation not represented:

GEORGE R. BRAY being first duly sworn, testified as follows:

ON BEHALF OF COMMISSIONER:

Q. What is your name?    A. George R. Bray.
Q. How old are you?    A. Twenty-seven years old.
Q. What is your postoffice address?    A. Warner.
Q. You appear here to-day in behalf of Charles Bray?    A. Yes sir.
Q. Did he claim to be a citizen by intermarriage of the Cherokee Nation? A. Yes sir.
Q. Through whom did he claim that right?    A. He married Jane C. Bertholf.
Q. Is he living or dead?    A. He is dead.
Q. When did he die?    A. June 20, 1904.
Q. When did he marry her?    A. July 21, 1869.
Q. Where?    A. Why, it was at William F McIntosh's house.
Q. In the Cherokee Nation?    A. No, in the Creek Nation.
Q. Was he married under Cherokee law?    A Yes sir.
Q. Did he get a Cherokee license?    A. Yes sir.
Q. Have you a copy of that license?    A. No sir.
Q. Where is it?    A. I don't know sir; I don't know whether the Commission has it here, or whether he lost it, or where it is, what did become of it.
Q. Did you ever see it?    A. No, I don't believe I ever did; I heard him say a long time ago that he got it.
Q. Where did he get that license; in what District?
A. I think it was in Canadian District.
Q. What relation are you to Charles Bray?    A. I am his son.
Q. You are a citizen by blood of the Cherokee Nation?    A. Yes sir.
Q. Is your mother living or dead?    A. Dead.

120

Q. When did she die?    A. She died January 13, 1888.

Q. Did your father ever marry again after her death in 1888?    A. No sir.

Q. Was he living with your mother at the time of her death in 1888?
A. Yes sir.

Q. Did they live together continuously as husband and wife, in the Cherokee Nation, from the time of their marriage until the time of her death?    [sic] Yes sir.

Q. Did they ever separate?    A. No sir.

Q. Was your mother ever married before she married your father, or do you know?
A. No sir, she was not.

Q. Was your father ever married before he married her?    A. No sir.

It appears from the records of this office that Charles Bray is identified on the 1880 roll, Canadian District, opposite No. 137, he being listed on Census card No. 1907.

Q. It will be necessary for you to furnish this office proof of the fact that your father was married to your mother according to Cherokee law, in 1869, and that your mother was at that time a recognized citizen by blood of the Cherokee Nation.

-------------------------------------------

The undersigned, being first duly sworn, states that as stenographer to the Commission to the Five Civilized Tribes she correctly recorded the testimony had in this case, and that the above and foregoing is a full, true and correct transcript of her stenographic notes thereof.

Lucy M. Bowman

Subscribed and sworn to before me this 4th day of January, 1907.

John E. Tidwell
Notary Public.

◇◇◇◇◇

*(The Affidavit below was originally handwritten on the microfilm and is typed as given.)*

Warner, Ind Ter
Jan 19th, 1907

John R Bertholf aged 53, on oath states that he was acquainted with Jane C Bertholf ever since he was a little child, also that he knew of her marriage to Charles Bray in 1869, and that she was a recognized citizen of the Cherokee Nation.

John R Bertholf

Subscribed and sworn to before me, a Notary Public for and in the Western District, Indian Territory this 19th day of Jan., 1907.

> Edmund J. Sapper
> Notary Public.
> My commission expires
> June 19th 1909.

◇◇◇◇◇

*(The Affidavit below was originally handwritten on the microfilm and is typed as given.)*

> Warner, Ind Ter
> Jan 18th, 1907

W. G. Fields, aged 60, on oath states that he was acquainted with Jane C Bertholf ever since 1866 also that he knew of her marriage to Charles Bray in 1869 and that she was a recognized citizen of the Cherokee Nation

> W G Fields

Subscribed and sworn to before me a Notary Public for and in the Western District of Indian Territory this 18th day of January 1907.

> Edmund J. Sapper
> Notary Public.
> My commission expires
> June 19th 1909.

◇◇◇◇◇

C. F. B.                                                      Cherokee 1907.

DEPARTMENT OF THE INTERIOR,
COMMISSIONER TO THE FIVE CIVILIZED TRIBES.
Muskogee, Indian Territory, January 25, 1907.

In the matter of the application for the enrollment of Charles Bray as a citizen by intermarriage of the Cherokee Nation.

SUPPLEMENTAL.

APPEARANCES:  Walter G. Fields for applicant.

Cherokee Nation represented by
W. W. Hastings, Attorney.

Walter G. Fields being first duly sworn by John E. Tidwell, Notary Public, testified as follows:

122

ON BEHALF OF COMMISSIONER.

| | | | |
|---|---|---|---|
| Q | What is your name? | A | Walter G. Fields. |
| Q | What is your age? | A | 60 years. |

Q   What is your post office address?

A   Warner, Indian Territory.

Q   You appear here to-day for the purpose of giving testimony relative to the right to enrollment of Charles Bray, as a citizen by intermarriage of the Cherokee Nation?

A   Yes sir.

Q   When did you first become acquainted with Charles Bray?

A   In the latter part of the summer or early in the fall of '69.

Q   Is he living at this time?    A   No sir; he's dead.

Q   Did you meet him in the Cherokee Nation?

A   Yes sir; I first met him in the Cherokee Nation.

Q   Was he married at the time you became acquainted with him?

A   Yes sir.

Q   What was his wife's name?

A   Her name prior to her marriage to Mr. Bray was Jane Bertholf.

Q   Is she living now?                              A   No sir; she's dead.

Q   When did she die?

A   In '87 or '88 as well as I remember.

Q   When did Charles Bray die?

A   About 2 years ago if I remember right.

Q   Did you know the wife of Charles Bray before he married her?

A   Yes sir.

Q   Was she a recognized citizen by blood of the Cherokee Nation at the time of their marriage?

A   Yes sir.

Q   Had she ever been married before she married Charles Bray?

A   No sir.

Q   Was he ever married to your knowledge before he married her?

A   Not to my knowledge.

Q   From the time of their marriage, did they live together as husband and wife continuously until her death?

A   Yes sir; they did.

Q   You knew them as husband and wife, residing together in the Cherokee Nation from 1869 on up until the time of her death?

A   Yes sir; but there was a space of time that they left Canadian District and moved over to Tahlequah; in that time I never saw Mrs. Bray but I was at Tahlequah at different times during out councils and I would meet Mr. Bray there every time and we would talk about his family.

Q   You never heard that there was any separation?

A   No sir; then they moved back down in the neighborhood where I lived.

Q   Did Charles Bray marry after her death?

A   No sir.

Q   Do you know of your own personal knowledge that Charles Bray has resided continuously in the Cherokee Nation since 1869?
A   Yes sir.
Q   If he ever has been out, you don't know it?
A   No sir; I don't know it; he was over at Tahlequah a few year but after he came back to Canadian District, I know he wasn't.
Q   During all these years, has he been recognized as a citizen by intermarriage of the Cherokee Nation?
A   Yes sir.
Q   Exercised all the rights and enjoyed all the privileges of that class of citizens?
A   Yes sir; he did.


John R. Bertholf being first duly sworn by John E. Tidwell, Notary Public, testified as follows:

ON BEHALF OF COMMISSIONER.

Q   What is your name?              A   John R. Bertholf.
Q   What is your age?              A   53.
Q   What is your post office address?
A   Checotah.
Q   You were acquainted with Charles Bray during his lifetime?
A   Yes sir.
Q   When did you get acquainted with him?
A   I first remember seeing him just a short time after his marriage.
Q   When was he married?
A   I can't say positively but it was about 1869 as well as I remember.
Q   You were not present at the marriage?
A   No sir.
Q   You were living in the neighborhood?
A   Well, I was living about 20 miles from there as well as I remember.
Q   It was the common report that he was married about that time?
A   Yes sir.
Q   Did you know his wife?              A   Yes sir.
Q   What was her name?
A   Jane Bertholf was her maiden name.
Q   Was she related to you?              A   Yes sir.
Q   What relation?              A   First cousin.
Q   She was a recognized citizen by blood of the Cherokee Nation at the time of their marriage?
A   Yes sir.
Q   She is dead now?              A   Yes sir.
Q   When did she die?
A   She's been dead 18 or 19 years.

Q   From the time of their marriage, did they live together as husband and wife until the time of her death?

A   Yes sir.

Q   Has he married since her death?

A   No sir.

Q   Has he lived in the Cherokee Nation continuously since their marriage?

A   Yes sir.

Q   Has it always been your understanding that Charles Bray secured a license and married his wife in accordance with the law of the Cherokee Nation?

A   Yes sir; I was always under that impression.

Q   You have every reason to believe that he did?

A   Yes sir; that he was married according to the laws of the Cherokee Nation.

Q   You have known him continuously since the time of his marriage until the time of his death?

A   Yes sir.

Q   Since his marriage has he to your personal knowledge exercised all the rights and enjoyed all the privileges of a citizen by intermarriage of the Cherokee Nation?

A   Yes sir.

Q   His right as that class of citizen to your knowledge has never been questioned?

A   No sir; not that I know of.

Q   Was he ever married prior to his marriage to his wife, Jane Bertholf?

A   No sir; not that I heard of.

Q   Was she ever married prior to her marriage to him?

A   No sir.

The undersigned being first duly sworn states that as stenographer to the Commission to the Five Civilized Tribes, she recorded the testimony taken in this case and that the foregoing is a full, true and correct transcript of her stenographic notes thereof.

Myrtle Hill

Subscribed and sworn to before me this the 31st day of January, 1907.

B.P. Rasmus
Notary Public.

◇◇◇◇◇

C. E. W. Cherokee 1907.

## DEPARTMENT OF THE INTERIOR,

## COMMISSIONER TO THE FIVE CIVILIZED TRIBES.

---------------------------

In the matter of the application for the enrollment of Charles Bray, as a citizen by intermarriage of the Cherokee Nation.

## D E C I S I O N

THE RECORDS OF THIS OFFICE SHOW: That at Fort Gibson, Indian Territory, August 24, 1900, application was received by the Commission to the Five Civilized Tribes for the enrollment of Charles Bray as a citizen by intermarriage of the Cherokee Nation. Further proceedings in the matter of said application were had at Muskogee, Indian Territory, October 7, 1902, and January 3 and 25, 1907.

THE EVIDENCE IN THIS CASE SHOWS: That the applicant herein, Charles Bray, a white man, was married in accordance with Cherokee law July 21, 1869, to one Jane Bray, nee Bertholf, since deceased, who at the time of said marriage was a recognized citizen by blood of the Cherokee Nation, whose name appears upon the Cherokee authenticated tribal roll of 1880, Canadian District, Page 5, No. 138; that since the time of said marriage the said Charles Bray and Jane Bray resided together as husband and wife and continuously lived in the Cherokee Nation until her death which occurred January 13, 1888; that since the time of said death the said Charles Bray has not married and continuously lived in the Cherokee Nation up to and including September 1, 1902. The applicant is identified upon the Cherokee authenticated tribal roll of 1880 and the Cherokee census roll of 1896 as an intermarried citizen of the Cherokee Nation.

IT IS, THEREFORE, ORDERED AND ADJUDGED: That in accordance with the decision of the Supreme Court of the United States, dated November 5, 1906, in the cases of Daniel Red Bird, et al., vs. the United States, Nos. 125, 126, 127, and 128, the said applicant, Charles Bray, is entitled under the provisions of Section 21 of the Act of Congress approved June 28, 1898 (30 Stats., 495), to enrollment as a citizen by intermarriage of the Cherokee Nation and his application for enrollment as such is accordingly granted.

Tams Bixby
Commissioner.

Dated at Muskogee, Indian Territory,
this    FEB 28 1907

◇◇◇◇◇

Cherokee
1907

Muskogee, Indian Territory, December 27, 1906.

George R. Gray,
Warner, Indian Territory.

Dear Sir:

November 6, 1906, the United States Supreme Court held that white persons who intermarried with Cherokee citizens according to Cherokee law prior to November 1, 1875, are entitled to enrollment and allotments of land as citizens of the Cherokee Nation.

You are advised that to properly determine the right of your deceased father, Charles Bray, to enrollment as a citizen by intermarriage of the Cherokee Nation, it will be necessary for you to appear before the Commissioner for the purpose of giving testimony as to the date of his marriage and whether or not his wife, by reason of his marriage to whom he claims the right to enrollment as a citizen by intermarriage of the Cherokee Nation, was a recognized Cherokee citizen at the time of his marriage to her, and whether or not he was married to her in accordance with Cherokee laws.

You are, therefore, directed to appear before the Commissioner at Muskogee, Indian Territory, at 9 o'clock A. M., on Thursday, January 3, 1907, and give testimony as above indicated.

Respectfully,

JMH

Acting Commissioner.

◇◇◇◇◇

Form No. 2.

## THE WESTERN UNION TELEGRAPH COMPANY.
------ INCORPORATED ------
### 24,000 OFFICES IN AMERICA.    CABLE SERVICE TO ALL THE WORLD.
ROBERT C. CLOWRY, President and General Manager.

| Receiver's No. | Time Filed | Check |
|---|---|---|
|  |  |  |

SEND the following message subject to the terms on back hereof, which are hereby agreed to.

Muskogee, Indian Territory,
January 19, 1907.        190

To    George R. Bray,

Warner, Indian Territory.

You are directed to appear before the Commissioner immediately with witnesses to establish the marriage of your parents.

Tams Bixby,

Commissioner.

O.B.G.R.

☞ READ THE NOTICE AND AGREEMENT ON BACK. ☜

*(Copy of original document from case.)*

◇◇◇◇◇

Cherokee 1907                    COPY

Muskogee, Indian Territory, February 28, 1907.

W. W. Hastings,
      Attorney for the Cherokee Nation,
         Muskogee, Indian Territory.

Dear Sir:

      There is enclosed herewith a copy of the decision of the Commissioner to the Five Civilized Tribes, dated February 28, 1907, granting the application for the enrollment of Charles Bray as a citizen by intermarriage of the Cherokee Nation.

Respectfully,

SIGNED *James Bixby*

Enc I-33                    Commissioner.

RPI

◇◇◇◇◇

Cherokee 1907

Muskogee, Indian Territory, February 28, 1907.

The Commissioner to the Five Civilized Tribes,
      Muskogee, Indian Territory.

Sir:

      Receipt is acknowledged of the testimony and of your decision enrolling Charles Bray as a citizen by intermarriage of the Cherokee Nation. Time for protesting said decision is waived and I consent that said person may be placed upon the schedule immediately.

Respectfully,
W. W. Hastings
Attorney for the Cherokee Nation.

◇◇◇◇◇

128

Cherokee 1907.

COPY

Muskogee, Indian Territory, February 28, 1907.

Charles Bray,
   Bennett, Indian Territory.

Dear sir[sic]:

There is enclosed herewith a copy of the decision of the Commissioner to the Five Civilized Tribes, dated February 28, 1907, granting the application for your enrollment as a citizen by intermarriage of the Cherokee Nation.

You will be advised when your name has been placed upon a schedule of citizens of the Cherokee Nation and approved by the Secretary of the Interior.

Respectfully,

SIGNED *Jams Bixby*

Enc. I-34
Commissioner.

RPI

---

**Cher IW 278**

◇◇◇◇◇

DEPARTMENT OF THE INTERIOR,<br>COMMISSION TO THE FIVE CIVILIZED TRIBES.<br>VINITA, I. T., SEPTEMBER 18th, 1900.

IN THE MATTER OF THE APPLICATION OF Daniel K. Wetzel, wife and child, for enrollment as citizens of the Cherokee Nation, and he being sworn by Commissioner, T.B. Needles, testified as follows:

Q What is your name?   A Daniel K. Wetzel.
Q What is your age?   A Fifty nine.
Q What is your Postoffice?   A Maysville, Arkansas.
Q What district do you live in?   A Delaware.
Q Are you a recognized citizen of the Cherokee Nation?   A Yes sir.
Q By blood or intermarriage?   A Intermarriage.
Q Your father and mother are non citizens?   A Yes sir.
Q What is the name of your wife?   A Martha A. McDonald; Wetzel now.
Q For whom do you apply for enrollment?   A My wife and daughter.
Q Do you apply for yourself?   A Yes sir.
Q What is your wifes[sic] fathers[sic] name?   A Collins McDonald.
Q Is he living?   A No sir.
Q Was he a Cherokee citizen by blood?   A Yes sir.

Q What degree of blood do you claim for your wife?
A About one eighth.
Q What is her age?    A Sixty; born in 1840.
Q When did you marry her according to Cherokee law?    A About 1871.
Q Is her name upon the authenticated roll of 1880?    A Yes sir.
Q Your name also?    A Yes sir.
Q Do you desire to enroll any children?    A One; I have four grand children; my son and his wife are both dead.
Q Do you want to enroll any children of your own?    A Yes sir; one.
Q What is its name?    A Lou Wetzel.
Q How old is she?    A Twenty two.
Q You have no children of your own under twenty one years of age?
A No sir/[sic]
Q All over twenty one?    A Yes sir.
Q What are the names of your grand children?    A Claud C. Wetzel.
Q How old is Claud C.?  A He is right at thirteen.
Q Next one?    A Ida May Wetzel.
Q How old?    A Eleven.
Q The next one?    A Oliver K. Wetzel., he is right at nine years old.
Q Next one?    A Edwin; six years old.
Q Are these children all living and living with you?    A Yes sir.
Q What is their father's name?    A Charles Wetzel.
Q Is he living?    A No sir.
Q Was he upon the roll of 1880?    A Yes sir.
Q What is their mother's name?    A Orlena Wetzel.
Q Was she a citizen by blood?    A No sir.
Q White woman?    A Yes sir.
Q Was Charles Wetzel a citizen by blood?    A Yes sir.
Q Have you any proof of the marriage between Charles, your son, and the mother of these children?    A No sir; none with me
    (1880 Roll, Page 497, #2136, D. Wetzel, Going Snake District)
    (1880 Roll, Page 497, #2137, Martha Wetzel, Going Snake Dis't)
    (1896 Roll, Page 593, #572, Daniel K. Wetzel, Delaware Dis't)
    (1896 Roll, Page 558, #3589, Martha Wetzel, Delaware Dis't)
    (1880 Roll, Page 497, #2139, Charley Wetzel, Going Snake Dis't)
Q Was Charley Wetzel's wife a citizen by blood?    A No sir.
Q But Charles mother, Martha Wetzel, was a Cherokee by blood?
A Yes sir.
    (1896 Roll, Page 558, #3591, Claude Wetzel, Delaware District)
    (1896 Roll, Page 558, #3592, Ida Wetzel, Delaware District)
    (1896 Roll, Page 558, #3593, Oliver Wetzel, Delaware District)
    (1896 Roll, Page 558, #3594, Eddie Wetzel, Delaware District)
Q Did the father and mother of these children die before 1896?
A Yes sir.
Q Are these children living, and living with you now?    A Yes sir.

Q  Have you any proof of the marriage between your son, Charles Wetzel, who was a Cherokee citizen by blood, and his wife, Orlena, who was a white person?    A  No sir; not now.

Q  You have no certificate of marriage, have you?    A  No sir.

The name of Daniel K. Wetzel and his wife, Martha Wetzel, appears upon the authenticated roll of 1880, as well as the census roll of 1896, and they being duly identified according to the page and number of the rolls, as indicated in the testimony, and having made satisfactory proof of their residence, the said Daniel K. Wetzel will be duly listed for enrollment as a Cherokee citizen by intermarriage; and his wife, Martha Wetzel, as a Cherokee citizen by blood.

David W. Harrison, being called and sworn, testified as follows:

Q  What is your name?    A  Harrison.

Q  Your first name?    A  David W.

Q  What is your age?    A  Fifty seven.

Q  What is your Postoffice?    A  Bluejacket.

Q  Are you a recognized citizen of the Cherokee Nation?    A  Yes sir.

Q  Did you know Charles Wetzel in his life time?    A  Yes sir.

Q  Did you know his wife, Orlena?    A  Yes sir.

Q  Do you know whether they were married or not?    A  They lived together as man and wife;  I was not at their wedding.

Q  Did they live together as man and wife until their death?
A  Yes sir.

Q  Were they recognized in the neighborhood as man and wife?
A  Yes sir.

Q  You did not see them married?    A  No sir.

Applicant recalled:

Satisfactory proof having been made of the marriage of Charles Wetzel and Orlena Petty, a white person, and the names of his children, Claud C. Wetzel, Ida May Wetzel, Oliver Wetzel and Eddie Wetzel, appearing on the census roll of 1896, and being duly identified as the chidren[sic] of Charles Wetzel, whose name appears on the authenticated roll of 1880, they will be duly listed for enrollment by this Commission as Cherokee citizens by blood.

---

The undersigned, being sworn, states that as stenographer to the Commission to the Five Civilized Tribes, he correctly recorded the testimony and proceedings in this case, and that the foregoing is a true and complete transcript of his stenographic notes thereof.

                                                  R R Cravens

Subscribed and sworn to before me
this 20th day of September, 1900.                TB Needles
                                                  C O M M I S S I O N E R .

# Cherokee Intermarried White 1906
## Volume X

JOR.
Cher. 2973.

Department of the Interior.
Commission to the Five Civilized Tribes.
Tahlequah, I. T., October 24, 1902.

SUPPLEMENTAL TESTIMONY in the matter of the application for the enrollment of DANIEL K. WETZEL as a citizen by intermarriage of the Cherokee Nation.

DANIEL K. WETZEL, being first duly sworn, and being examined, testified as follows:

BY COMMISSION: What is your name?    A  Daniel K. Wetzel.
Q  How old are you?    A  Sixty-two.
Q  What is your post office address?    A  Mayesville, Arkansas.
Q  You are a white man, are you?    A  Yes sir.
Q  Have you heretofore made application to this Commission for enrollment as a citizen by intermarriage of the Cherokee Nation?
A    Yes sir.
Q  What is the name of your wife?    A  Martha Wetzel.
Q  Is she living?    A  Yes sir.
Q  Is she a Cherokee by blood?    A  Yes sir.
Q  Do you claim your right to enrollment by reason of your marriage to her?  A  Yes sir.
Q  When were you and she married?    A  We were married in the Nation. We came from the State, and then we were married in the Nation according to law about 1869.
Q  You were first married to her under state law, then married her according to Cherokee law in the Cherokee Nation in 1869?
A  Yes sir.
Q  Does your name appear upon the roll of 1880?    A  Yes sir.
Q  Were you ever married before you married your present wife?
A  No sir.
Q  Was she ever married before she married you?    A  No sir.
Q  You are her first husband and she is your first wife?    A  Yes sir
Q  Have you and she lived together continuously since your marriage?
A  Yes sir.
Q  Were you living together on the 1st day of September, 1902?
A  Yes sir.
Q  Never been separated at all?    A  No sir.
Q  Have you resided in the Cherokee Nation continuously since you married her?
A  Yes sir, never lived anywhere else.
Q  How long has your wife resided in the Cherokee Nation?    A  Since 1869.
Q  Continuously?    A  Yes sir.
Q  Neither one of you have been out for any purpose within the past four years?
A  No sir.
Q  You made application for the enrollment of some children, did you[sic]

132

A  Yes sir, grand children.
Q  How many?    A  Four.
Q  Are all of those children living at this time?    A  Yes sir.

This testimony will be filed with and made a part of the record in the matter of the application for the enrollment of Daniel K. Wetzel as a citizen by intermarriage of the Cherokee Nation, Cherokee straight card field No. 2973.

----------------

Wm. Hutchinson, being first duly sworn, states that as stenographer to the Commission to the Five Civilized Tribes he correctly recorded the testimony and proceedings in this case, and that the foregoing is a true and complete transcript of the stenographic notes thereof.

Wm Hutchinson

Subscribed and sworn to before me this 12th day of November, 1902.

BC Jones N.P.

◇◇◇◇◇

JOR                                                                           Cherokee 2973.

DEPARTMENT OF THE INTERIOR,
COMMISSION TO THE FIVE CIVILIZED TRIBES,
CHEROKEE LAND OFFICE.
Tahlequah, I. T., June 1, 1905.

---

In the matter of the application of Daniel K. Wetzel for the enrollment of himself as a citizen by intermarriage, and his wife, Martha, and grand-children, Claud C., Ida May, Oliver K., and Edwin Wetzel, as citizens by blood of the Cherokee Nation. No. 2973.

---

DANIEL K. WETZEL, being duly sworn by J. O. Rosson, a Notary Public, and examined by the Commission, testified as follows:---

Q    What is your name?    A  Daniel K. Wetzel's the way its[sic] on the roll.
Q    How old are you?    A  I'm 64 years old.
Q    What is your post-office?    A  Maysville, Arkansas.
Q    You are an intermarried citizen of the Cherokee Nation?    A  Yes sir.
Q    Your wife [sic] named Martha?    A  Yes sir.
Q    She's living?    A  Yes sir.
Q    You applied for the enrollment of some grand-children, Claud C., Ida May, Oliver K. and Edwin Wetzel, did you?    A  Yes sir.

Q   Are they all living?   A  Yes sir.

Q   Is their father your son?   A  Yes sir.

Q   What is his name?   A  Charley Wetzel.

Q   Did he have a middle name?   A  Yes sir. I think it was Charley C. I can't tell you positively what his middle name was.

Q   How long has he been dead?   A  8 or 9 years. I can't tell you exactly.

Q   What is the name of your oldest child?   A  Ida I don't know what's her middle name.

Q   Is she living?   A  Yes sir.

Q   What was you[sic] next child's name?   A  Lizzie.

Q   Is she living?   A  No sir. She's dead.

Q   Who is the older, Lizzie or Charley?   A  Charley's the oldest.

Q   Did Charley come next to Ida?   A  Yes sir.

Q   What is the next child after Lizzie?   A  Emma.

Q   And the next one?   A  Minnie.

Q   And the next?   A  Jennie.

Q   Jennie is after Emma?   A  Yes sir. Jennie's after Emma and then Luvena.

Q   Did you have a child to die just older than Lue?   A  Yes sir.

Q   What was its name?   A  I don't beliene[sic] I can tell you.

Q   Was it a boy or girl?   A  It was a girl, right small. I don't remember it now.

Q   Your son, Charley, the father of these grand-children, is just younger than Ida and older than Lizzie?   A  Yes sir.

BY THE COMMISSION:

It is shown by the copy of the 1880 authenticated roll of citizens of the Cherokee Nation that Charley Wetzel, father of the grand-children of the applicant, is duly identified upon said roll along with the members of the applicant's family.

Q   Was your son, Charley, born in the Cherokee Nation?   A  No. He was born in the State of Georgia.

Q   Did you come to the Cherokee Nation with him?   A  Yes sir. I brought him when he was a baby

Q   Did he reside in the Cherokee Nation continuously from prior to 1880 until the time of his death?   A  Yes sir.

Q   During that period he never made hi[sic] home anywhere else?   A  No sir.

Q   What is the name of the mother of these children?   A  Arlena[sic] Wetzel.

Q   She was a white woman?   A  Yes sir.

Q   Who died first, she or your son?   A  My son died first. About one year.

Q   These children were all born prior to the death of your son?   A  Yes sir.

Q   Do you know anything about the marriage of your son and his wife, Arlena?

A   Yes sir.

Q   When were they married?   A  They were married in Goingsnake District at an old school house.

Q   Did they have a license?   A  Yes sir.

Q   Do you know whether they got a marriage certificate from the minister who married them?   A No sir. I don't.
Q   You never saw it?   A No sir.
Q   Were you present at their marriage?   A Yes sir.
Q   What is the name of the preacher that married them?   A Ewing.
Q   Full name?   A I don't remember his full name.
Q   Did your son and Arena live together continuously from the time they married until he died?   A Yes sir.
Q   Have these children lived in the Cherokee Nation continuously all of their lives?
A   Yes sir.

---

Joe Chambers, being duly sworn, states that as stenographer to the Commission to the Five Civilized Tribes, he correctly recorded the testimony in this case, and that the above and foregoing is a true and complete copy of his stenographic notes thereof.

Joe Chambers

Subscribed and sworn to before
me this 14th day of June, 1905.

JO Rosson
Notary Public.

JC

◇◇◇◇◇

LGD                                                                    Cherokee 2973.

DEPARTMENT OF THE INTERIOR,
COMMISSIONER TO THE FIVE CIVILIZED TRIBES.

Muskogee, January 3, 1907.

In the matter of the application of DANIEL K. WETSEL[sic] for enrollment as a citizen by intermarriage of the Cherokee Nation.

Daniel K. Wetsel[sic], being first duly sworn by B. P. Rasmus, a notary public, testified as follows:

Q   What is your name?   A Daniel K. Wetsel.
Q   What is your age?   A 66 years old.
Q   What is your postoffice address?   A Maysville, Arkansas.
Q   You claim to be a citizen by intermarriage of the Cherokee Nation?   A Yes sir.
Q   Through whom do you claim your rights?   A My wife, Martha C. McDonald.
Q   When were you married to her?   A In 1863.
Q   Where were you married to her?   A In the state of Georgia.
Q   What time in 1863?   A December, I think.
Q   Who married you?   A Gideon.

# Cherokee Intermarried White 1906
## Volume X

Q   Did you ever remarry after you came to the Cherokee Nation?   A Yes sir.
Q   When did you marry the second time?   A In 1869.
Q   When did you remove to the Cherokee Nation?   A In 1868.
Q   Then you remarried in 1869?   A Yes.
Q   Did you have a license?   A Yes sir.
Q   Where is it?   A I dont[sic] know, we lost it.
Q   When?   A About twenty years ago.
Q   Did you make search for it?   A No much, for I didnt[sic] think it would amount to much.
Q   What District did you get your license in?   A Goingsnake District.
Q   When did you get your license?   A In 1869.
Q   Who was the clerk who issued your license?   A Head Beck.
Q   Is he living?   A No.
Q   Who married you the second time?   A George Whitmire.
Q   Is he dead?   A Yes sir.
Q   Is there anyone who knew you at the time of your second Marriage?   A Yes, Walter Whitmire.

The applicant is identified on the 1880 Cherokee roll, Goingsnake District, opposite No. 2136. His wife, through whom he claims the right to enrollment, is identified on said roll in said district opposite No. 2137. She is also identified upon the final roll of citizens by blood of the Cherokee Nation opposite No. 23711.

Q   When was your wife admitted to citizenship?   A I dont[sic] know positively, but I think it was about 1870.
Q   Under decree of court or council admitting her?   A No sir, didn't need any. My wife's parents came with her and they put her on the roll.
Q   When was she first enrolled?   A In 1870.
Q   Is your wife here?   A Yes sir.

Witness excused.

Martha Wetsel, being first duly sworn by B. P. Rasmus, a notary public, testified as follows:

Q   What is your name?   A Martha Wetsel.
Q   What is your age?   A 66 years old.
Q   What is your postoffice address?   A Maysville, Arkansas.
Q   Are you a citizen of the Cherokee Nation?   A Yes sir.
Q   By blood?   A Yes sir.
Q   What relation are you to Daniel K. Wetsel?   A His wife.
Q   When were you married to him?   A Have been married twice, last time in 1869, first time in 1863. First time in Murray County, Georgia.
Q   How long after you were married until you left there?
A   Married in 1863 and left there in 1868.
Q   You came to the Cherokee Nation then?   A Came in 1869.

Q  When were you first admitted to citizenship in the Cherokee Nation?  A  Soon after we came. My father attended to it, Collins McDonald.

Q  When were you first enrolled?  A  I cant[sic] tell you the year

Q  Did you draw any money in the seventies as a Cherokee citizen?  A  Yes sir.

Q  You were married again in 1869?  A  Yes sir.

Q  Under the Cherokee law?  A  Yes, in May, 1869.

Q  Did you and your husband get a marriage license?  A  Yes.

Q  Were you ever married before you married Daniel K. Wetsel?  A  No sir.

Q  Was he ever married before he married you?  A  No sir.

Q  Have you lived together continuously as husband and wife since your marriage up to the present time?  A  Yes sir.

Q  Who married you the second time?  A  George Whitmire. He was District Judge.

Q  What district?  A  Goingsnake.

Q  Who issued your license?  A  Head Beck, the clerk.

Q  Have you your license?  A  No, it was lost.

Q  How long since you have had it?  A  About 15 years.

Q  Have you searched for it recently?  A  Yes, several times. It was recorded, though.

Witness excused.

Walt Whitmire, being first duly sworn by B. P. Rasmus, a notary public, testified as follows:

Q  What is your name?  A  Walt Whitmire.

Q  How old are you?  A  54 years old.

Q  What is your postoffice address?  A  Westville, I. T.

Q  Are you a citizen of the Cherokee Nation?  A  Yes.

Q  Are you acquainted with Daniel K. Wetsel?  A  Yes.

Q  Are you acquainted with Martha Wetsel, his wife?  A  Yes.

Q  How long have you known them?  A  A[sic]  First I got acquainted with them when they moved on my father's place in 1869.

Q  Do you know anything about their marriage after they came to the Cherokee Nation?
A  Yes.

Q  Who married them?  A  George Whitmire.

Q  Do you know they were married?  A  Yes.

Q  Under a Cherokee license, do you know?  A  Yes, Head Beck was clerk at that time.

Q  Did you see the license?  A  Yes.

Q  Was Martha Wetsel considered a citizen of the Cherokee Nation at that time?
A  Yes.

Q  Was Daniel K. Wetsel considered a citizen of the Cherokee Nation ever since his marriage to Martha Wetsel?  A  Yes.

Q  He exercised all rights as a citizen?  A  Yes.

Q  He voted?  A  Yes.

Q  He held property in the Cherokee Nation?  A  I dont[sic] know.

Witness excused.

Ed Walkingstick, being first duly sworn by B. P. Rasmus, a notary public, testified as follows:

Q   What is your name?   A  Ed Walkingstick.
Q   How old are you?   A  57 years old.
Q   What is your postoffice address?   A  Baron, I. T.
Q   Are you a citizen by blood of the Cherokee Nation?   A  Yes
Q   Are you acquainted with Daniel K. Wetsel?   A  Yes.
Q   Are you acquainted with his wife, Martha Wetsel?   A  Yes.
Q   How long have you known them?   A  Since 1869.
Q   Do you know of their second marriage in 1869?   A  I have heard of it, but was not present.
Q   Has Martha Wetsel been considered a citizen of the Cherokee Nation ever since you have known her?   A  Yes.
Q   Have they lived together continuously as husband and wife ever since you knew them up to the present time?   A  Yes.

Witness excused.
Demie T. Stubblefield, being first duly sworn, on oath states that as stenographer to the Commission to the Five Civilized Tribes she reported the proceedings in the above case, and that the above and foregoing is a true and correct transcript of her stenographic notes thereof.

Demie T Stubblefield

Subscribed and sworn to before me this, January 4, 1907.

Edward Merrick
Notary Public.

E C M                                                                    Cherokee 2973.

DEPARTMENT OF THE INTERIOR,
COMMISSION TO THE FIVE CIVILIZED TRIBES.

In the matter of the application for the enrollment of Daniel K. Wetzel as a citizen by intermarriage of the Cherokee Nation.

D E C I S I O N

THE RECORDS OF THIS OFFICE SHOW:  That at Vinita, Indian Territory, September 18, 1900 application was received by the Commission to the Five Civilized

Tribes for the enrollment of Daniel K. Wetzel as a citizen by intermarriage of the Cherokee Nation. Further proceedings in the matter of said application were had at Tahlequah, Indian Territory, October 24, 1902 and June 3, 1903 and at Muskogee, Indian Territory, January 3, 1907.

THE EVIDENCE IN THIS CASE SHOWS: That the applicant herein, Daniel K. Wetzel, a white man, was married in accordance with Cherokee law about the year 1869 to one Martha Wetzel, hee McDonald, who was at the time of said marriage a recognized citizen by blood of the Cherokee Nation, who is identified on the Cherokee authenticated tribal roll of 1880, Going Snake District No. 2137 as a native Cherokee. It is further shown that the said Daniel K. Wetzel and Martha Wetzel had been previously married in the State of Georgia in 1863, and upon their removal to the Cherokee Nation the said Martha Wetzel was admitted to citizenship therein by the duly constituted authorities thereof about 1869. It is further shown that from the time of said marriage the said Daniel K. Wetzel and Martha Wetzel resided together as husband and wife and continuously lived in the Cherokee Nation up to and including September 1, 1902. Said applicant is identified on the Cherokee authenticated tribal roll of 1880 and the Cherokee census roll of 1896 as an intermarried citizen of the Cherokee Nation.

IT IS, THEREFORE, ORDERED AND ADJUDGED: That in accordance with the decision of the Supreme Court of the United States, dated November 5, 1906, in the cases of Daniel Red Bird, et al. vs. the United States, Nos. 125, 126, 127, and 128, the said applicant, Daniel K. Wetzel is entitled, under the provisions of Section Twenty-one of the Act of Congress approved June 28, 1898 (30 Stats. 495), to enrollment as a citizen by intermarriage of the Cherokee Nation, and his application for enrollment as such is accordingly granted.

Tams Bixby<br>Commissioner.

Dated at Muskogee, Indian Territory,
this    FEB 27 1907

◇◇◇◇◇

Cherokee
2973.

Muskogee, Indian Territory, February 19, 1907.

Special

Daniel K. Wetezel[sic],
     Maysville, Arkansas.

Dear Sir:

The Commissioner sent you this day a telegram as follows:

"Intermarried case incomplete, appear immediately to establish admission of wife to citizenship, also date of your marriage."

## Cherokee Intermarried White 1906
## Volume X

The Act of Congress approved April 26, 1906, provides that the Secretary of the Interior shall have no jurisdiction to approve the enrollment of any person as a citizen of the Cherokee Nation after March 4, 1907.

This matter, therefore, demands your immediate attention.

Respectfully,

HJC                                                                    Commissioner.

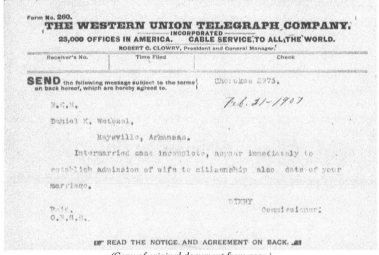

*(Copy of original document from case.)*

Cherokee
2973.

COPY

Muskogee, Indian Territory, February 27, 1907.

W. W. Hastings,
  Attorney for the Cherokee Nation,
    Muskogee, Indian Territory.

Dear Sir:

There is enclosed herewith a copy of the decision of the Commissioner to the Five Civilized Tribes, dated February 27, 1907, granting the application for the enrollment of Daniel K. Wetzel as a citizen by intermarriage of the Cherokee Nation.

Respectfully,

SIGNED *Jams Bixby*

Encl. HJ-130.
HJC                                              Commissioner.

◇◇◇◇◇

Cherokee
2973.

Muskogee, Indian Territory, February 27, 1907.

The Commissioner to the Five Civilized Tribes,
    Muskogee, Indian Territory.

Sir:

Receipt is acknowledged of the testimony and of your decision enrolling Daniel K. Wetzel as a citizen by intermarriage of the Cherokee Nation. Time for protesting said decision is waived and I consent that said person may be placed upon the schedule immediately.

Respectfully,
W. W. Hastings
Attorney for Cherokee Nation.

◇◇◇◇◇

Cherokee
2973.                                            COPY

Muskogee, Indian Territory, February 27, 1907.

Daniel K. Wetzel,
    Maysville, Arkansas.

Dear Sir:

There is enclosed herewith a copy of the decision of the Commissioner to the Five Civilized Tribes, dated February 27, 1907, granting your application for enrollment as a citizen by intermarriage of the Cherokee Nation.

You will be advised when your name has been placed upon a schedule of citizens of the Cherokee Nation and approved by the Secretary of the Interior.

Respectfully,

SIGNED *Tams Bixby*

Encl. HJ-112.
HJC                                                    Commissioner.

---

**Cher IW 279**

<><><><><>

Department of the Interior,
Commission to the Five Civilized Tribes,
Vinita, I.T.  September 22, 1900.

In the matter of the application of James A. Thompson for the enrollment of his mother-in-law, Elizadath Taylor, as a Cherokee citizen; being sworn and examined by Commissioner Needles he testified as follows:

Q    What is your name?    A  James A. Thompson.
Q    How old are you?    A  Fifty-one.
Q    What is your post-office address?    A  Vinita.
Q    What is the name of your mother-in-law?    A  Elzada Taylor.
Q    What is her age?    A  Fifty-seven.
Q    What is her post-office?    A  Vinita.
Q    What is her district?    A  Cooweescoowee.
Q    Is she a citizen of the Cherokee Nation by blood?    A  No sir, by adoption.  She married Richard Cowan in 1872 I think.
Q    What is the reason that Elzada Taylor is not here herself, on account of bodily infirmities, and unable to be here?    A  She could come out, but it would be a heap of trouble.
Q    She is old and feeble is she?    A  Yes sir, not very old, but she is very fleshy and can't get around hardly.
1880 roll  page 241  #658 Elsade[sic] Cowan, Delaware District;
Q    When did she marry Taylor?    A  She married him-- I dis remember.
Q    Can't you think about what year it was?    A  No sir, it was in 1880 sometime.
1896 roll  page 326  #983 Elyada[sic] Taylor  Cooweescoowee District.

Examined by Cherokee Representative W. W. Hastings:
Q    What was her second husband's name?    A  David Taylor
Q    Is he alive?    A  No sir, he died in April.
Q    He is a Cherokee by blood?    A  Yes sir
1880 roll for Elzada Taylor's last husband, page 185    #2865 David Taylor, Sr., Cooweescoowee District, native Cherokee.

Com'r Needles:    The name of Elzada Taylor appears upon the authenticated roll of 1880 as Elsade Cowan; it is averred that she has been married since to one David

Taylor, who was a Cherokee citizen by blood, and whose name appears upon the authenticated roll of 1880 as indicated in the testimony; said David Taylor now being deceased; the name of Elzada Taylor also appears upon the census roll of 1896, and being fully identified according to page and number of the rolls as indicated, said Elzada Taylor will be duly listed for enrollment by this Commission as a Cherokee citizen by intermarriage.

M.D. Green, being first duly sworn, states that as stenographer to the Commission to the Five Civilized Tribes he correctly recorded the testimony and proceedings in this case and that the foregoing is a true and complete transcript of his stenographic notes thereof.

MD Green

Subscribed and sworn to before me this 24 day of September 1900.

TB Needles
Commissioner.

◇◇◇◇◇

Statement of Applicant Taken Under Oath.

## CHEROKEE BY BLOOD AND ADOPTION.

Date **SEP 22 1900** 1900.

Name **Vinita I.T.**

District............................ Year ............ Page ............ No. ............

Citizen by blood ............ Mother's citizenship ............

Intermarried citizen ............

Married under what law............................ Date of marriage ............

License (**57**)............................ Certificate............

Wife's name.......... **Elzada Taylor**

District.......... **DELAWARE.** ............Year **1880** ....Page **241**...No. **658**

Citizen by blood..........Mother's citizenship............

Intermarried citizen..........**Yes**

Married under what law............................Date of marriage............

License ............................Certificate............

Names of Children:

| | Dist. | Year | Page | No. | Age |
|---|---|---|---|---|---|
| | Dist. | Year | Page | No. | Age |
| | Dist. | Year | Page | No. | Age |
| | Dist. | Year | Page | No. | Age |
| | Dist. | Year | Page | No. | Age |

**1 on 1880 roll as Elsade Cowan**

**#3310**

◇◇◇◇◇

Cher
Supp'l to # 3310

Department of the Interior,
Commission to the Five Civilized Tribes,
Muskogee, I. T., October 22, 1902.

In the matter of the application of ELZADA TAYLOR, for the enrollment of herself as a citizen by intermarriage of the Cherokee Nation.

ELZADA TAYLOR, being duly sworn and examined by the Commission, testified as follows:

Q    What is your name ?    A  Elzada Taylor.
Q    How old are you ?    A  Sixty two.
Q    What is your post office address ?    A  Vinita.
Q    Are you a white man[sic] ?    A  Yes sir.
Q    Is your name on the 1880 roll as an adopted citizen ?
A    Yes sir, it's on the 1880 roll.
Q    What was your husband's name in 1880 ?    A  Richard Cowan.
Q    Is he the husband through whom you claim your right to citizenship ?
A    I claim through both.
Q    Was Richard Cowan your first husband ?    A  Yes sir.
Q    Is he dead ?    A  Yes sir.
Q    When did he die ?    A  He's been dead seventeen years.
Q    Did you live with him from 1880 up to the time he died ?
A    Yes sir, I lived with him from the time I married him until he died.
Q    When did you marry Taylor ?    A  I married him in 1890.
Q    What is his first name ?    A  David.
Q    Is David Taylor a Cherokee by blood ?    A  Yes sir.
Q    How long had he been living in the Cherokee Nation when you married him ?
A    Well he has been here ever since--I just forget when he come, but he's been here for over thirty years, forty years I reckon.
Q    Are you living with Taylor now ?    A  He is dead now.
Q    When did he die ?    A  He has been dead about three years next April.
Q    Did you live with Taylor from the time you married him until he died ?
A    Yes sir.
Q    Have you married again since his death ?    A  No sir.
Q    You were married just twice then ?    A  Yes sir.
Q    Your home has never been anywhere else during that time ?    A  No sir.

-------------------

E. C. Bagwell, on oath states that, as stenographer to the Commission to the Five Civilized Tribes, he correctly recorded the testimony and proceedings had in the above entitled cause, and that the foregoing is an accurate transcript of his stenographic notes thereof.

E.C.Bagwell

Subscribed and sworn to before me this November 29, 1902.

BC Jones
Notary Public.

◇◇◇◇◇

Cherokee 3310.

## DEPARTMENT OF THE INTERIOR,
## COMMISSIONER TO THE FIVE CIVILIZED TRIBES.
## MUSKOGEE, I. T., JANUARY 30, 1907.

In the matter of the application for the enrollment of ELZADA TAYLOR as a citizen by intermarriage of the Cherokee Nation.

ELZADA TAYLOR, being first duly sworn by John E. Tidwell, a Notary Public, testified as follows:

ON BEHALF OF THE COMMISSIONER:

Q  What is your name?  A Elzada Taylor.
Q  Your age?  A 66.
Q  Your postoffice?  A Vinita, Indian Territory.
Q  You claim the right to enrollment as a citizen by intermarriage of the Cherokee Nation, do you?  A Yes sir.
Q  You are a white woman, are you, not possessed of any Indian blood?  A  Yes sir, I am a white woman.
Q  Your claim to the right to enrollment is solely by virtue of your marriage to a citizen of the Cherokee Nation?  A Yes sir.
Q  What is the name of the citizen through whom you claim your right?  A  Richard Cowen.
Q  When were you married to Richard Cosen[sic]?  A  I was married in 1865, October 3.
Q  At the time you married Richard Cowen was he a recognized citizen by blood of the Cherokee Nation?  A Yes sir.
Q  Where were you married to him?  A In Illinois, in Woodford County; here is the certificate.

Applicant presents a certificate of County Clerk of Woodford County, Illinois, showing that Richard Cowen was married to Beda Allen on October 3, 1865.

145

Q   Mrs. Taylor, are you the same person name in this certificate as Beda Allen?
A   Yes sir, I am the same person. He misspelled it when he made that out.

Q   When did you remove to the Cherokee Nation?   A '70, I think it was '70, as well as I remember; he was down here before we moved here; he was in and out.

Q   When did Richard Cowen die?   A He died in '81.

Q   From the time of your removal to the Cherokee Nation in 1870 until the death of Richard Cowen in 1881, did you reside together as husband and wife and live continuously in the Cherokee Nation?   A Yes sir.

Q   Had you been married before you married Richard Cowen?   A Yes sir, I was married before I married him.

Q   How many times?   A Just once.

Q   Was that first husband living at the time you married Richard Cowen?   A No sir, time of the war he was killed.

Q   Had Richard Cowen been married before he married you?   A No sir.

Q   When Richard Cowen came back to the Cherokee Nation in 1870 was he readmitted to citizenship?   A Yes sir, he was.

Q   Have you any documentary evidence showing his readmission?
A   Well it is on the rolls in Washington.

Q   What we are talking about his admission by the Cherokee Council or some Cherokee tribal authorities?   A Yes sir.

Q   You haven't a copy of that?   A No sir, I haven't got it; I wouldn't say for sure what year we moved in but I think it was then; my little girl was two or three years old and she was born in 1869.

Q   After the death of Richard Cowen you married again?   A Yes sir.

Q   What is the name of that husband?   A David Taylor.

Q   Is he living?   A No sir, he is not living.

Q   When did he die?   A In 1900.

Q   At the time you married David Taylor was he a reocgnized[sic] citizen by blood of the Cherokee Nation?   A Yes sir.

Q   From the time of your marriage to him until his death you continued to reside in the Cherokee Nation, did you?   A Yes sir, I haven't been out.

Q   You haven't been out of the Cherokee Nation since you moved here in 1870?
A   No sir.

Q   You haven't married since the death of Mr. Taylor?   A No sir I can't say whether it was '70 just the exact time, I can't remember.

Q   Where was your husband, Richard Cowen, born?   A He was born in the Nation.

Q   And did he continue to live in the Nation up until the time of the war?
A   Yes sir, he did.

Q   He entered the war did he?   A Yes sir.

Q   After the war he returned to the Cherokee Nation?   A Yes sir, after we were married awhile he come right in and as soon as we could we moved in and have been here ever since, and he died over here on Cow Skin Prairie.

Q   It was your understanding after your return to the Cherokee Nation after the war he was readmitted to citizenship?   A Yes sir, before we moved in we had that fixed up.

# Cherokee Intermarried White 1906
## Volume X

Q   You were married in 1865, how long was it before he made the first trip back to the Cherokee Nation?    A  It was either 6 or 7 years I guess.

Q   Did he make any trips down here in the meantime?    A  He made a trip, yes sir, he went south with a drove of cattle and mules and he come back through here.

Q   Which years was that?    A  It was about '72 I guess, as well as I remember; I can't remember very good.

Q   That was before you moved to the Cherokee Nation?    A  Yes sir, that was before I moved.

Q   When did you move to the Cherokee Nation?    A  I moved here, my child was about three years old; she was born in '69.

Q   That would make you moving to the Cherokee Nation in about 1872?    A   I don't know.

Q   It is important, of course, that we fix these dates as nearly correct as we can?    A  That is what I am trying to do as near correct as I can do it.

Q   You say you had a daughter born in 1869, and she was about three years old at the time you moved to the Cherokee Nation, so that would make it about 1872 that you moved here, but up until the time you moved here in 1872, your husband, Richard Cowen, considered Illinois his home, did he?    A  Well we come back as far as Missouri and stopped awhile with my people, and then we come on down first to South West City and then over on the Prairie there and lived there awhile, and then went to Vinita I expect about 25 years ago.

Q   You were living in the Cherokee Nation prior to November 1, 1875, were you?    A  Oh, yes sir.

Q   Do you know whether or not your husband exercised the rights of a Cherokee citizens[sic] at the time he came here in 1870, that is did he vote, take part in the elections?  A  Yes sir.

Q   Did he ever hold any office in the Cherokee Nation?    A  No sir, he didn't hold any office; he voted and was recognized as a citizen.

Q   He exercised the same rights and privilege every other citizen of the Nation exercise?    A  Yes sir; I guess you know Mr. Dave Taylor, I don't guess you do, but Campbell Taylor, he was his Uncle, and this John Taylor at Claremore.

Q   Do you know any one who is living at this time what[sic] would know of your husband, Richard Cowen, being a recognized citizen before 1875?    A  Well the rolls will show I reckon that he was recognized; I understood that this certificate is plenty; all of them up around there knows he was a citizen; they told me that if I had this paper I wouldn't need any witnesses; I could have brought witnesses; they said if I needed them they would come down.

Q   What District were you living in in 1880?    A  Delaware.

The applicant, Elzada Taylor, is identified on the Cherokee Authenticated Tribal roll of 1880 Delaware District, page 241, No. 658 as Elsade Cowan, and on the Cherokee Census roll of 1896, Cooweescoowee District, page 326, No. 983 as an intermarried citizen of the Cherokee Nation. The applicant's husband, Richard Cowan, is identified on the Cherokee Authenticated roll of 1880?[sic] Delaware District, page 241, No. 657 as a native Cherokee.

# Cherokee Intermarried White 1906
## Volume X

------------------------oOo------------------------

Geo. H. Lessley, being first duly sworn, states that as stenographer to the Commissioner to the Five Civilized Tribes, that he reported the proceedings had in the above entitled cause, and that the above and foregoing is a true and correct transcript of his stenographic notes thereof.

Geo H Lessley

Subscribed and sworn to before me this 31st day of January, 1907.

John E. Tidwell
Notary Public.

◇◇◇◇◇

E.C.M.                                                                                        Cherokee 3310.

## DEPARTMENT OF THE INTERIOR,
## COMMISSIONER TO THE FIVE CIVILIZED TRIBES.
## MUSKOGEE, I. T., FEBRUARY 21, 1907.

------------------------

In the matter of the application for the enrollment of ELZADA TAYLOR as a citizen by intermarriage of the Cherokee Nation.

ETTA BIRDS, being first duly sworn by Walter W. Chappell, Notary Public, testified as follows:

ON BEHALF OF THE COMMISSIONER:

Q    What is your name?     A Etta Birds.
Q    What is your name[sic]?     A 46.
Q    What is your post office address?     A Vinita.
Q    Are you here today for the purpose of giving testimony relative to the right of Elzada Taylor to enrollment as a citizen by intermarriage of the Cherokee Nation?     A Yes sir.
Q    You are acquainted with the applicant, Elzada Taylor, are you?
     A Yes sir.
Q    Were you acquainted with her husband?     A No sir.
Q    Have you lived in the same neighborhood with them for a good many years?
     A Yes sir, for the last 18 or 20 years, but my father, Mr. Hitchcock here, knew them better than I did.
Q    They you simply desire to testify that your father, Mr. Hitchcock, who is here today, is acquainted with Elzada Taylor and her husband?     A Yes sir.

( Witness excused ).

I. B. HITCHCOCK, being first duly sworn by Walter W. Chappell,
Notary Public, testified as follows:

Q   What is your name?   A  I. B. Hitchcock.
Q   What is your age?   A  82.
Q   What is your post office address?   A  Vinita.
Q   Do you appear here today for the purpose of giving testimony relative to the right of
Elzada Taylor to enrollment as a citizen by intermarriage of the Cherokee Nation?
A  Yes sir, for Mrs. Taylor, I didn't know her given name.
Q   How long have you been acquainted with the applicant, Mrs. Taylor?
A  Since way back in '74 or '75 or '6; I had heard of them before that.
Q   Was she married at that time?   A  Yes sir.
Q   What was the name of her husband?   A  Dick, or Richard Cowan.
Q   She was living with a man by the name of Richard Cowan when you became
acquainted with them?   A  Yes sir.
Q   Were they recognized as husband and wife in the community?
A  Yes sir, and were the father and mother of 2 children.
Q   Is Richard Cowan dead now?   A  So I have been told, I suppose he is
Q   Has she remarried since his death?   A  Yes sir.
Q   What is the name of her last husband?   A  Dave Taylor; he is dead too.
Q   Since you became acquainted with her in 1874 can you testify as to whether or not
she has lived in the Cherokee Nation since then?   A  I think I can safely testify
that she has lived in the Cherokee Nation all the time; it is the only home she has
had.
Q   Do you know whether or not Richard Cowan was a citizen by blood of the Cherokee
Nation?   A  So called, by reputation.
Q   Were you acquainted with him in 1874?   A  Not before '73 or '744; I heard of him
in '73, and became acquainted with him personally in '74.

( Witness excused ).

J. A. THOMPSON, being first duly sworn by Walter W. Chappell,
Notary Public, testified as follows:

Q   What is your name?   A  J. A. Thompson.
Q   What is your age?   A  56.
Q   What is your post office address?   A  Vinita.
Q   Do you appear here today for the purpose of giving testimony relative to the right of
Elzada Taylor to enrollment as a citizen by intermarriage of the Cherokee Nation?
A  Yes sir.
Q   How long have you been acquainted with Elzada Taylor?
A  Since 1874.
Q   What was the name of her husband in 1874?   A  Richard Cowan.
Q   Was he a recognized citizen by blood of the Cherokee Nation at that time?
A  Yes sir.
Q   Were you acquainted with him prior to that time?   A  No sir.
Q   Then, you do not know whether or not he had been out of the Cherokee Nation
before that time?   A  Yes sir.

Q   Lived out of the Nation prior to that time, had he?   A   I think so, during the war.

Q   Did he return to the Cherokee Nation immediately after the war?
    A   In 1869, I think.

Q   Was he readmitted to citizenship?   A   That was my understanding.

Q   He is dead , is he?   A   Yes sir.

Q   Since his death has his wife remarried?   A   Yes sir.

Q   Whom did she marry?   A   Dave Taylor.

Q   Is he dead?   A   Yes sir.

Q   When did he die?   A   About 3 years ago.

Q   Since you became acquainted with this applicant in 1874, has she remained a
    resident of the Cherokee Nation continuously?   A   Yes sir.

Q   Was her last husband, Dave Taylor, a Cherokee by blood?   A   Yes sir.

Q   They were never separated before his death?   A   No sir.

BY W. W. HASTINGS, Attorney for Cherokee Nation;

Q   About what time did Richard Cowan die?   A   In '77 or '78.

_____ ( Witness excused ). _____

     The undersigned, upon oath states that, as stenographer to the Commissioner to the Five Civilized Tribes, she correctly reported the above and foregoing testimony, and that the same is a full, true and complete transcript of her stenographic notes thereof.

Sarah Waters

Subscribed and sworn to before me this 23d day of February, 1907.

Frances R Lane<br>Notary Public.

◇◇◇◇◇

*(Copy of original document from case.)*

◇◇◇◇◇

E C M                                                      Cherokee 3310.

## DEPARTMENT OF THE INTERIOR,
## COMMISSIONER TO THE FIVE CIVILIZED TRIBES.

In the matter of the application for the enrollment of ELZADA TAYLOR as a citizen by intermarriage of the Cherokee Nation.

## D E C I S I O N

THE RECORDS OF THIS OFFICE SHOW:   That at Vinita, Indian Territory September 22, 1900 application was received by the Commission to the Five Civilized Tribes for the enrollment of Elzada Taylor as a citizen by intermarriage of the Cherokee Nation.   Further proceedings in the matter of said application were had at Muskogee, Indian Territory, October 22, 1902, January 30 and February 21, 1907.

THE EVIDENCE IN THIS CASE SHOWS:   That the applicant herein, Elzada Taylor, a white woman, married in the state of Illinois, October 3, 1865, one Richard Cowen, since deceased, who is identified on the Cherokee authenticated tribal roll of 1880, Delaware District No. 657 as a native Cherokee marked "Dead".   It is further shown that in 1872 the said Richard Cowen and Elzada Cowen removed to the Cherokee Nation where they resided together as husband and wife until the death of said Richard Cowen, which occurred in 1885.   It is also shown that upon their removal to the Cherokee Nation the said Richard Cowen made application and was re-admitted to citizenship therein by the duly constituted authorities of said Nation about the year 1872.   It is also shown that in 1890 the said Elzada Cowen was married to one David Taylor, since deceased, who was at the time of said marriage a recognized citizen by blood of the Cherokee Nation, who is identified on the Cherokee authenticated tribal roll of 1880, Cooweescoowee district No. 2865 as a native Cherokee.   It is further shown that from the time of said marriage until the death of said David Taylor, which occurred in 1900, the said David Taylor and Elzada Taylor resided together as husband and wife and continuously lived in the Cherokee Nation.   That after the death of said David Taylor the said Elzada Taylor remained unmarried and continuously lived in the Cherokee Nation up to and including September 1, 1902   Said applicant is identified on the Cherokee authenticated tribal roll of 1880 and the Cherokee census roll of 1896 as an intermarried citizen of the Cherokee Nation.

IT IS, THEREFORE, ORDERED AND ADJUDGED:   That in accordance with the decision of the Supreme Court of the United States, dated November 5, 1906, in the cases of Daniel Red Bird, et al. vs. the United States, Nos. 125, 126, 127, and 128, the said applicant, Elzada Taylor, is entitled, under the provisions of Section Twenty-one of the Act of Congress approved June 28, 1898 (30 Stats. 495), to enrollment as a citizen by intermarriage of the Cherokee Nation, and her application for enrollment as such is accordingly granted.

Tams Bixby

Commissioner.

Dated at Muskogee, Indian Territory,
this    FEB 27 1907

◇◇◇◇◇

PGR

COMMISSIONERS:
HENRY L. DAWES,
TAMS BIXBY,
THOMAS B. NEEDLES,
C. R. BRECKINRIDGE.

ALLISON L. AYLESWORTH,
SECRETARY.

ADDRESS ONLY THE
COMMISSION TO THE FIVE CIVILIZED TRIBES.

DEPARTMENT OF THE INTERIOR,
COMMISSION TO THE FIVE CIVILIZED TRIBES.

**Cherokee No. 3310**

Muskogee, Indian Territory,    **September 30th**   ,1902

**Elzada Taylor,**
**Vinita, Indian Territory.**

**Dear Madam:**

The Act of Congress, approved July 1, 1902, and entitled "An Act To provide for the enrollment of the lands of the Cherokee Nation, for the disposition of town sites therein, and for other purposes," (Public No. 241), provides that "the roll of citizens of the Cherokee Nation shall be made as of September first, nineteen-hundred and two."

In accordance with said provision, you are hereby notified that the Commission to the Five Civilized Tribes will be at its offices at Muskogee, Indian Territory, until Friday, October 31, 1902, inclusive, for the purpose of affording you an opportunity to show that you have not, between the date of the original application for your enrollment and Sept 2, 1902, forfeited your right as a citizen by intermarriage of the Cherokee Nation.

This evidence should be introduced immediately, as it is necessary in determining your right to share in the allotment of the lands of the Cherokee Nation, and until the same is furnished no further action can be taken looking toward your final enrollment as an intermarried citizen.

Yours truly,

Tams Bixby
Acting Chairman.

◇◇◇◇◇

152

# Cherokee Intermarried White 1906
## Volume X

Cherokee
3310.

Muskogee, Indian Territory, December 27, 1906.

Elzada Taylor,
    Vinita, Indian Territory.

Dear Madam:

    November 6, 1906, the United States Supreme Court held that white persons who intermarried with Cherokee citizens according to Cherokee law prior to November 1, 1875, are entitled to enrollment and allotments of land as citizens of the Cherokee Nation.

    You are advised that to properly determine your right to enrollment as a citizen by intermarriage of the Cherokee Nation, it will be necessary for you to appear before the Commissioner for the purpose of giving testimony as to the date of your marriage and whether or not your husband, by reason of your marriage to whom you claim the right to enrollment as a citizen by intermarriage of the Cherokee Nation, was a recognized Cherokee citizen at the time of your marriage to him.

    You are therefore directed to appear before the Commissioner at Muskogee, Indian Territory, at 9 o'clock A. M., on Friday, January 4, 1907, and give testimony as above indicated.

          Respectfully,

H.J.C.                                Acting Commissioner.

◇◇◇◇◇

Cherokee
3310

Muskogee, Indian Territory, January 22, 1907

Elzada Taylor,
    Vinita, Indian Territory.

Dear Madam:

    Replying to your letter of January 7, in reference to your right to enrollment as a citizen by intermarriage of the Cherokee Nation, you are advised that the supreme[sic] Court of the United States, by its decision of November 5, 1906, held that white persons who intermarried according to Cherokee law with Cherokee citizens, prior to November 1, 1875, are entitled to enrollment as citizens by intermarriage of the Cherokee Nation.

If you claim to be entitled to enrollment under the Court's decision, you should appear at once before the Commissioner at March Indian Territory, and submit such testimony as you desire relative to your marriage to your Cherokee husband by reason of your marriage to whom you claim the right to enrollment as March the Cherokee Nation, and as to the date of your marriage to him.

The Act of March 1906 provides that the March the Interior shall have no jurisdiction to approve the enrollment of any person as a citizen of the Cherokee Nation after March 4, 1907, and the matter of your enrollment should, therefore, receive your immediate attention.

Respectfully,

L M B                                            Commissioner.

◇◇◇◇◇

E.C.M.

Cherokee
3310.

Muskogee, Indian Territory, February 4, 1907.

Special.

Executive Secretary of the Cherokee Nation,
        Tahlequah, Indian Territory.

Dear Sir:

You are requested to forward to this office at once a certified copy of the record showing the admission to citizenship of Richard Cowen about 1872.

Respectfully,

HJC.                                          Commisioner[sic].

◇◇◇◇◇

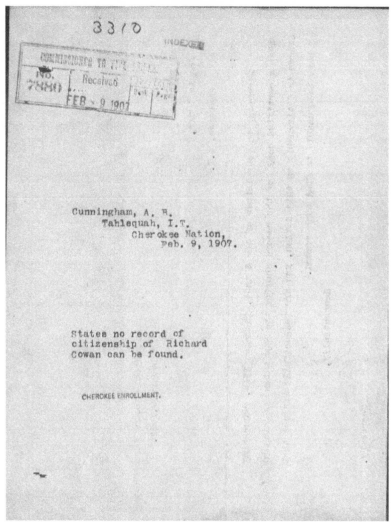

3310

Cunningham, A. B.
Tahlequah, I.T.
Cherokee Nation,
Feb. 9, 1907.

States no record of
citizenship of Richard
Cowan can be found.

CHEROKEE ENROLLMENT.

*(Copy of original document from case.)*

W. C. ROGERS, Principal Chief
D. M. FAULKNER, Assistant Chief
W. W. HASTINGS, National Attorney
J. H. COVEL, Interpreter

EXECUTIVE DEPARTMENT

A. B. CUNNINGHAM, Executive Secretary
C. J. HARRIS, Assistant Secretary
W. H. WALKER, Assistant Secretary

**CHEROKEE NATION**

**TAHLEQUAH, INDIAN TERRITORY**

3310

February,9,1907.

Tams Bixby,

Commissioner,

Muskogee, I.T.

Sir:-

Referring to your letter of the 4 inst, Cherokee 3310, requesting that a certified copy of the record showing the admission of Richard Cowen to Citizenship in the Nation, you are respectfully advised that I have been unable to find such record.

Respectfully,

A B Cunningham

Secretary.

◇◇◇◇◇

**THE WESTERN UNION TELEGRAPH COMPANY.**
──── INCORPORATED ────
**23,000 OFFICES IN AMERICA. CABLE SERVICE TO ALL THE WORLD.**

This Company TRANSMITS and DELIVERS messages only on conditions limiting its liability, which have been assented to by the sender of the following message. Errors can be guarded against only by repeating a message back to the sending station for comparison, and the Company will not hold itself liable for errors or delays in transmission or delivery of Unrepeated Messages, beyond the amount of tolls paid thereon, nor in any case where the claim is not presented in writing within sixty days after the message is filed with the Company for transmission.
This is an UNREPEATED MESSAGE, and is delivered by request of the sender, under the conditions named above.
ROBERT C. CLOWRY, President and General Manager.

**RECEIVED** at

No. 4 ks sd jn Ck. 20 paid govt.

Muskogee, I.T. Feb. 20th, 1907.

Elseada Taylor,

Vinita, I.T.

Inter married case incomplete appear immeaditely as witness to establish date of marriage to Cowan,

Bixby,

Commissioner,...... 140PM.

*(Copy of original document from case.)*

◇◇◇◇◇

# Cherokee Intermarried White 1906
## Volume X

Form No. 260.

**THE WESTERN UNION TELEGRAPH COMPANY.**
INCORPORATED
23,000 OFFICES IN AMERICA.   CABLE SERVICE TO ALL THE WORLD.
ROBERT C. CLOWRY, President and General Manager.

| Receiver's No. | Time Filed | Check |
|---|---|---|
| | | Cherokee 3310 |

SEND the following message subject to the terms on back hereof, which are hereby agreed to. Muskogee, Indian Territory, February 20, 1907

Elzada Taylor,

Vinita, Indian Territory.

Intermarried case incomplete. Appear immediately with witnesses to establish date of marriage to Cowan.

Bixby,

Commissioner

O.B.G.R.Paid

☞ READ THE NOTICE AND AGREEMENT ON BACK. ☜

*(Copy of original document from case.)*

◇◇◇◇◇

Cherokee 3310

Special

Muskogee, Indian Territory, February 20, 1907

Elzada Taylor,
Vinita, Indian Territory;

Dear Madam:

The Commissioner sent you this day a telegram as follows:

"Intermarried case incomplete. Appear immediately with witnesses to establish date of marriage to Cowan."

The Act of Congress approved April 26, 1906, provides that the Secretary of the Interior shall have no jurisdiction to approve the enrollment of any person as a citizen of the Cherokee Nation after March 4, 1907.

This matter, therefore, demands your immediate attention.

Respectfully,

MMP

Commissioner.

157

◇◇◇◇◇

*(Copy of original document from case.)*

◇◇◇◇◇

Cherokee
3310

Muskogee, Indian Territory, February 27, 1907.

W. W. Hastings,
      Attorney for the Cherokee Nation,
            Muskogee, Indian Territory.

Dear Sir:

      There is enclosed herewith a copy of the decision of the Commissioner to the Five Civilized Tribes, dated February 27, 1907, granting the application for the enrollment of Elzada Taylor, as a citizen by intermarriage of the Cherokee Nation.

Respectfully,

SIGNED *Jams Bixby*
Commissioner.

Encl. C-19
LMC

◇◇◇◇◇

Cherokee 3310.

Muskogee, Indian Territory, February 27, 1907.

The Commissioner to the Five Civilized Tribes,
    Muskogee, Indian Territory.

Sir:

Receipt is acknowledged of the testimony and of your decision enrolling Elzada Taylor, as an intermarried citizen of the Cherokee Nation. Time for protesting said decision is waived, and I consent that said person may be placed upon the schedule immediately.

Respectfully,

W. W. Hastings
Attorney for Cherokee Nation.

◇◇◇◇◇

COPY

Cherokee
    3310.

Muskogee, Indian Territory, February 27, 1907.

Elzada Taylor,
    Vinita, Indian Territory.

Dear Madam:

Thee is enclosed herewith a copy of the decision of the Commissioner to the Five Civilized Tribes, dated February 27, 1907, granting your application for enrollment as a citizen by intermarriage of the Cherokee Nation.

You will be advised when your name has been placed upon a schedule of citizens of the Cherokee Nation and approved by the Secretary of the Interior.

Respectfully,

SIGNED *Tams Bixby*
Commissioner.

Encl. C-18
LMC

---

**Cher IW 280**

◇◇◇◇◇

# Cherokee Intermarried White 1906
## Volume X

DEPARTMENT OF THE INTERIOR.
COMMISSION TO THE FIVE CIVILIZED TRIBES.
VINITA, I. T., SEPTEMBER 25th, 1900.

IN THE MATTER OF THE APPLICATION OF John H. Clark and wife for enrollment as citizens of the Cherokee Nation, and he being sworn by Commissioner, T. B. Needles, testified as follows?

Q What is your name?     A John H. Clark.
Q What is your age?     A Sixty.
Q What is your Postoffice?     A Grove.
Q What district do you live in?     A Delaware.
Q Are you a recognized citizen of the Cherokee Nation?     A Yes sir.
Q By blood or intermarriage?     A By blood.
Q For whom do you apply?     A Myself and wife.
Q What is the name of your wife?     A Elizabeth Calrk[sic]
Q What was her name before you married herM[sic]     A Elizabeth Sutton.
Q When did you marry her?     A June, 1883.
Q Have you a certificate of marriage?     A Yes sir.
    The applicant presents a certificate of marriage, certifying that he was married to one, Miss Elizabeth Sutton, according to the laws of the Cherokee Nation on the 24th of June, 1883.
Q Is your wife a Cherokee by blood?     A Yes sir.
Q Have you any children?     A No sir.
Q What is the age of your wife?     A She is thirty nine years old.
Q What is the name of her father?     A John Sutoon[sic].
Q Is he living?     A No sir; he is dead.
Q What is the name of her mother?     A Mary Sutton.
Q Is she living?     A No sir.
    (1800 Roll, Page 79, #506, John Clark, Cooweescoowee D'st)
    (1896 Roll, Page 567, #75, John (C) Clark, Delaware D'st)
    (1896 Roll, Page 450, #612, Elizabeth Clark, Delaware D'st)

By Mr. W. W. Hastings, Cherokee Represenative[sic]:
Q Do you know when your wife's mother moved to South West City, Missouri?
A I think it was about - . She is here; she can tell; I think it was along in 1870 some time.
Q Do you know when they returned to the Cherokee Nation?
A 1881, I believe.

Elizabeth Clark, being called, testified as follows:
Q What is your name?     A Elizabeth Clark.
Q What is your age?     A Thirty nine.
Q What is your Postoffice?     A Grove.
Q Are you a recognized citizen of the Cherokee Nation?     A Yes sir.\
Q By blood?     A Yes sir.

Q What degree of blood do you claim?   A One eighth.

Q What was your name before you were married?   A Sutton.

Q What is your father's name?   A John Sutton.

Q Your mother's name?   A Mary Sutton.

Q Your name is not found on the roll of 1880; do you know why?

A My mother moved to South West City, to send us to school.

Q When did she move there?   A In 1872.

Q How long did she live there?   A Until 1881.

Q She never was readmitted after she returned?   A They said it was no use: We had not lost our citizenship: We had property in the Cherokee Nation: She talked to the Clerk and the Judge and they said we had not lost our citizenship.

Q They knew at that time, did they not, that your name was not on the roll of 1880?

A I do not know.


By Mr. W. W. Hastings, Cherokee Represenative[sic]:

Q How far is South West City over the line?   A About a half of a mile from where we lived.

Q How old are you now?   A Thirty nine.

Q You were twenty years old when you came back?   A Yes sir.

Q When did your father die?   A In 1865,

Q And your mother moved over there?   A Yes sir.

Q Your mother owned property over on this side?   A Yes sir.

Q A farm?   A Yes sir.

Q Owned it when you lived there?   A Yes sir.

Q Where?   A On Wet Prairie.

Q You owned this farm all of the time you were over there in South West City going to school?   A Yes sir.


By the Commission?[sic]

Q Have you any brothers or sisters?   A Yes sir.

Q Are their names upon the authenticated roll of 1880?   A Yes sir; one brother is; my youngest brother was living with my mother.


Q[sic] By Cherokee Represenative[sic], W. W. Hastings:

Q Is George your full brother?   A Yes sir.

Q Is W. H. your full brother?   A Yes sir.


Q[sic] By the Commission:

Q Where were they living in 1880?   A In the Nation.

Q They were not living in South West City with you?   A No sir.

Q Were they older than you?   A Yes sir.

Q Where did you draw your strip money in 1894?   A Here in Vinita.

   (1894 Roll,  Page 364,  #440,  Lizzy Clark, Delaware District)


   The name of John H. Clark appears upon the authenticated roll of 1880, as well as the census roll of 1896.

Q  How long have yiu[sic] lived in the Territory?    A  Since 1871.
Q  Continuously?    A  Yes sir.

The name of John H. Clark appears upon the authenticated roll of 1880, as well as the census roll of 1896; and having made satisfactory proof as to his residence, being duly identified, the said John H. Clark will be listed for enrollment as a Cherokee citizen by blood.

He avers that he was married to one, Elizabeth Sutton, a Cherokee citizen by blood, in 1883, and the name of the said Elizabeth Sutton appears upon the census roll of 1896, as well as the pay roll of 1894, but it is not found on the authenticated roll of 1880.  She testifies, according to her statement in the testimony, as a reason why her name does not appear on the authenticated roll of 1880.  Satisfactory proof having been made that said Elizabeth Sutton is a Cherokee citizen by blood, entitled to citizenship, and the said Elizabeth Clark will be duly listed for enrollment as a Cherokee citizen by blood.

------------------

The undersigned, being sworn, states that as stenographer to the Commission to the Five Civilized Tribes, he correctly recorded the testimony and proceedings in this case, and that the foregoing is a true and complete transcript of his stenographic notes thereof.

R R Cravens

Subscribed and sworn to before me
this 25th day of September, 1900.

C R Breckinridge
COMMISSIONER.

<><><><><>

Cherokee 3424.

Department of the Interior,
Commission to the Five Civilized Tribes,
Muskogee, I. T., October 9, 1902.

In the matter of the application of John H. Clark for the enrollment of himself as a citizen by intermarriage, and for the enrollment of his wife, Elizabeth Clark, as a citizen by blood of the Cherokee Nation:  he being sworn and examined by the Commission, testified as follows:

Q  What is your name?    A  John H. Clark.
Q  How old are you?    A  Sixty-three.
Q  What is your postoffice?    A  Echo.
Q  It isn't Grove now is it?    A  No sir.
Q  You are a white man?    A  Yes sir.
Q  You are on the authenticated tribal roll of 1880 as an intermarried white?    A  Yes sir.

Q  What was the name of your wife at that time?    A  Nancy.

Q  Is she dead?    A  Yes sir, she is dead.

Q  When did she die?    A  Died in '81.

Q  Were you living with her when she died?    A  Yes sir.

Q  You hadn't been separated?    A  No sir.

Q  Have you married again?    A  Yes sir.

Q  When did you marry?    A  I married in 1882.

Q  Who did you marry?    A  Elizabeth Sutton.

Q  Is she a Cherokee by blood?    A  Yes sir.

Q  Is she living?    A  Yes sir.

Q  You have been living with her ever since you married her?    A  Yes sir.

Q  You have never made your home outside of the Cherokee Nation for the past twenty-two years?    A  No sir, not since '71.

Q  How long has your present wife lived in the Cherokee Nation? A  She was raised here.

Q  Born --------A  She was born and raised here.

Q  Lived here all her life? A  Pretty much, only when she was young going to school.

-------------------------------

The undersigned, being duly sworn, states that as stenographer to the Commission to the Five Civilized Tribes he correctly recorded tehe testimony and proceedings in this case, and that the foregoing is a true and correct transcript of his stenographic notes thereof.

E.G. Rothenberger

Subscribed and sworn to before me this 15th day of December, 1902.

BC Jones
Notary Public.

◇◇◇◇◇

ECM                                                                    Cherokee 3424.

## DEPARTMENT OF THE INTERIOR,
## COMMISSIONER TO THE FIVE CIVILIZED TRIBES.

---

In the matter of the application for the enrollment of JOHN H. CLARK as a citizen by intermarriage of the Cherokee Nation.

## D E C I S I O N

THE RECORDS OF THIS OFFICE SHOW:  That at Vinita, Indian Territory, September 25, 1900 application was received by the Commission to the Five Civilized Tribes for the enrollment of John H. Clark as a citizen by intermarriage of the Cherokee

Nation. Further proceedings in the matter of said application were had at Muskogee, Indian Territory, October 9, 1902.

THE EVIDENCE IN THIS CASE SHOWS: That the applicant herein, John H. Clark, a white man, was married in accordance with Cherokee law December 3, 1871 to one Nancy Clark, nee Hamilton, since deceased, who was at the time of said marriage a recognized citizen by blood of the Cherokee Nation, who is identified on the Cherokee authenticated tribal roll of 1880, Cooweescoowee District No. 507 as a native Cherokee marked "Dead". It is further shown that from the time of said marriage until the death of said Nancy Clark, which occurred in 1881, the said John H. Clark and Nancy Clark resided together as husband and wife and continuously lived in the Cherokee Nation. It is also shown that on June 24, 1883 the said John H. Clark was married to one Elizabeth Clark, nee Sutton, who was at the time of said marriage a recognized citizen by blood of the Cherokee Nation, who is identified on the "Strip Payment Roll" of 1894 as "Lizzie Clark", and whose name appears upon the approved partial roll of citizens by blood of the Cherokee Nation opposite No. 8369, but whose name does not appear on the Cherokee authenticated tribal roll of 1880, because at the time it was taken the said Elizabeth Clark was temporarily residing out of the Cherokee Nation. Said absence therefrom is not considered to have been sufficient to cause a forfeiture of her citizenship in the Cherokee Nation. It is further shown that from the time of said marriage the said John H. Clark and Elizabeth Clark resided together as husband and wife and continuously lived in the Cherokee Nation up to and including September 1, 1902. Said applicant is identified on the Cherokee authenticated tribal roll of 1880 and the Cherokee census roll of 1896 as an intermarried citizen of the Cherokee Nation.

IT IS, THEREFORE, ORDERED AND ADJUDGED: That in accordance with the decision of the Supreme Court of the United States, dated November 5, 1906, in the cases of Daniel Red Bird, et al. vs. the United States, Nos. 125, 126, 127, and 128, the said applicant, John H. Clark is entitled, under the provisions of Section Twenty-one of the Act of Congress approved June 28, 1898 (30 Stats. 495), to enrollment as a citizen by intermarriage of the Cherokee Nation, and his application for enrollment as such is accordingly granted.

Tams Bixby

Commissioner.

Dated at Muskogee, Indian Territory,
this    FEB 26 1907

◇◇◇◇◇

| | |
|---|---|
| *REFER IN REPLY TO THE FOLLOWING:* | **DEPARTMENT OF THE INTERIOR,** |
| Cherokee 3424. | **COMMISSIONER TO THE FIVE CIVILIZED TRIBES.** |

ECM                                    Muskogee, Indian Territory, February 12, 1907.

John H. Clark,
     Echo, Indian Territory.

Sir:

     You are directed to appear before the Commissioner immediately upon receipt of this letter to give testimony relative to your right to enrollment as a citizen by intermarriage of the Cherokee Nation, the record in your case being insufficient, it not being shown through whom you claim the right to enrollment as a citizen by intermarriage of the Cherokee Nation.

Respectfully,

Commissioner.

GHC.

◇◇◇◇◇

Cherokee
3424.

Muskogee, Indian Territory, February 26, 1907.

W. W. Hastings,
     Attorney for the Cherokee Nation,
          Muskogee, Indian Territory.

Dear Sir:

     There is enclosed herewith a copy of the decision of the Commissioner to the Five Civilized Tribes, dated February 26, 1907, granting the application for the enrollment of John H. Clark as a citizen by intermarriage of the Cherokee Nation.

Respectfully,

Commissioner.

Encl. HJ-121.
HJC

◇◇◇◇◇

Cherokee
3424.

Muskogee, Indian Territory, February 26, 1907.

The Commissioner to the Five Civilized Tribes,
Muskogee, Indian Territory.

Sir:

Receipt is acknowledged of the testimony and of your decision enrolling John H. Clark as a citizen by intermarriage of the Cherokee Nation. Time for protesting said decision is waived and I consent that said person may be placed upon the schedule immediately.

Respectfully,

W. W. Hastings
Attorney for the Cherokee Nation.

◇◇◇◇◇

Cherokee
3424

Muskogee, Indian Territory, February 26, 1907.

John H. Clark,
Echo, Indian Territory.

Dear Sir:

There is enclosed herewith a copy of the decision of the Commissioner to the Five Civilized Tribes, dated February 26, 1907, granting your application for enrollment as a citizen by intermarriage of the Cherokee Nation.

You will be advised when your name has been placed upon a schedule of citizens of the Cherokee Nation and approved by the Secretary of the Interior.

Respectfully,

Encl. HJ-119.                                          Commissioner.
HJC

**Cher IW 281**

◇◇◇◇◇

# Cherokee Intermarried White 1906
## Volume X

DEPARTMENT OF THE INTERIOR,

COMMISSIONER TO THE FIVE CIVILIZED TRIBES.

In the matter of the application for the enrollment of

ROBERT A. PRATHER

As a citizen by intermarriage of the Cherokee Nation.

Cherokee 4014

File with Cher. D. 316.

DEPARTMENT OF THE INTERIOR,
COMMISSION TO THE FIVE CIVILIZED TRIBES,
VINITA, I.T., OCTOBER 3rd, 1900.

In the matter of the application of Caroline C. Prather and husband for enrollment as citizens of the Cherokee Nation, and she being sworn and examined by Commissioner T.B. Needles, testified as follows:

Q What is your name?  A Caroline C. Prather.
Q How old are you?  A Sixty-eight.
Q What is your postoffice?  A Vinita.
Q What district do you live in?  A Delaware.
Q Are you a citizen by blood?  A Yes, sir.
Q Do you want to enroll any one byt[sic] yourself?  A Yes, sir; my husband.
Q Is he not here?  A No, sir; he is sick in bed.
Q What is his name?  A Robert A. Prather.
Q White man?  A Yes, sir.
Q How long have you been married to him?  A Thirty three or thirty four years.
Q How old is your husband?  A He is seventy three. Will be next May.
    (1896 roll, page 517, #2416, Edath[sic] C. Prather, Delaware D'st)
    (1896 Roll, page 585, #420, Robert A. Prather, Delaware D'st)
Q How long have you lived in the Cherokee Nation?  A About thirty five years.
Q Right along; continuously?  A Yes, sir, never lived out.

The applicant presents a certified copy, issued from the Executive Department of the Cherokee Nation, July 13th, 1886, said certificate being signed by W. P. Boudenot, Executive Secretary, under the seal of the Nation, certifying that Caroline C. Prather and family were admitted to citizenship.

Afterwards a certified is presented, certifying that the said Caroline C. Prather and family were summoned to appear before the Commission to try and determine applications for citizenship and show cause why their admission was not obtained by fraud.

Said applicants did appear before the Commission on the 27th of June, 1887; the case was investigated and the following verdict was rendered: "We, the Commission on Citizenship, fail to find that fraud or briberty[sic] has been resorted to by the said Prathers in obtaining their citizenship in the Cherokee Nation, on December 19th, 1870. We find for the defendants in this case." Signed by J. T. Adair, Chairman, D. W. Lipe and H. C. Barnes, Commissioners, certified to by William M. Gulliger, Assistant Executive Secretary, under the seal of the Nation.

It appears that because said charge of fraud, the names of the applicants were not placed on the authenticated roll of 1880. Their names are found upon the census roll of 1896, according to the page and number of the rolls as indicated in the testimony. The applicant avers under oath that she was married to one Robert A. Prather about the year 1873, according to the laws of the Cherokee Nation, and that she has lived with him continuously ever since. Proof being satisfactory as to the citizenship of the said Caroline C. Prather and Robert A. Prather, her husband, she will be duly listed for enrollment as a Cherokee citizen by blood, and the said Robert A. Prather as a citizen by intermarriage.

---

The undersigned, being sworn, states that as stenographer to the Commission to the Five Civilized Tribes he correctly recorded the testimony and proceedings in this case, and that the foregoing is a true and cokplete[sic] transcript of his stenographic notes thereof.

(Signed) R. R. Cravens.

Sworn to and subscribed before me this 7th day of October, 1900.

(Signed) C. R. Breckinridge,
Commissioner.

----oooOOOooo----

J. O. Rosson, being first duly sworn, states that as stenographer to the Commission to the Five Civilized Tribes he correctly recorded the testimony and proceedings in this case, and that the foregoing is a true and complete transcript of his stenographic notes thereof.

JO Rosson

Subscribed and sworn to before me this October 11th, 1901.

T B Needles

Commissioner.

◇◇◇◇◇

To be filed in Straight Cherokee #4014, Robert A. Prather et al.

Department of the Interior,
Commission to the Five Civilized Tribes,
Vinita, I.T., October 16th, 1901.

SUPPLEMENTAL TESTIMONY in the matter of the enrollment of Lenora Prather, et al, as Cherokee citizens; introduced on part of applicants.

APPEARANCES:
Mr. P. S. Davis, Attorney for Applicants;
Mr. J. L. Baugh, of Counsel for Cherokee Nation.

ROBERT A. PRATHER, being duly sworn by Commissioner Needles, testified as follows on part of applicants:

MR. DAVIS:    State your name to the Court?    A  Robert A. Prather.

Q  How old are you, Mr. Prather?    A  I will be 76 in May.

Q  Are you the applicant in case No. 4014, Robert A. Prather, et al?

A  I reckon I am.

Q  That is the number of the case, No. 4014, you are the applicant there?

A  Yes, sir.

Q  What is the name of your wife?    A  Caroline Prather.

Q  I will ask you if your and your wife, Caroline Prather, had a son by the name of Richard L. Prather?    A  Yes, sir, Richard Lewis Prather.

Q  At the time of the death of your son, Richard L. Prather, was he married to a woman named Lenora Prather, and living with her?    A  I didn't see them married, but they was living, he was living with a woman, Lenora, she was considered his wife. They was married I think at Claremore.

Q  Mr. Prather, in your case, 4014, you offered as exhibits to the Commission certain citizenship papers issued to you and your wife in '86 and in 1870; I will ask you, if at the time you and your wife were admitted to citizenship, Richard L. Prather was admitted and included in these same papers?    A  Yes, sir, his name was on the papers.

Q  I will ask you if you ever turned over to me as attorney for Lenora Prather these same original papers that were offered as exhibits in your case, No. 4014?    A  I suppose I never turned over but one batch to you.

Q  They are the same papers you turned over to me?    A  I suppose they are.

Q  You say that Caroline C. Prather is the mother of Richard L. Prather?    A  Yes, sir.

Q  And you are the father of Richard L. Prather?    A  Yes, sir, we raised him.

MR. BAUGH:  Why, Mr. Prather, were you folks admitted in '86?

A  Well, we passed through that, there was a re-examination called and we passed through successfully as I know.

Q  You were admitted in '70?     A  We was admitted by the Daniels Court in '71.

Q  Your wife was the only one that was admitted at that time?

A  I guess so, I wasn't there.

Q  Now then, isn't it a fact you were accused back in 1886 before the Commission court, and that the Cherokee Nation alleged that fraud had been practiced in your case, in 1870; in the case of your wife?     A  Yes, sir.

Q  In the examination of that case and the findings of the court wasn't it this, that they found that no fraud had been practiced in the admission of the person who was admitted, that was your wife?

> Mr. Davis:  I object to this question for the reason that it is incompetent, immaterial and irrelevant, that these papers are the best evidence, certified copies of which is filed in case D. #16, they show what was done.
>
> Commissioner:  Objection will be noted and witness answer.
>
> Mr. Baugh:  The Cherokee Nation proposes to make that as a foundation and to show that the persons that were placed on the certificate at the time were placed there without any authority, or without the authority of the court itself.

Q  Is that a fact?     A  I don't know.

Q  Well, the case was simply tried upon the question of fraud itself in the admission of your wife, wasn't it?     A  I don't know, the papers are here.

Q  Did you go with your wife and them to make a new application for citizenship in 1886?     A  I don't think that I did, I might but I don't recollect it.

> PRESTON S. DAVIS, being duly sworn by Commissioner Needles:  testified as follows in behalf of the applicants:

> Mr. David:  I desire to state that the papers mentioned in the testimony in case #4014, Robert A. Prather, et al, the originals were turned over to me as attorney for Lenora Prather, the wife of Richard L. Prather, and certified copies of the same were made by me, that same certified copies of said papers, certified to by me as a notary public, are now on file in case D. #16; and that said papers show upon their face that Richard L. Prather was admitted at the time his mother, Caroline C. Prather, was admitted to citizenship in the Cherokee Nation; that those certified copies are correct and were duly compared by me in all respects with the original papers here filed by me as attorney of the applicant.

> COM'R NEEDLES:  Where are the original papers?     A  Mr. Prather has
them.

> Com'r Needles:  The testimony taken will be made a part of the record in the case at bar, and upon the request of the attorney for the Cherokee Nation will be made part of the record in the case of Robert A. Prather, et al, No. 4014.

Mr. Davis: I desire to introduce in evidence that portion of the amendments of the Constitution of the Cherokee Nation relating to citizenship in said Nation by intermarriage, as found at the beginning of the compilation of the Cherokee laws of 1892, and is amendment of Article three, section Five, pages 33 and 34, compiled laws of the Cherokee Nation, edition of 1892.

Com'r Needles: It will be done.

---0000::0000---

J. O. Rosson, being first duly sworn, states that as stenographer to the Commission to the Five Civilized Tribes he correctly recorded the testimony and proceedings in this case, and the foregoing is a true and complete transcript of his stenographic notes thereof.

(Signed) J. O. Rosson.

Subscribed and sworn to before me this October 21st, 1901.

(Signed) T. B. Needles,
Commissioner.

Arthur G. Croninger, being duly sworn, states that as stenographer to the Commission to the Five Civilized Tribes he made the foregoing copy, and that the same is a true and complete copy of the original transcript.

Arthur G. Croninger

Subscribed and sworn to before me this 11th day of December, 1901.

T B Needles
Commissioner.

◇◇◇◇◇◇

Cherokee 4014.

Department of the Interior,
Commission to the Five Civilized Tribes,
Muskogee, I. T., October 3, 1902.

In the matter of the application of Robert A. Prather for the enrollment of himself as an intermarried citizen, and for the enrollment of his wife, Caroline C. Prather, as a citizen by blood of the Cherokee Nation.

Preston S. Davis, being sworn and examined by the Commission, testified as follows:
Q What is your name?     A Preston S. David.

Q  What is your age?    A  Thirty-two years old this coming November.

Q  Are you acquainted with Robert A. Prather?    A  Yes sir.

Q  How long have you know him?    A  I have known him since 1883.

Q  What is his wife's name?    A  Caroline.

Q  Has Robert A. Prather and his wife, Catherine[sic], lived together all the time since you have known them as husband and wife?    A  Yes sir, both living and living together now as husband and wife.

Q  Living together on the first day of September, 1902?    A  Yes sir.

Q  Never have separated?    A  No sir, never have separated.

Q  Do you know whether Robert A. Prather was married to his wife, Catherine C., under a Cherokee license?    A  He was, and applied to the Cherokee citizenship Commission and was duly admitted before that Commission and the record of the same is on file in his application before this Commission.

Q  Has his marriage license been filed?    A  Yes sir; and also has his admission to citizenship before the Cherokee Commission been filed.

Q  Where has Robert A. Prather and his wife, Catherine C. lived for the last eight years?    A  Vinita.

Q  Cherokee Nation?    A  Yes sir, living there now.

Q  Is there any other statement you wish to make?    A  No sir, I believe not.

————————————

The undersigned, being duly sworn, states that as stenographer to the Commission to the Five Civilized Tribes he correctly recorded the testimony and proceedings in this case, and that the foregoing is a true and correct transcript of his stenographic notes thereof.

E.G. Rothenberger

Subscribed and sworn to before me this 4th day of October, 1902.

BC Jones
Notary Public.

◇◇◇◇◇

Cherokee 4014.

DEPARTMENT OF THE INTERIOR,
COMMISSION TO THE FIVE CIVILIZED TRIBES.
Muskogee, I. T., October 30, 1902.

In the matter of the application of Robert A. Prather for the enrollment of himself as a citizen by intermarriage, and for the enrollment of his wife, Caroline C. Prather, as a citizen by blood, of the Cherokee Nation.

SUPPLEMENTAL PROCEEDINGS.

L. S. ROBINSON, being sworn, testified as follows:

By the Commission,

Q What is your name?    A Robinson; L. S. Robinson.
Q How old are you?    A I am fifty-one years old.
Q What is your postoffice address?    A Big Cabin.
Q You appear for the purpose of giving some testimony in the matter of the application of Robert A. Prather and his wife?    A I suppose just himself.
Q Well, it is both of them.  The matter of his application for both?
A Yes, sir.
Q What is the reason Robert A. Prather is not before the Commission?
A Dr. Clinkscales says an abscess on his lungs.
Q Is Dr. Clinkscales the attending physician?    A Yes, sir.
Q Is Mr. Prather confined to the house?    A Nearly all the time.
Q Is he a very old man?    A Yes, sir, close to eighty years old, I think.  He is between seventy-five and eighty.
Q How long have you known Robert A. Prather?    A Well, I guess I have known him for eight years.
Q Eight years?    A Yes, sir, I married his daughter seven years ago.
Q Known him since then?    A Yes, sir.
Q Has Robert A. Prather and his wife, Caroline, lived together since you have known them as husband and wife?    A Yes, sir.
Q They never have been separated?    A No, sir.
Q They were living together as husband and wife on the first day of September, 1902?
A Yes, sir.
Q And both living at the time?    A yes, sir.
Q Have they lived in the Cherokee Nation for the last eight years?
A I expect for the last forty.
Q Well, so far as you know?    A Yes, sir.

Retta Chick, being first duly sworn, states that, as stenographer to the Commissioner to the Five Civilized Tribes, she recorded the testimony and proceedings

173

in the matter of the foregoing application, and that the above is a true and complete transcript of her stenographic notes thereof.

Retta Chick

Subscribed and sworn to before me this 9th day of December, 1902.

PG Reuter
Notary Public.

◇◇◇◇◇

J.

Cherokee 4014

Cherokee Allotment_____

Department of the Interior,
Commission to the Five Civilized Tribes,
Cherokee Land Office,

Tahlequah, I.T., August 10, 1903.

In the matter of the application of Robert A. Prather for the enrollment of himself as a citizen by intermarriage, and for the enrollment of his wife, Caroline C. Prather, as a citizen by blood of the Cherokee Nation.

## SUPPLEMENTAL TESTIMONY.

HOWARD L. PRATHER, being duly sworn and examined by the Commission, testified as follows:

Q What is your name?   A Howard L. Prather.
Q How old are you?   A I am 41.
Q What is your postoffice address?   A Grove.
Q Are you a citizen by blood of the Cherokee Nation?   A Yes sir.
Q You present here a power of attorney signed by R. A. Prather and Caroline Prather, authorizing you to select allotments for them in the Cherokee Nation. Are R. A. Prather and Caroline Prather related to you?   A Yes sir.
Q What relation?   A Father and mother.
Q Are they citizens of the Cherokee Nation?   A Yes sir.
Q What is your father's correct name?   A Robert A. Prather.
Q What is your mother's correct name?   A Caroline Prather.
Q Has she an initial?   A C. Aint[sic] C but they always got it that way; it is P for Phoebe.
Q Then the R. A. Prather and the Caroline Prather who sign this power of attorney are the same people as your parents, Robert A. and Caroline C. Prather, are they?
A Yes sir.

Q Why aren't they here to select their own allotments?    A They are not able; been sick in bed for over a year; sick most of the time.

Q Are they old and feeble?    A Yes sir; father is 78 and mother is 73.

Q They are both of them too infirm from old age to appear here?    A Yes sir.

+++++++++++++++++++++++++

Mable F. Maxwell, being duly sworn, states that, as stenographer to the Commission to the Five Civilized Tribes, she correctly recorded the supplemental testimony in this case, and that the above is a true and complete transcript of her stenographic notes thereof.

Mable F. Maxwell

Subscribed and sworn to before me
this 10th day of August, 1903.

Samuel Foreman
Notary Public.

◇◇◇◇◇

E.C.M.

Cherokee ~~4041~~.
4014

DEPARTMENT OF THE INTERIOR,
COMMISSIONER TO THE FIVE CIVILIZED TRIBES.
Muskogee, I. T., February 15, 1907.

In the matter of the application for the enrollment of Robert A. Prather as a citizen by intermarriage of the Cherokee Nation.

W. W. Hastings representing the Cherokee Nation.

Howard L. Prather being first duly sworn by Frances R. Lane, a Notary Public for the Western District of Indian Territory, testified as follows:

By the Commissioner:

Q What is your name?    A Howard L. Prather.

Q Your age?    A Forty-five.

Q What is your postoffice address?    A Grove, I. T.

Q You appear here today for the purpose of testifying relative to the right of Robert A. Prather to enrollment as a citizen by intermarriage of the Cherokee Nation ?    A yes sir, what I know?[sic]  I wasn't very old at that time.

Q What relation are you to Robert A. Prather?

A He is my father.

Q Was Robert A. Prather the husband of a Cherokee by blood?

A Yes sir.

Q What was her name?    A Caroline Prather.

Q When were Caroline C. Prather and Robert A. Prather married?

A They were married--I don't know exactly how long. I was about nine years old when they got married the second time.

Q I mean in accordance with the Cherokee law?    A That was bout 1870-- '69 or '70.

> Book S. of Marriage Records, Delaware district, for the years 1868 to 1874 inclusive, on page indexed as T. opposite No. 42, the following entry is found:
> "This is to certify by me that Robert A. Prather, a white man, was licensed to marry Caroline Rogers, a female Cherokee on the ____ day of February, 1869, and the license executed and returned February 14, 1869, being with according to the Act passed by the National Council bearing date October 15, 1855 in regard to white men marrying in this Nation.
> (Signed) T. J. McGhee<br>Clerk Delaware District Court.<br>Cherokee Nation."

Q Mr. Prather, do you know when your mother was admitted to citizenship in the Cherokee Nation?    A Not exactly because I was young; it was along about 1869 or '70; we come to the Territory in 1867, and it was sometime a year or two afterwards.

Q Was your mother admitted to citizenship when you first came to the Territory?

A We had been here about a year.  It was a year or two year before she got the certificate.

Q Had she been admitted to citizenship about the time you father married her in accordance with Cherokee law?    A Yes sir.

Q She had been admitted then?    A Yes sir.

Q You offer in evidence here today, a certified copy showing that Caroline Prather was admitted to citizenship on December 19, 1870?    A I don't know nothing about that; I was too young to know anything about that; I was only nine years old.  That was after she was made a citizen I suppose, that she was married according to the Cherokee law; after she was made a citizen.

Q Now, Mr. Prather, I will ask you if there were not some charges of fraud preferred against their admission to citizenship in 1870?

A Not that I know of--later on there was.

Q Were these charges sustained.[sic]  A No, I think not.

By Mr. Hastings:

Q You offer in evidence a certified copy of your mother's re-admission to citizenship on December 19, 1870?    A I don't know anything about that.  I was so young then.

Q I will ask you if you desire to offer that in evidence?    A The main thing I was aiming at was the time they got married.

Q I am asking you if you desire to offer in evidence the certified copy which you have referred to?    A Yes sir.

> By the Commissioner: The same will be accepted and made a part of the record herein.

There is also offered in evidence a copy of the docket in the case of the Cherokee Nation vs. Robert A. Prather and Caroline Prather, in which said parties were charged with fraud in obtaining their admission to citizenship in the Cherokee Nation. Said case was called and tried and determined on August 11, 1887, the committee on citizenship finding that there was no fraud in said admission.

The copy of the docket entry in this case will be accepted and made a part of the record herein.

------

Frances R. Lane upon oath states that as stenographer to the Commission to the Five Civilized Tribes she reported the testimony in the above entitled cause and that the above and foregoing is a true and correct transcript of her stenographic notes thereof.

Frances R Lane

Subscribed and sworn to before me this February 15, 1907.

Walter W. Chappell
Notary Public.

◇◇◇◇◇

JOURNAL   CONTINUED   1870.

Monday morning Dec. 19th, 1870, Court met pursuant to adjournment, with all present: Docket of Delaware District continued and the case of the Cherokee Nation Vs. Caroline Prather being announced as ready for trial, was taken up and in absence of witnesses documentary evidence was produced for examination: Court then adjourned to 2, P.M.

2, o'clock P.M. Court met pursuant to appointment and the above case continued, and after the consideration of the testimony, make the following decision: " That Caroline C. Prather is a Cherokee by blood and entitled to full rights and privileges of a Cherokee citizen".

Executive Department, Cherokee Nation,
Tahlequah, Ind. Terr. Aug. 21-1900
I, A. B. Cunningham, Assistant Executive Secretary, of the Cherokee Nation do hereby certify that the above and foregoing is a true and correct transcript of page 6 of the record of the Supreme Court of the Cherokee Nation, acting as a "Court of Commission: to try and decide the rights of persons returned on the census rolls whose rights to Cherokee Citizenship is doubtful: Chief Justice R. B. Daniel, Jno. S. Vann and Red-Bird Sixkiller

composing said "Court of Commission", with W. H. Turner Clerk and Johnson Foreman Atty. for the Cherokee Nation.

 In Witness Whereof, I hereunto set my hand and affix the seal of the Cherokee Nation, the day and date above written.

A. B. Cunningham

Assistant Executive Secretary, C.N.

◇◇◇◇◇

*(The Affidavit below was originally handwritten on the microfilm and is typed as given.)*

2nd Recording Dist
Indian Territory

Grove  February 5" 1907

 Personally appeared before me a notary in and for said Dist. and Territory. Howard L. Prather age 45 years whose Post Office and residence is Grove, Ind Territory to me well known and entitled to credit who after being duly sworn declares as follows:  I was at the home of my father, Robert A Prather, One mile west of Maysville Ark in the Cherokee Nation in the year about 1870 when my father remarried my mother, Caroline C. Prather according to the laws of the Cherokee Nation existing at that time.  I was then about nine years old.  There were present at the wedding James Allen Thompson and wife, now deceased, John Millers wife, now living, whose Post office is Needmore. Knows about the marriage being in the neighborhood at the time.

Howard L. Prather

The within affidavit subscribed and sworn to this

*(illegible)* 5 day of February A.D. 1907.

G.S. Remsen

Notary Public

My Coms Expires May 2d 1908.

◇◇◇◇◇

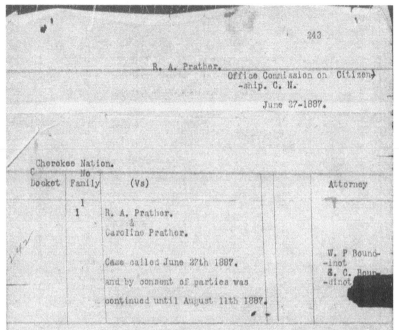

243

R. A. Prather.

Office Commission on Citizen-
-ship. C. N.

June 27-1897.

Cherokee Nation.

| Docket | Family | (Vs) | | Attorney |
|---|---|---|---|---|
| 1 | 1 | R. A. Prather. & Caroline Prather. Case called June 27th 1887. and by consent of parties was continued until August 11th 1887. | | W. P Bound- -inot S. C. Boud- -inot |

the above case was tried August 11th 1887. and has since that time
been awaiting the action of the Commission on Citizenship upon the
charge of fraud & bribery having been used in securing the judgement
on the Commission, granting said Prathers Citizenship in the Cherokee
Nation( See, 18th sec, of an act of Dec, 8th 1886.)

The case was duly tried and the Nations Att'y Hon R. F. Wyly. used
every endeavor to ferret out the fraud charge.
alledged

This case was tried and admitted to citizenship Dec 19th 1870. by
the Bob Daniels Court of Commission.

The witnesses in this are all about dead, and the original testimony
upon which the Commission based their opinion has nearly all been lost
in consequence of which , The Attorney for the Nation had but little
margin to work on.

*(continued below)*

179

We the Commission on Citizenship fail to find that fraud or bribery
had been resorted to by said Prathers in obtaining their citizenship
in the Cherokee Nation, on Dec, 19th 1870-
We find for the defendants in this cause.

J. T. Adair, Chairman Commission

D. W. Lipe, Commissioner.

H. C. Barnes, Commissioner.

Office Com- on Citizenship,

Tahlequah. I, T. Nov,1st 1888.

I, William M. Gulager , Assistant Executive Secretary hereby certify
that the above is a true and literal copy of the page given and
is now a matter of record in this Department.

Given this 15th, 1896.

*William M. Gulager*

Assistant Executive Secretary.

*(Copy of original document from case.)*

◇◇◇◇◇

*(The below typed as given.)*

Vinita, Ind. Ter.
Febuary 2nd. 19o7.

On this 2nd. day of February 19o7 personally appeared before me a Notary Public for the
Northern District, Ind. Ter., Mrs John Parks nee ~~Mollie Rogers~~ Margarette Prather and
stated that she is a citizen of the Cherokee Nation Ind. Ter. and that she is a daughter of
RobertAaPrather and Edith Caroline Prrather Nee ( Edith Caroline Rogers).
. and I am 52 years old.
She further states that her father and her mother were married prior to 1875 under the
laws of the Cherokee Nation Ind. Ter and that she was present at there second marriage
under said laws of the Cherokee Nation, Ind. Ter., and that her ~~parents~~ father then lived
continuosly in the Cherokee Nation Ind. Ter. near ~~Grove,~~ Vinita, until his death in June
19o6.

Margrett J Prather

))))))))

I do solmnly swear that the above statement is true and correct to the best of my knowledge and belief.

Margrett J Prather

Sworn to and subscribed before me this 2nd, day of Febuary 19o7.

R.V. McSpadden<br/>Notary Public.

My Com Epries Feb 7th, 191o.

T.W.L.                                                                                          Cherokee  4014

## DEPARTMENT OF THE INTERIOR

## COMMISSIONER TO THE FIVE CIVILIZED TRIBES

In the matter of the application for the enrollment of Robert A. Prather as a citizen by intermarriage of the Cherokee Nation the Cherokee Nation.

## D E C I S I O N

THE RECORDS OF THIS OFFICE SHOW:   That at Vinita, Indian Territory, October 3, 1900, application was received by the Commission to the Five Civilized Tribes for the enrollment of Robert A. Prather as a citizen by intermarriage of the Cherokee Nation.  Further proceedings in the matter of said application were had at Vinita, Indian Territory, October 16, 1901, Muskogee, Indian Territory, October 3, 1902, and October 30, 1902, Tahlequah, Indian Territory, August 10, 1903 and Muskogee, Indian Territory, February 15, 1907.

THE EVIDENCE IN THIS CASE SHOWS:   That the applicant herein, Robert A. Prather, a white man, was married in accordance with Cherokee law in February, 1869, to his wife, Caroline C. Prather, nee Rogers, who was at the time of said marriage a recognized citizen by blood of the Cherokee Nation, her name being found opposite No. 9698 on the approved partial roll of citizens of the Cherokee Nation.  It is further shown that from the time of said marriage the said Robert A. Prather and the said Caroline C. Prather resided together as husband and wife and continuously lived in the Cherokee Nation up to and including September 1, 1902. The said Robert A. Prather is identified on the 1896 Cherokee census roll, Delaware District, No. 420, Page 585.  It further appears that on December 19, 1870 the Supreme Court of the United States held that white persons who intermarried with Cherokee citizens, according to Cherokee law, prior to November 1, 1875, are entitled to enrollment and allotments of land as citizens of the Cherokee Nation. Cherokee Nation sitting as a "Court of Commission" to try and decide the rights of persons returned on the census roll whose rights to Cherokee citizenship were doubtful, found "That Caroline C. Prather is a Cherokee by blood and entitled to full rights and privileges of a Cherokee citizen". The Cherokee Nation contends herein that this was an admission of the said Caroline C. Prather and for that reason it was incumbent upon the applicant to show a marriage in accordance with Cherokee tribal law subsequent to said December 19, 1870 and prior to November 1, 1875. It is the opinion of the Commissioner however, that such was not an admission of Mrs Prather to citizenship in the Cherokee Nation, but a judgment or finding of fact that Caroline C. Prather was a citizen by blood of said Nation and that therefore, there is nothing in said finding of the Court of Commission inconsistent with the finding heretofore made that Caroline C. Prather was, at the time of her marriage to Robert A. Prather, a recognized citizen by blood of the Cherokee Nation.

IT IS THEREFORE ORDERED AND ADJUDGED: That in accordance with the decision of the Supreme Court of the United States, dated November 5, 1906, in the cases of Daniel Red Bird, et al., vs. the United States, Nos. 125, 126, 127, and 128, the said applicant, Robert A. Prather is entitled, under the provisions of Section 21 of the Act of Congress approved June 28, 1898 (30 Stats. 495), to enrollment as a citizen by intermarriage of the Cherokee Nation, and his application for enrollment as such is accordingly granted.

Tams Bixby

Commissioner.

Dated at Muskogee, Indian Territory,
this     FEB 27 1907

◇◇◇◇◇

Cherokee                       COPY
4014

Muskogee, Indian Territory, February 27, 1907.

W. W. Hastings,
      Attorney for the Cherokee Nation,
          Muskogee, Indian Territory.

Dear Sir:

There is enclosed herewith a copy of the decision of the Commissioner to the Five Civilized Tribes, dated February 27, 1907, granting the application for the enrollment of Robert A. Prather as a citizen by intermarriage of the Cherokee Nation.

Respectfully,

SIGNED *Tams Bixby*

Encl. HJ-134.                               Commissioner.
HJC

◇◇◇◇◇

Cherokee
4014

Muskogee, Indian Territory, February 27, 1907.

The Commissioner to the Five Civilized Tribes,
Muskogee, Indian Territory.

Sir;

Receipt is acknowledged of the testimony and of your decision enrolling Robert A. Prather as a citizen by intermarriage of the Cherokee Nation. Time for protesting said decision is waived and I consent that said person may be placed upon the schedule immediately.

Respectfully,

W. W. Hastings
Attorney for Cherokee Nation

◇◇◇◇◇

Cherokee
4014.

COPY

Muskogee, Indian Territory, February 27, 1907.

Mrs. Geo. Ella Robinson,
Big Cabin, Indian Territory.

Dear Madam:

There is enclosed herewith a copy of the decision of the Commissioner to the Five Civilized Tribes, dated February 27, 1907, granting the application for the enrollment of Robert A. Prather as a citizen by intermarriage of the Cherokee Nation.

You will be advised when the name of said applicant has been placed upon a schedule of citizens of the Cherokee Nation and approved by the Secretary of the Interior.

Respectfully,

SIGNED *Tams Bixby*

Encl. HJ-131.                                      Commissioner.
HJC

# Cherokee Intermarried White 1906
## Volume X

**Cher IW 282**

DEPARTMENT OF THE INTERIOR,
COMMISSION TO THE FIVE CIVILIZED TRIBES,
VINITA, I.T., OCTOBER 4th, 1900.

In the matter of the application of William Harrison Brown for the enrollment of himself and children as citizens of the Cherokee Nation; said Brown being sworn by Commissioner T. B. Needles, testified as follows:

Q What is your name?    A William Harrison Brown.
Q How old are you?    A Close to 55.
Q What is your post office?    A Kennison.
Q What is your district?    A Cooweescoowee.
Q Are you a recognized citizen of the Cherokee Nation?    A By adoption, yes, sir.
Q Whom do you apply for enrollment?    A W. H. Brown and three children.
Q What is your wife's name?    A My wife is dead.
Q She had a name before she died?    A Georgia Ann.
Q When were you married to her?    A I was married to her in 1871.
Q Is her name upon the roll of 1880?    A Yes, sir.
Q Is your name upon the roll of 1880?    A Yes, sir.
Q What is the name of your children?    A Frank Brown.
Q How old is he?    A 19.
Q What is the name of the next one?    A Mary Brown, 15.
Q Next one?    A Mamie[sic] Brown, 13.

> 1880 enrollment;  page 65, #160, Wm. Brown,  Cooweescoowee.
> 1880 enrollment;  page 65, #161, Ga. Brown,　　　　"
> 1896 enrollment;  page 297, #154,  William Brown,　　"
> 1896 enrollment;  page 112, #394,  Frank Brown,　　　"
> 1896 enrollment;  page 112, #395,  Mary Brown,　　　"
> 1896 enrollment;  page 112, #397,  Mamie Brown,　　　"

Q Did you[sic] wife die before 1896?    A Yes, sir.
Q These children alive and living with you?    A Yes, sir.
Q You have not married since?    A No, sir.
Q Still a widower, are you?    A Yes, sir.

Com'r Needles:--The name of William H. Brown appears upon the authenticated roll of 1880 as well as the census roll of 1896. The name of his children, Frank, Mary and Mamie, appear upon the census roll of 1896. They all being duly identified and having made satsifactory[sic] proof as to their residence, said William H. Born[sic] will be duly listed for enrollment as a Cherokee citizen by intermarriage and his children, Frank, Mary and Mamie, as Cherokee citizens by blood.

184

---oooOOOooo---

J. O. Rosson, being first duly sworn, states that as stenographer to the Commission to the Five Civilized Tribes, he correctly recorded the testimony and proceedings in this case, and the foregoing is a true and complete transcript of his stenographic notes thereof.

J.O. Rosson

Subscribed and sworn to before me this 9th day of October, 1900.

C R Breckinridge
Commissioner.

◇◇◇◇◇

### DEPARTMENT OF THE INTERIOR.
Commission to the Five Civilized Tribes.
Muskogee, Indian Territory, October 6th, 1902.

In the matter of the application of William H. Brown for the enrollment of himself as a citizen by intermarriage of the Cherokee Nation and for the enrollment of his children, Frank, Mary and Nannie Brown, as citizens by blood of the Cherokee Nation.

Supplemental to #4171.

Applicant appears in person.
Cherokee Nation by J. C. Starr.

WILLIAM H. BROWN, being duly sworn, testified as follows:
Examination by the Commission.
Q. What is your name, please?   A. W. H. Brown--William H. Brown.
Q. What is your age at this time?   A. I am nearly 57.
Q. What is your post office?   A. Kinnison[sic].
Q. Are you the same William H. Brown who made application to this Commission for enrollment as an intermarried citizen on October 4th, 19oo[sic]?   A. Yes, sir.
Q. What is your wife's name?   A. Georgia Ann Brown.
Q. Is she living or dead?   A. She is dead.
Q. When did she die?   A. She has been dead 16 years.
Q. When were you married to her?   A. I was married in '72.
Q. Under a Cherokee license?   A Yes, sir.
Q. Were you ever married prior to your marriage to this wife?
A. No, sir.

Q. Was she ever married prior to her marriage to you?
A. Yes, sir.
Q. How many times had she been married?    A. Once.
Q. Was that husband living or dead when you married her?
A. He was dead.
Q. Did you and your wife live together from the time of your marriage, all the time up until her death?    A. Yes, sir.
Q. Have you ever married any other woman since your marriage to this wife?
A. No, sir.
Q. Were you still a widower and single on the first of September, 1902?    A. Yes, sir.
Q. How long have you lived in the Cherokee Nation?    A. I have lived in the Cherokee Nation about 33 years.
Q. Have you lived in the Cherokee Nation all the time for the last 20 years?
A. Yes, sir.
Q. Are these children, Frank, Mary and Mamie, your children by your Cherokee wife?
A. Yes, sir. Mamie ain't the right name of that last one.
Q. What is the right name of this last child?    A. Nannie.
Q. You want the name put down as Nannie and not Mamie?    A. Yes, sir.
Q. Have these children lived in the Cherokee Nation from the time they were born up to the present time?    A. Yes, sir.
Q. All the time?    A. All the time.
Q. Never lived anywhere else?    A No, sir.
Q. Are they all living at this time?    A. Was yesterday morning.

Jesse O. Carr, being first duly sworn, states that as stenographer to the Commission to the Five Civilized Tribes he reported the above entitled case and that the foregoing is a true and complete transcript of his stenographic notes thereof.

Jesse O. Carr

Subscribed and sworn to before me this 3rd day of November, 1902.

BC Jones
Notary Public.

DEPARTMENT OF THE INTERIOR,
COMMISSION TO THE FIVE CIVILIZED TRIBES.
AUXILIARY CHEROKEE LAND OFFICE.

Muskogee, Indian Territory, March 22, 1905.

In the matter of the allotment of land to Nannie Brown, minor, cherokee[sic] Card No. 4171, Approved Roll No. 24461.

Larkin Brown, citizen brother, Cherokee Card No. 4129, Approved Roll No. 9964, being sworn, testified as follows:

Examination by the Commission:

Q    What is your name?    A Larkin Brown.
Q    How old are you?    A 30.
Q    What is your post office?    A Kinnison[sic], Indian Territory.
Q    What is the name of your father?    A William H. Brown.
Q    What is the name of your mother?    A Georgia A. Brown.
Q    Are you father and mother living?    A No sir.
Q    Are you a citizen by blood of the Cherokee Nation?    A Yes sir.
Q    Have you selected an allotment of land?    A Yes sir.
Q    What is your object in appearing at the Land Office today?
A    To designate land as an allotment for my minor sister, Nannie Brown
Q    Is Nannie Brown the daughter of William H. Brown and Georgia A. Brown?
A    Yes sir.
Q    You testified that your father and mother were both dead?    A Yes sir
Q    Who has Nannie Brown been living with since the death of her father and mother?
A    With me.
Q    Are the lands you desire allotted to Nannie Brown improved?    A Yes sir.
Q    Are these lands you wish allotted to her part of your home place?
A    Yes sir.
Q    Has any guardian been appointed for Nannie Brown?    A No sir.
Q    Do the land you wish allotted to her lay west of Grand river?    A Yes sir.
Q    Has any previous filing been made for her?    A No sir.

WITNESS EXCUSED.

Blanch Ashton upon oath states that as stenographer to the Commission to the Five Civilized Tribes she accurately recorded the testimony in the above entitled cause and that the foregoing is a correct transcript of her notes thereof.

Blanch Ashton

Subscribed and sworn to before me this 22nd day of March, 1905.

*(Name Illegible)*

◇◇◇◇◇

E.C.M.                                                    *Cherokee 4171.*

## DEPARTMENT OF THE INTERIOR,
## COMMISSIONER TO THE FIVE CIVILIZED TRIBES.

------------------------

In the matter of the application for the enrollment of William H. Brown as a citizen by intermarriage of the Cherokee Nation.

## D E C I S I O N .

THE RECORDS OF THIS OFFICE SHOW: That at Vinita, Indian Territory, October 4, 1900, application was received by the Commission to the Five Civilized Tribes for the enrollment of William H. Brown as a citizen by intermarriage of the Cherokee Nation. Further proceedings in the matter of said application were had at Muskogee, Indian Territory October 6, 1902.

THE EVIDENCE IN THIS CASE SHOWS: That the applicant herein, William H. Brown, a white man, was married in accordance with Cherokee law in 1871 to his wife, Georgia Ann Brown who was, at the time of said marriage, a recognized citizen by blood of the Cherokee Nation, who is identified on the Cherokee authenticated tribal roll of 1880, Cooweescoowee District, No. 161, as a native Cherokee marked "dead". It is further shown that from the time of said marriage until the death of said Georgia Ann Brown, the said William H. Brown and Georgia Ann Brown resided together as husband and wife and continuously lived in the Cherokee Nation. That after the death of said Georgia Ann Brown the said William H. Brown remained unmarried and continuously lived in the Cherokee Nation up to and including September 1, 1902. Said applicant is identified on the Cherokee authenticated tribal roll of 1880, and on the Cherokee census roll of 1896 as a citizen by intermarriage of the Cherokee Nation.

IT IS, THEREFORE, ORDERED AND ADJUDGED: That in accordance with the decision of the Supreme Court of the United States, dated November 5, 1906, in the case of Daniel Red Bird et al., vs. the United States, Nos. 125, 126, 127 and 128, the said applicant, William H. Brown is entitled, under the provisions of Section 21 of the Act of Congress approved June 28, 1898 (30 Stats. 495), to enrollment as a citizen by intermarriage of the Cherokee Nation, and his application for enrollment as such is accordingly granted.

Tams Bixby
Commissioner.

Dated at Muskogee, Indian Territory,
this    FEB 28 1907

◇◇◇◇◇

# Department of the Interior.
## COMMISSIONER TO THE FIVE CIVILIZED TRIBES.

---

*In the matter of the death of*     **William H Brown**

a citizen of the     **Cherokee**     Nation, who formerly resided at or near

    **Kinnison**[sic]     , Ind. Ter., and died on the     **29**     day of

**June**     , **1903**

---

**AFFIDAVIT OF RELATIVE.**

**Western Dist**
**Ind. Ter.**

I,     **Larkin Brown**     , on oath state that I am     **33**
years of age and a citizen by     **blood**     , of the     **Cherokee**     Nation;
that my postoffice address is     **Kinnison**[sic]     , Ind. Ter.; that I am
    **Son**     of     **William H Brown**
who was a citizen, by     **Intermarriage**     , of the     **Cherokee**     Nation
and that said     **William H Brown**     died on the     **29**     day of
**June**     , **1903**

                **Larkin Brown**

WITNESSES TO MARK:

Subscribed and sworn to before me this to before me this **21st** day of     **August**     , 1907

             **John E. Tidwell**
             Notary Public.

---

**AFFIDAVIT OF ACQUAINTANCE.**

I, _____ , on oath state that I am _____
years of age, and a citizen by _____ of the _____ Nation;
that my postoffice address is _____ , Ind. Ter.;
that I was personally acquainted with _____
who was a citizen, by _____ , of the _____ Nation;
and that said _____ died on the _____ day of
_____ , 1____

WITNESSES TO MARK:

Subscribed and sworn to before me this to before me this _____ day of _____, 190____

Notary Public.

◇◇◇◇◇

Form No. 260.

# THE WESTERN UNION TELEGRAPH COMPANY.
### ———— INCORPORATED ————
**23,000 OFFICES IN AMERICA.    CABLE SERVICE TO ALL THE WORLD.**
ROBERT C. CLOWRY, President and General Manager.

| Receiver's No. | Time Filed | | Check |
|---|---|---|---|

**SEND** the following message subject to the terms on back hereof, which are hereby agreed to.    Cherokee 4171.

C.F.B.                                        Muskogee, I.T., February 12, 1907.

William H. Brown,

        Kennison, Indian Territory,

        Intermarried case incomplete, appear immediately with

witnesses to establish date of marriage.

                                BIXBY

                                        Commissioner.

Paid.
O.B.G.R.

☞ READ THE NOTICE AND AGREEMENT ON BACK. ☜

*(Copies of original documents from case.)*

Form No. 260.

# THE WESTERN UNION TELEGRAPH COMPANY.
### ———— INCORPORATED ————
**23,000 OFFICES IN AMERICA.    CABLE SERVICE TO ALL THE WORLD.**
ROBERT C. CLOWRY, President and General Manager.

| Receiver's No. | Time Filed | Check |
|---|---|---|

**SEND** the following message subject to the terms on back hereof, which are hereby agreed to.

☞ READ THE NOTICE AND AGREEMENT ON BACK. ☜

*(Transcription of above telegram given below.)*

Commissioner

Our tarriff[sic] does not show Kennison I.T. What do you want done with this message. If you can show where to dia[sic] it please do so.

Lane

◇◇◇◇◇

Cherokee 4171

Muskogee, Indian Territory, February 28, 1907.

W. W. Hastings,
Attorney for the Cherokee Nation,
Muskogee, Indian Territory.

Dear Sir:

There is enclosed herewith a copy of the decision of the Commissioner to the Five Civilized Tribes, dated February 28, 1907, granting the application for the enrollment of William H. Brown, as a citizen by intermarriage of the Cherokee Nation.

Respectfully,

SIGNED *Tams Bixby*

Encl. H-61
JMH

Commissioner.

◇◇◇◇◇

Cherokee 4171

Muskogee, Indian Territory, February 28, 1907.

The Commissioner to the Five Civilized Tribes,
Muskogee, Indian Territory.

Sir:

Receipt is acknowledged of the testimony and of your decision enrolling William H. Brown as a citizen by intermarriage of the Cherokee Nation. Time for protesting said decision is waived, and I consent that said person may be placed upon the schedule immediately.

Respectfully,

W.W. Hastings
Attorney for Cherokee Nation.

◇◇◇◇◇

Cherokee 4171.                    COPY

Muskogee, Indian Territory, February 28, 1907.

William H. Brown,
    Kinnison[sic], Indian Territory.

Dear Sir:

There is enclosed herewith a copy of the decision of the Commissioner to the Five Civilized Tribes, dated February 28, 1907, granting your application for enrollment as a citizen by intermarriage of the Cherokee Nation.

You will be advised when your name has been placed upon a schedule of citizens of the Cherokee Nation and approved by the Secretary of the Interior.

Respectfully,

SIGNED *Tams Bixby*
Encl. H-60                         Commissioner.
    JMH

◇◇◇◇◇

Cherokee
    4171

Muskogee, Indian Territory, March 26, 1907

Frank Brown,
    Welch, Indian Territory.

Dear Sir:

This office is in receipt of your letter of February 18, 1907, relative to the right to enrollment as a citizen by intermarriage of the Cherokee Nation, of your father, William H. Brown, deceased.

In reply you are advised that the application of William H. Brown for enrollment as a citizen by intermarriage of the Cherokee Nation, was granted by the Department February 28, 1907, and his name now appears opposite Number 262 on a schedule of such citizens approved by the Secretary of the Interior.

# Cherokee Intermarried White 1906
## Volume X

Respectfully,

L M B                                     Acting Commissioner

---

**Cher I W 283**

◇◇◇◇◇

DEPARTMENT OF THE INTERIOR,
COMMISSION TO THE FIVE CIVILIZED TRIBES,
CLAREMORE, I. T., OCTOBER 22d, 1900.

In the matter of the application of Marshall Mann for the enrollment of himself wife and child as citizens of the Cherokee Nation; said Mann being sworn and examined by Commissioner T. B. Needles, testified as follows:

Q   What is your name?   A   Marshall Mann.
Q   What is your age?   A   50.
Q   What is your post office address?   A   Chouteau.
Q   What district do you line in?   A   Cooweescoowee.
Q   Are you a recognized citizen of the Cherokee Nation?   A   Yes, sir.
Q   By blood or intermarriage?   A   Intermarriage.
Q   For whom do you apply for enrollment?   A   Myself, wife and daughter.
Q   What is your wife's name?   A   Pauline.
Q   When were you married to her?   A   1873.
Q   What is the name of your child?   A   Lola.
Q   How old is Lola?   A   15.
Q   Was Pauline a white person of indian[sic]?   A   Indian.
Q   Lola alive and living with you at this time?   A   Yes, sir.
Q   How long have you lived in the Cherokee Nation?   A   28 years.
Q   Lived continuously with your wife since that time?   A   Yes, sir.
Q   She is aoive[sic] now?   A   Yes, sir.

> 1880 enrollment;   page 285, #1668, Marshall Mann, Delaware.
> 1880 enrollment;   page 285, #1669, Pauline Mann, Delaware.
> 1896 enrollment;   page 824, #121, Marshall Mann, Going Snake.
> 1896 enrollment;   page 767, #1342, Pauline Mann, Going Snake.
> 1896 enrollment;   page 767, #1343, Lola Mann, Going Snake.

Com'r Needles:--The name of Marshall Mann appears upon the authenticated roll of 1880 as an intermarriage[sic] white and also appears upon the census roll of 1896. The name of his wife, Pauline, appears upon the authenticated roll of 1880 as a Cherokee citizen by blood, and her name also appears upon the census roll of 1896, as well as the name of his daughter, Lola. They all being deuly[sic] identified according to the page and number of the rolls as indicated in the testimony, and having made satisfactory proof as to their residence, said Marshall Mann will be duly listed for enrollment as a Cherokee

193

citizen by intermarriage, and his wife, Pauline, and his daughter, Lola, as Cherokee citizen[sic] by blood.

---oooOOOooo---

J. O. Rosson, being first sworn, states that as stenographer to the Commission to the Five Civilized Tribes, he correctly recorded the testimony and proceedings in this case, and the flregoing[sic] is a true and complete transcript of his stenographic notes thereof.

J.O. Rosson

Subscribed and sworn to before me this 23d day of October, 1900.

TB Needles
Commissioner.

◇◇◇◇◇

C.F.B.                                                        Cherokee 4735

## DEPARTMENT OF THE INTERIOR,

## COMMISSIONER TO THE FIVE CIVILIZED TRIBES
## MUSKOGEE, IND. TER., JANUARY 4, 1907.

In the matter of the application for the enrollment of MARSHALL MANN as a citizen by a citizen by intermarriage of the Cherokee Nation:

APPEARANCES:

Applicant represented by Pauline Mann:

Cherokee Nation by H. M. Vance, on behalf of Attorney, W. W. Hastings:

PAULINE MANN being first duly sworn by B. P. Rasmus, a Notary Public, testified as follows:

On Behalf of Commissioner:

Q.   What is your name?   A.  Pauline Mann.
Q.   What is your age?    A.  Fifty-three.
Q.   What is your postoffice address?    A.  Muskogee.
Q.   Are you a citizen by blood of the Cherokee Nation?
A.   Yes sir.
Q.   Are you married?   A.  Yes sir.
Q.   Is your husband living or dead?   A.  He is dead.
Q.   Was he a Cherokee by blood or a white man?   A.  He was a white man.

Q. You appear here to-day for the purpose of giving testimony relative to the right to enrollment of your deceased husband, Marshall Mann, as a citizen by intermarriage of the Cherokee Nation, do you?    A. Yes sir.

Q. When were you married to him?    A. The 24th day of March, 1873.

Q. Where were you living at the time you married him?

A. Webbers Falls, Canadian District.

Q. Was he a resident of the Indian Territory at that time?

A. Yes sir; he had been here about a year.

Q. Did he secure a license and marry you in accordance with the laws of the Cherokee Nation?    A. Yes sir.

Q. Was the license issued in Canadian District?    A. Yes sir.

Q. Were you ever married before you married him?    A. No sir.

Q. Was he ever married before he married you?    A. No sir.

Q. From the time of your marriage did you and he continuously live together as husband and wife, in the Cherokee Nation, until his death?    A. Yes sir.

Q. Do you remember the exact date of his death?    A. The 31st day of October, 1902.

The applicant, Marshall Mann, is identified on the Cherokee authenticated tribal roll of 1880 Delaware District No. 1668. His wife, Pauline Mann, is included in an approved partial roll of citizens by blood of the Cherokee Nation, opposite No. 11360.

Q. Have you any evidence of a documentary character showing your marriage to your husband, Marshall Mann?

A. No, I had the license, and our house burned down, and it was burned with everything we had.

Q. Are you sure the license was issued in Canadian District?

A. Yes sir, we were living at Webbers Falls.

Q. In 1873?    A. Yes sir; in 1873.

-------------------------------------------------------

The undersigned, being first duly sworn, states that as stenographer to the Commission to the Five Civilized Tribes she correctly recorded the testimony taken in this case, and that the above and foregoing is a full, true and correct transcript of her stenographic notes thereof.

Subscribed and sworn to before me this the 4th day of January, 1907.

John E. Tidwell
Notary Public.

Cherokee 4733.

DEPARTMENT OF THE INTERIOR,
COMMISSION TO THE FIVE CIVILIZED TRIBES,
Webbers Falls, Indian Territory,
February 23, 1907.

------------------------------

In the matter of the application for the enrollment of MARSHALL MANN as a citizen by intermarriage of the Cherokee Nation.

------------------------------

J. L. McCORKLE, being first duly sworn by H. L. Sanders, a Notary Public, testified as follows:

ON BEHALF OF THE COMMISSIONER:

Q    What is your name?
A    J. L. McCorkle.
Q    What is your age?
A    I was born in 1837.
Q    Mr. McCorkle, are you a citizen of the Cherokee Nation?
A    Not so regarded.
Q    Were you at one time a citizen of the Cherokee Nation?
A    So regarded.
Q    Did you ever hold any official position in the Cherokee Nation?
A    I was Clerk of the District Court, Canadian district from 1869 to 1874.
Q    While acting in that capacity did you issue a marriage license to Marshall Mann, a white man, to marry Miss Pauline McCoy, a citizen by blood of the Cherokee Nation?
A    Yes sir.
Q    When was that license issued?
A    On the 22nd day of March, 1873.
Q    When were they married?
A    On the 24th day of March, 1873.
Q    Mr. McCorkle, how do you fix the date of their marriage?
A    From some old papers in my possession.  Then when Marshall Mann left this country he owed me $75.00; that makes me remember all about him.
Q    What is the nature of these papers?    Are they parts of records that you kept while clerk of the District Court?
A    They are parts of the records not turned over to my successor.  They were among some old scraps in a trunk that I had, and which I came across in making a search for information.

Q   Now Mr. McCorkle, you can swear positively that this paper which you hand me is a part of a leaf taken from a record of the marriage license iddued[sic] by you while acting as Clerk of the District Court of Canadian District?

A   Yes sir. I had received a letter from Mrs. Mann and made a search for the license, and upon finding it made a note on this paper. I have not now got the original, I don't know where it is.

Q   After their marriage was Marshall Mann recognized as a citizen of the Cherokee Nation?

A   Yes sir.

Q   Did they reside together as husband and wife as long as you knew them?

A   Yes sir.

Q   Mr. McCorkle, will you let the Commissioner have this memorandum now in your possession?

A   Yes sir.

ON BEHALF OF THE COMMISSIONER:

The witness here presents a copy taken from the record of marriage licenses issued by the Clerk of the District Court of Canadian District, showing a license to have been issued to Marshall Mann on the 22nd day of March, 1873, and solemnized on the 24th day of March, 1873, and recorded on the 27th day of March, 1873.

(WITNESS EXCUSED)

ROBERT T. HANKS, being first duly sworn by H. L. Sanders, a Notary Public, testifies as follows:

ON BEHALF OF THE COMMISSIONER:

Q   What is your name[sic]

A   Robert T. Hanks.

Q   What is your age?

A   67.

Q   Were you present at the marriage of Marshall Mann and Pauline Mann?

A   I don't think I was.

Q   When did you first become acquainted with Marshall Mann?

A   Well, a good many years ago.

Q   Was it prior to November 1, 1875?

A   Oh yes.

Q   Well Mr. Hanks, while you were not present at the marriage, you are willing to swear it was prior to November 1, 1875, are you?

A   Yes sir, I am, and I think it was either in 1872 or 1873.

Q   Is his wife, Pauline Mann, a Cherokee?

A   Yes.

Q    Was he recognized as a citizen of the Cherokee Nation before his marriage to his wife, Pauline?

A    No sir.

Q    Then it was by virtue of his marriage to his wife, Pauline, that he became a citizen of the Cherokee Nation, was it?

A    Yes sir.

Q    Were either of them ever married before their marriage in 1873?

A    I never heard they was.

Q    From the date of their marriage until the death of Marshall Mann did they continuously reside together as husband and wife and live in the Cherokee Nation?

A    Well, you see, they moved away from here, but I always heard they did. As long as they were here they did.

Q    Now Mr. Hanks, you are willing to swear positively that they were married before November 1, 1875, are you?

A    Yes sir.

Q    And that they were married under a license issued by the authorities of the Cherokee Nation?

A    I did'nt[sic] see the license, but they had to get one before they could marry.

Q    Was Mrs. Mann born and raised in the Cherokee Nation?

A    Yes sir, she was.

(WITNESS EXCUSED.)


E. C. Motter, being first duly sworn, doth depose and say that the above and foregoing are the original questions propounded by him to, and the answers returned thereto by Robert T. Hanks and J. L. McCorkle, the above named witnesses.

E.C. Motter

Subscribed and sworn to before me this 25th day of February, 1907.

Walter W. Chappell
Notary Public.


This certifies that the undersigned, being duly sworn, states that as stenographer to the Commission to the Five Civilized Tribes she reported the proceedings had in the above entitled cause and that the above and foregoing is a full, true and correct transcript of her stenographic notes thereof.

Georgia Coberly

Subscribed and sworn to before me this 25th day of February, 1907.

Oliver C Hinkle
Notary Public.

C.F.B.                                                        Cherokee 4735

## DEPARTMENT OF THE INTERIOR,
### COMMISSIONER TO THE FIVE CIVILIZED TRIBES.
### MUSKOGEE, IND. TER. FEBRUARY 23, 1907.

Supplemental proceedings in the matter of the application for the enrollment of Marshall Mann as a citizen by intermarriage of the Cherokee Nation.

Mrs. W. N. Martin, being first duly sworn by Mrs. Lyman K. Lane, notary public, testified as follows:

Q.  What is your name?    A. Mrs. W. N. Martin.
Q.  What is your age?    A. I am fifty-three years old.
Q.  What is your postoffice address?    A. Muskogee.
Q.  You appear here today for the purpose of giving testimony relative to the right to enrollment of Marshall Mann as a citizen by intermarriage of the Cherokee Nation, do you?
A   I do.
Q.  Is Marshall Mann living at this time?    A He is not.
Q.  How long has he been dead?    A. Well, I am sure I don't know. He has been dead a long time.
Q.  A matter of two or three years?    A. I don't know how long it has been. I remember when he died.
Q.  How long had you known him prior to his death?    A. I had known him ever since before his marriage.
Q.  He was the husband of Pauline Mann?    A. He was the husband of Pauline Mann.
Q.  Mrs. Mann's maiden name was McCoy, was it?    A. It was.
Q.  Do you know when Marshall and Pauline Mann were married?
A.  I do.
Q.  Will you give me the date of their marriage?    A. The 24th day of March '73.
Q.  Were you present at the marriage ceremony?    A. I was.
Q.  You are not able, are you, to give personal testimony as to whether or not Marshall Mann secured a license to marry his wife, Pauline Mann in accordance with the law of the Cherokee Nation?    A. Yes, he was married according to Cherokee law.
Q.  But what I want to know is if you can state positively that he secured a license. Did you see the license?    A. The license was read at his wedding.
Q.  How long had you known him prior to that time?    A. Well sometime, I can't tell exactly how long.
Q.  Pauline Mann was his first wife, was she?    A. She was, I think.
Q.  And he was her first husband?    A. He was.
Q.  You have known them continuously since then, have you, or until the time of the death of Marshall Mann?    A. Yes, I have known them, and known the family. They lived in a different part of the country from where I lived. I lived Muskogee and they lived in the Cherokee Nation.

Q. You never heard Marshall Mann's rights as a citizen by intermarriage of the Cherokee Nation, questioned?    A. Never.

Q. You state that you were present at the ceremony?    A. I was at the wedding.

Q. And that you heard the license read?    A. Yes sir, the license was read at the wedding. They were married by a District Judge. Judge Taylor, and it was the custom to read the license.

Mattie M. Pace, being first duly sworn, states that as stenographer to the Commission to the Five Civilized Tribes, she reported the proceedings had in the foregoing cause, and that the same is a full, true and correct transcript of her stenographic notes thereof.

Mattie M Pace

Subscribed and sworn to before me this February 23, 1907.

Walter W. Chappell
Notary Public.

◇◇◇◇◇

E C M                                    Cherokee 4735.

## DEPARTMENT OF THE INTERIOR,
## COMMISSIONER TO THE FIVE CIVILIZED TRIBES.

In the matter of the application for the enrollment of MARSHALL MANN as a citizen by intermarriage of the Cherokee Nation.

## D E C I S I O N

THE RECORDS OF THIS SHOW:  That at Claremore, Indian Territory, October 22, 1900 application was received by the Commission to the Five Civilized Tribes for the enrollment of Marshall Mann as a citizen by intermarriage of the Cherokee Nation. Further proceedings in the matter of said application were had at Muskogee, Indian Territory, January 4, 1907 and February 23, 1907 and at Webbers Falls, Indian Territory, February 23, 1907.

THE EVIDENCE IN THIS CASE SHOWS:  That the applicant herein, Marshall Mann, a white man, was married in accordance with Cherokee law March 24, 1873 to his wife, Pauline Mann, nee McCoy, who was at the time of said marriage a recognized citizen by blood of the Cherokee Nation, who is identified on the Cherokee authenticated tribal roll of 1880, Delaware District No. 1669 as a native Cherokee, and whose name is included on the approved partial roll of citizens by blood of the Cherokee Nation opposite No. 11360.  It is further shown that from the time of said marriage the said Marshall Mann and Pauline Mann resided together as husband and wife and continuously lived within the domain of the Five Civilized Tribes up to and including September 1, 1902. Said applicant is identified on the Cherokee authenticated tribal roll of 1880 and the Cherokee census roll of 1896 as an intermarried citizen of the Cherokee Nation.

IT IS, THEREFORE, ORDERED AND ADJUDGED: That in accordance with the decision of the Supreme Court of the United States, dated November 5, 1906, in the cases of Daniel Red Bird, et al. vs. the United States, Nos. 125, 126, 127, and 128, the said applicant, Marshall Mann is entitled to enrollment, under the provisions of Section Twenty-one of the Act of Congress approved June 28, 1898 (30 Stats., 495), to enrollment as a citizen by intermarriage of the Cherokee Nation, and his application for enrollment as such is accordingly granted.

Tams Bixby<br>Commissioner.

Dated at Muskogee, Indian Territory,
this    FEB 27 1907

◇◇◇◇◇

Cherokee
4735.

Muskogee, Indian Territory, December 29, 1906.

Pauline Mann,
    Muskogee, Indian Territory.

Dear Madam:

November 6, 1906, the United States Supreme Court held that white persons who intermarried with Cherokee citizens according to Cherokee law prior to November 1, 1875, are entitled to enrollment and allotments of land as citizens of the Cherokee Nation.

You are advised that to properly determine the right to enrollment as a citizen by intermarriage of the Cherokee Nation, of your deceased husband, Marshall Mann, it will be necessary for you to appear before the Commissioner for the purpose of giving testimony as to the date of your marriage and whether or not his wife, by reason of his marriage to whom he claims the right to enrollment as a citizen of the Cherokee Nation, was a recognized citizen of the Nation at the time of his marriage to her, and whether or not he was married in accordance with Cherokee laws.

You are therefore directed to appear before the Commissioner at Muskogee, Indian Territory, at 9 o'clock A. M., on Friday, January 4, 1907, and give testimony as above indicated.

Respectfully,

H.J.C.                                                    Acting Commissioner.

◇◇◇◇◇

Cherokee
4735.

COPY

Muskogee, Indian Territory, February 27, 1907.

W. W. Hastings,
        Attorney for the Cherokee Nation,
                Muskogee, Indian Territory.

Dear Sir:

      There is enclosed herewith a copy of the decision of the Commissioner to the Five Civilized Tribes, dated February 27, 1907, granting the application for the enrollment of Marshall Mann as a citizen by intermarriage of the Cherokee Nation.

Respectfully,

SIGNED *James Bixby*

Encl. HJ-135.
    HJC                                            Commissioner.

◇◇◇◇◇

Cherokee
4735.

Muskogee, Indian Territory, February 27, 1907.

The Commissioner to the Five Civilized Tribes,
        Muskogee, Indian Territory.

Sir:

      Receipt is acknowledged of the testimony and of your decision enrolling, Marshall Mann as a citizen by intermarriage of the Cherokee Nation. Time for protesting said decision is waived and I consent that said person may be placed upon the schedule immediately.

Respectfully,

W. W. Hastings
Attorney for Cherokee Nation.

Cherokee                                    <u>COPY</u>
4735.

Muskogee, Indian Territory, February 27, 1907

Pauline Mann,
        Muskogee, Indian Territory.

Dear Madam:

        There is enclosed herewith a copy of the decision of the Commissioner to the Five Civilized Tribes, dated February 27, 1907, granting the application for the enrollment as a citizen by intermarriage of the Cherokee Nation of your deceased husband Marshall Mann.

        You will be advised when the name of your husband, Marshall Mann has been placed upon a schedule of citizens of the Cherokee Nation and approved by the Secretary of the Interior.

                                    Respectfully,

                                    SIGNED  *Tams Bixby*
Encl. HJ-133.
    HJC                                    Commissioner.

---

**Cher IW 284**

◇◇◇◇◇

### DEPARTMENT OF THE INTERIOR.
### COMMISSION TO THE FIVE CIVILIZED TRIBES.
### CLAREMORE, I.T., OCTOBER 29th, 1900.

IN THE MATTER OF THE APPLICATION OF Isaac P. Howell for the enrollment of himself, wife and one child as citizens of the Cherokee Nation, and he being sworn and examined by Commissioner, C. R. Breckinridge, testified as follows:

Q   What is your full name?   A  Isaac P. Howell.
Q   How old are you?   A  Fifty three.
Q   What is your Postoffice?   A  Texana[sic].
Q   In what district do you live?   A  Canadian.
Q   Do you apply for the enrollment of yourself and family?
A   Yes sir.
Q   Have you a wife?   A  Yes sir.

Q   How many children have you?   A  One.
Q   Are you a Cherokee by blood?   A  No sir.
Q   Is your wife a Cherokee by blood?   A  Yes sir.
Q   Let me see your marriage license and certificate?   A  I have not got them.
Q   Are you on the roll of 1880?   A  Yes sir.
Q   When were you married?   A  In 1871, or '72.
Q   Are you living now with the same wife you married then?
A   Yes sir.
Q   Have you and she continued to live in the Cherokee Nation since 1880?   A  Yes
sir; came here about 1868 I think.
Q   Give me the name of your wife?   A  Rebecca Howell.
Q   How old is she?   A  Fifty four years old.
Q   Give me the name of her father?   A  I can not give you his full name: Woods.
Q   Is he dead?   A  Yes sir.
Q   Do you remember her mother's given name?   A  Edy.
Q   Is she dead?   A  Yes sir.
Q   Give me the name of your child?   Emmett Lee Howell.
Q   How old is the child?   A  Sixteen years old.
Q   He is living now, is he?   A  Yes sir.

(1880 Roll, Page 439, #829, Isaac Howell, Going Snake D'st)
(1880 Roll, Page 439, #830, Beckey Howell, Going Snake D'st)
(1896 Roll, Page 88, #106, Isaac P. Howell, Canadian D'st)
(1896 Roll, Page 32, #864, Beckie Howell, Canadian D'st)
(1896 Roll, Page 32, #865, Emmett L. Howell, Canadian D'st)

Q   Your wife has lived in the Cherokee Nation all her life, has she?
A   No sir; she was born in the Cherokee Nation, but was taken out when she was little:
Me and her were married and I moved back here in 1868.
Q   Have you lived here ever since?   A  Yes sir.

The applicant applies for the enrollment of himself, his wife and one child: His wife is
identified on the rolls of 1880 and 1896, as a native Cherokee: She has lived in the
Cherokee Nation since 1868, and will be listed now for enrollment as a Cherokee by
blood.

The applicant married his wife in 1871, or 1872. He is identified on the rolls of
1880 and 1896, as an adopted white. He has lived with her in the Cherokee Nation eve
since their marriage, and he will be listed for enrollment as a Cherokee by intermarriage.

The child, Emmett Lee Howell, a minor, is identified on the roll of 1896: He is living
now, and will be listed for enrollment as a Cherokee by blood.

--------------------------------

The undersigned, being sworn, states that as stenographer to the Commission to the
Five Civilized Tribes, he correctly recorded the testimony and proceedings in this case,
and that the foregoing is a true and complete transcript of his stenographic notes thereof.

R R Cravens

Subscribed and sworn to before
me this 29th day of October, 1900.

C R Breckinridge
COMMISSIONER.

◇◇◇◇◇

Cherokee 5037.

Department of the Interior,
Commission to the Five Civilized Tribes,
Muskogee, I. T., September 29, 1902.

In the matter of the applicayion[sic] of Isaac P. Howell for the enrollment of himself as a citizen by intermarriage, and for the enrollment of his wife, Rebecca, and child, Emmett L. Howell, as citizens by blood of the Cherokee Nation; he being sworn and examined by the Commission, testified as follows:

Q    What is your name?    A  Isaac P. Howell.
Q    What is your age at this time?    A  About 54.
Q    What is your postoffice?    A  Texanna.
Q    Are you the same Isaac P. Howell for whom application was made to the Commission on October 29, 1900?    A  Yes sir.
Q    You claim as an intermarried citizen?    A  Yes sir.
Q    What is your wife's name?    A  Rebecca.
Q    She a citizen by blood?    A  Yes sir.
Q    When were you and she married?    We were married in '67.
Q    You never have been married to any other woman since your marriage to her?
A    No sir.
Q    Are you her first husband?    A  No sir.
Q    Had she been married before that?    A  Yes sir.
Q    Was her husband living or dead when you married her?    A  Dead.
Q    How many time had she been married?    A  Just the once.
Q    Is she your first wife?    A  No sir.
Q    How many times had you been married before?    A  Once before.
Q    Was your first wife dead?    A  No sir, she was living.
Q    Had you been divorced from her before you married this woman?    A  Yes sir.
Q    Where?    A  In Dallas County, Arkansas.
Q    Did you file a copy of the decree of the divorce when you made your application?
A    Yes.
Q    Have you and your wife Rebecca lived together as husband and wife continuously since you were married?    A  Yes sir.
Q    Never have been separated?    A  No sir.
Q    Are you living together as husband and wife now?    A  Yes sir.
Q    And were living together on the first day of September, 1902?    A  Yes sir.
Q    How long have you lived in the Cherokee Nation?    A  Been here ever since '68.

Q   Continuously since that time?      A  Yes sir, except out on a visit a week or so at a time.

Q   And your wife has lived here in the Cherokee Nation ever since your marriage?

A   Yes sir.

Q   Is your wife Rebecca and your son Emmett L., living at this time?   A  Yes sir.

----------------------------

The undersigned, being duly sworn, states that as stenographer to the Commission to the Five Civilized Tribes he correctly recorded the testimony and proceedings in this case, and that the foregoing is a true and correct transcript of his stenographic notes thereof.

                                                  E.G. Rothenberger

Subscribed and sworn to before me this 16th day of October, 1902.

                                        BC Jones
                                                Notary Public.

                        ◇◇◇◇◇

## DEPARTMENT OF THE INTERIOR.
## COMMISSION TO THE FIVE CIVILIZED TRIBES.
## AUXILIARY CHEROKEE LAND OFFICE.

                          Muskogee, Indian Territory, March 3, 1905.

In the matter of the allotment of land to Rebecca Howell and her minor son Emmett L. Howell, Cherokee Card No. 5037, Approved Roll Nos. 12043 and 12044.

Emmett L. Howell being sworn, testified as follows:

Examination by the Commission:

Q   What is your name?    A  Howell.

Q   Full name?    A  Emmett L. Howell.

Q   How old are you?    A  20.

Q   What is the name of your father?    A  Isaac P. Howell.

Q   What is the name of your mother?    A  Rebecca Howell.

Q   What is your post office?    A  Texanna.

Q   Is your father living?    A  No sir.

Q   Is your mother living?    A  Yes sir.

Q   What is your object in appearing at the Land Office today?

A   To designate lands for an allotment for my mother and myself.

Q   Are there any improvements on the land that you want to designate as allotments for your mother and yourself?    A  Yes sir.

Q   Home place you are living on?    A  Yes sir.

Q   Since the death of your mother[sic] do you represent your mother in all business matters?   A  Yes sir.

Q   Has she requested you to make these designations for herself?   A  Yes sir.

Q   Has she given you any written authority?   A  Yes sir.

> Witness offers Power of Attorney executed by Rebecca Howell dated February 25, 1905, wherein she appoint Lee H. Howell her minor son, her lawful attorney for the purpose of filing her allotment in the Cherokee Nation.

Q   Is the Rebecca Howell who executed this Power of Attorney your mother?

A   Yes sir.

Q   Are you identical with the Lee H. Howell named in this Power of Attorney?

A   Yes sir.

Q   In the Power of Attorney which you offer your mother states that she is physically unable to leave home, is this the reason that she does not make personal selection?

A   Yes sir.

Q   How long has she been in this condition?   A  About 20 years off and on.

Q   She is an invalid then?   A  Yes sir, sometimes she is able to be up and sometimes she is not.

Q   Do the lands lay west of the Grand river?   A  Yes sir.

Q   Has any previous application been made for lands for either your mother or yourself?   A  No sir.

Q   This is first application?   A  Yes sir.          (WITNESS EXCUSED)

Blanch Ashton upon oath states that as stenographer to the Commission to the Five Civilized Tribes she accurately recorded the testimony in the above entitled cause and that the foregoing is a correct transcript of her stenographic notes thereof.

Blanch Ashton

Subscribed and sworn to before me this the 3rd day of March, 1905.

WS Hawkins
Notary Public.

◇◇◇◇◇

*(The Affidavit below was originally handwritten on the microfilm and is typed as given.)*

*Texanna, I. T.*     Feb 20"          *190* 7

To whom it may concern:

This to certify that I, Rebecca Howell a citizen of the Cherokee Nation and on Cherokee Roll No. 12043, was born in the year of 1841, was married to Isaac P. Howell 1867 in the state of Ark. and again under the Cherokee law in 1871 by Judge Thornton in Goingsnake Dist.

207

Ind Terr. John Thornton was Clerk who issued the license and I further certify that I was a recognized citizen of the Cherokee Nation at the time I was married to Isaac P. Howell and that we were married under the Cherokee Law.

| | | her |
|---|---|---|
| Wit to Mark | { J.R. Whisenhunt | Rebecca x Howell |
| | { Ethel Quinton | mark |

Subscribed and sworn to before me a Notary Public this 20 day of Feb 1907

My com expires Feb 1" 1909

D. Ogden
Notary Public

◇◇◇◇◇

E. C. M.                                                                        Cherokee 5037.

DEPARTMENT OF THE INTERIOR,
COMMISSIONER TO THE FIVE CIVILIZED TRIBES.
Muskogee, Indian Territory, February 26, 1907.

In the matter of the application for the enrollment of Isaac P. Howell as a citizen by intermarriage of the Cherokee Nation.

Cherokee Nation represented by W. W. Hastings.

------------------------

Noah Whisenhunt being first duly sworn by Walter W. Chappell, a Notary Public, testified as follows:

ON BEHALF OF COMMISSIONER.

Q   What is your name?                    A   Noah Whisenhunt.
Q   What is your age?                     A   73 years old.
Q   What is your post office address?
A   Oolagah, Indian Territory.
Q   You appear here today for the purpose of giving testimony relative to the right of Isaac P. Howell to enrollment as a citizen by intermarriage of the Cherokee Nation?
A   Yes sir.
Q   Through whom does he claim his right to enrollment as a citizen of the Cherokee Nation?
A   Rebecca Woods,-- her maiden name was. She was a widow --
Q   When was he married to Rebecca Woods?
A   He was first married in Arkansas.
Q   When was he married in the Cherokee Nation?
A   In '71; that was when he was married but I don't know for certain only I was living right by him; I never seen him married.

208

# Cherokee Intermarried White 1906
## Volume X

Q    Was he married under a license issued by the authorities of the Cherokee Nation?
A    That was my understanding.
Q    In what district was he married?
A    Going Snake District.
Q    Secured his license in Going Snake District?
A    Yes sir; John Thornton was the Clerk.
Q    Was Rebecca his first wife?
A    No sir; he had been married once before in Arkansas.
Q    To whom?                              A    I forget her name.
Q    Was she a Cherokee or white woman?            A    White woman.
Q    Was she dead at the time he married Rebecca?
A    I think so.
Q    Was she the only woman he was ever married to besides Rebecca?
A    Yes sir.
Q    Is Rebecca living now?
A    She is; just is alive though.
Q    Is Isaac P. Howell alive?
A    No sir; he's dead.
Q    When did he die?
A    He's been dead-- I don't know the dates exactly; He's been dead nearly two years; it
     will be two years this fall sometime.
Q    You don't know much about this first marriage of his, do you?
A    No sir.
Q    You don't know whether he was ever divorced from his wife or whether she ws a
     white woman or whether she died?
A    She died.


BY MR. HASTINGS.

Q    This man indicates in his original testimony that he was perhaps divorced from her;
     you don't know about that, do you?
A    No sir.
Q    Did you ever know his first wife?
A    O yes, I have seen her.
Q    How far did she live from you?
A    Two or three miles; in the same neighborhood.
Q    You knew they separated?                  A    Yes.
Q    Then you were just guessing that she was dead?
A    I heard she was; I didn't know.
Q    You didn't know that she was dead before his marriage to Rebecca?
A    No, I didn't know it.

Q    Wasn't Isaac P. Howell first married over in Arkansas to Rebecca and then
     afterwards married in the Cherokee Nation?
A    Yes sir.

Q   What was Howell's wife's maiden name?
A   Rebecca Woods.
Q   She had never been married before she married Howell?
A   Yes sir.
Q   What was her first husband's name?
A   Kirk.
Q   Was Kirk living---
A   No sir; he was killed in time of the war.
Q   She had only been married to one man, Kirk, before she married Howell?
A   That's right.
Q   Do you know when Howell came to the Cherokee Nation?
A   Yes sir.
Q   When?
A   He came to the Cherokee Nation about '68.
Q   Did his wife live in the Cherokee Nation prior to the war?
A   She was born and partly raised here and then they moved to Arkansas, and after the war, they came back in '68.
Q   Is it your understanding that they moved to Arkansas about the beginning of the war?
A   No sir; it was away[sic] before the war.
Q   Do you know whether she was admitted after they came back here or not?
A   Yes sir.
Q   When?
A   I can't give you the exact time at all; they was admitted in '68 or '69.
Q   Mr. Whisenhunt, do you know anything about that second marriage in the Cherokee Nation?
A   I do not only from hearsay.
Q   Did you hear that they were married the second time and in the Cherokee Nation?
A   Yes sir; I heard they got license and went to Judge Thornton and got married; and he was always recognized by the Courts; he sat on juries and voted; I know that to be true. I never saw his license and never saw him married.

BY THE COMMISSIONER.

An examination of the records of persons admitted to Cherokee citizenship since 1866, shows on Page 13, the name of "Isaac Howell, December 5, '69, re-admitted, unconditional."

There is here presented in evidence, an affidavit signed by Rebecca Howell, which is accepted and made a part of the record herein as follows:

"Texanna, I. T., Feb. 20th, 1907.

To whom it may concern:
This to certify that I, Rebecca Howell a citizen of the Cherokee Nation and on Cherokee Roll No. 12043, was born in the year of 1841, was married to

Isaac P. Howell 1867 in the state of Ark. and again under the Cherokee Law in 1871 by Judge Thornton in Goingsnake District, Ind. Terr. John Thornton was Clerk who issued the license and I further certify that I was a recognized citizen of the Cherokee Nation at the time I was married to Isaac P. Howell and that we were married under the Cherokee Law.

her<br>
Rebecca  x  Howell<br>
mark

J. R. Whisenhunt

Wit. to Mark

Ethel Quinton.

Subscribed and sworn to before me a Notary Public, this 20 day of Feb. 1907.

D. Ogden<br>
Notary Public.

(SEAL)

My Com. expires Feb. 1st, 1909.

--------------------

The undersigned on oath states that she reported the testimony in this case and that the foregoing is a true and correct transcript of her stenographic notes thereof.

Myrtle Hill

Subscribed and sworn to before me this the 26th day of February, 1907.

Walter W. Chappell<br>
Notary Public.

◇◇◇◇◇

E C M                                               Cherokee 5037.

## DEPARTMENT OF THE INTERIOR,
## COMMISSIONER TO THE FIVE CIVILIZED TRIBES.

In the matter of the application for the enrollment of ISAAC P. HOWELL as a citizen by intermarriage of the Cherokee Nation.

## D E C I S I O N

THE RECORDS OF THIS OFFICE SHOW: That at Claremore, Indian Territory, October 29, 1900 application was received by the Commission to the Five Civilized Tribes for the enrollment of Isaac P. Howell as a citizen by intermarriage of the Cherokee Nation. Further proceedings in the matter of said application were had at Muskogee, Indian Territory, September 29, 1902, March 3, 1905 and February 26, 1907.

THE EVIDENCE IN THIS CASE SHOWS: That the applicant herein, Isaac P. Howell, a white man, was married in the state of Arkansas in 1867 to his wife, Rebecca Howell, nee Woods, who is identified on the Cherokee authenticated tribal roll of 1880, Going Snake District No. 830 as a native Cherokee, and whose name appears upon the approved partial roll of citizens by blood of the Cherokee Nation opposite No. 12043. It is further shown that subsequent to the said marriage of the said Isaac P. Howell and Rebecca Howell they removed to the Cherokee Nation, whereupon, the said Isaac P. Howell was on December 5, 1869 re-admitted to citizenship therein by the duly constituted authorities of said Nation. The record of said re-admission is construed to have included that of his wife, the said Rebecca Howell. The evidence also shows the said Isaac P. Howell and Rebecca Howell to have been re-married in accordance with Cherokee law in 1871. It is also shown that from the time of their said removal the said Isaac P. Howell and Rebecca Howell resided together as husband and wife and continuously lived in the Cherokee Nation up to and including September 1, 1902. It appears also that the said Isaac P. Howell had been married prior to his marriage to the said Rebeca Howell to a woman from whom he claims to have been divorced, and it is a presumption of law in favor of the validity of the second marriage that the said Isaac P. Howell was divorced from his first wife before his marriage to Rebecca Howell. Said applicant is identified on the Cherokee authenticated tribal roll of 1880 and the Cherokee census roll of 1896 as an intermarried citizen of the Cherokee Nation.

IT IS, THEREFORE, ORDERED AND ADJUDGED: That in accordance with the decision of the Supreme Court of the United States, dated November 5, 1906, in the cases of Daniel Red Bird, et al. vs. the United States, Nos. 125, 126, 127, and 128, the said applicant, Isaac P. Howell is entitled, under the provisions of Section Twenty-one of the Act of Congress approved June 28, 1898 (30 Stats. 495), to enrollment as a citizen by intermarriage of the Cherokee Nation, and his application for enrollment as such is accordingly granted.

Tams Bixby
Commissioner.

Dated at Muskogee, Indian Territory,
this      FEB 27 1907

◇◇◇◇◇

Cherokee
5037

Muskogee, Indian Territory, December 28, 1906.

Isaac P. Howell,
        Texanna, Indian Territory.

Dear Sir:

November 6, 1906, the United States Supreme Court held that white persons who intermarried with Cherokee citizens according to Cherokee law prior to November 1, 1875, are entitled to enrollment and allotments of land as citizens of the Cherokee Nation.

You are advised that to properly determine your right to enrollment as a citizen by intermarriage of the Cherokee Nation, it will be necessary for you to appear before the Commissioner for the purpose of giving testimony as to the date of your marriage and whether or not your wife, by reason of your marriage to whom you claim the right to enrollment as a citizen of the Cherokee Nation, was a recognized citizen of the Cherokee Nation at the time of your marriage to her, and whether or not you were married to her in accordance with Cherokee laws.

You are therefore directed to appear before the Commissioner at Muskogee, Indian Territory, at 9 o'clock A. M., on Friday, January 4, 1907, and give testimony as above indicated.

                                        Respectfully,

H.J.C.                                        Acting Commissioner.

◇◇◇◇◇

**Form No. 260.**

## THE WESTERN UNION TELEGRAPH COMPANY.
INCORPORATED
#### 23,000 OFFICES IN AMERICA.    CABLE SERVICE TO ALL THE WORLD.
ROBERT C. CLOWRY, President and General Manager.

| Receiver's No. | Time Filed | | Check |
|---|---|---|---|

**SEND** the following message subject to the terms on back hereof, which are hereby agreed to.  Cherokee 5037.

C.F.R.    Muskogee, I.T., February 12, 1907.

Isaac P. Howell,

Texanna, Indian Territory.

Intermarried case incomplete appear immediately with witnesses to establish date of marriage.

Bixby
Commissioner.

Paid.
C.F.C.R.

☞ READ THE NOTICE AND AGREEMENT ON BACK. ☜

*(Copy of original document from case.)*

◇◇◇◇◇

Cherokee
5037.

Muskogee, Indian Territory, February 12, 1907.

Special

Isaac P. Howell,
Texanna, Indian Territory.

Dear Sir:

The Commissioner sent you this day a telegram as follows:

"Intermarried case incomplete, appear immediately with witnesses to establish date of marriage".

The Act of Congress approved April 26, 1906, provides that the Secretary of the Interior shall have no jurisdiction to approve the enrollment of any person as a citizen of the Cherokee Nation after March 4, 1907.

This matter, therefore, demands your immediate attention.

Respectfully,

HJC                                                Commissioner.

◇◇◇◇◇

Cherokee 5037

Muskogee, Indian Territory, February 27, 1907.

W. W. Hastings,
    Attorney for the Cherokee Nation,
        Muskogee, Indian Territory.

Dear Sir:

There is enclosed herewith a copy of the decision of the Commissioner to the Five Civilized Tribes, dated February 27, 1907, granting the application for the enrollment of Isaac P. Howell as a citizen by intermarriage of the Cherokee Nation.

Respectfully,

Encl. E-27                                     Commissioner.

  BLE

◇◇◇◇◇

Cherokee 5037.

Muskogee, Indian Territory, February 27, 1907.

The Commissioner to the Five Civilized Tribes,
    Muskogee, Indian Territory.

Sir:

Receipt is acknowledged of the testimony and of your decision enrolling Isaac P. Howell as a citizen by intermarriage of the Cherokee Nation. Time for protesting said decision is waived, and I consent that said person may be placed upon the schedule immediately.

Respectfully,

W. W. Hastings
Attorney for Cherokee Nation.

◇◇◇◇◇

Cherokee 5037

Muskogee, Indian Territory, February 27, 1907.

Isaac P. Howell,
    Texanna, Indian Territory.

Dear Sir:

    There is enclosed herewith a copy of the decision of the Commissioner to the Five Civilized Tribes, dated February 27, 1907, granting the application for your enrollment as a citizen by intermarriage of the Cherokee Nation.

    You will be advised when your name has been placed upon a schedule of citizens of the Cherokee Nation and approved by the Secretary of the Interior.

Respectfully,

Encl. E-28                                     Commissioner.
  BLE

---

**Cher IW 285**

◇◇◇◇◇

E
Cher D 2025

Department of the Interior,
Commission to the Five Civilized Tribes,
Muskogee, I. T., June 30, 1902.

    In the matter of the application of JAMES BULLETT, ET AL., for enrollment as citizens of the Cherokee Nation:

    EMMET STARR, being duly sworn and examined by the Commission, testified as follows:

Q    What is your name ?   A  Emmet Starr.
Q    What is your age ?    A  Thirty one years.
Q    What is your post office address ?   A Claremore, I. T.
Q    You are a citizen by blood of the Cherokee Nation ?
A    Yes sir, I am.
Q    You are so recognized ?   A  Yes sir.

Q   For whom do you desire to make application for enrollment   ?

A   For the following names persons on the 1896 Cherokee roll, their families and descendants:

Q   Are there any other persons for whom you desire to make application for enrollment?

A   I desire to apply for the following named persons on the 1880 Cherokee roll, their families and their descendants:

**Hugh Holland, page 769, # 1051, Tahlequah District; Ad. White.**

E. C. Bagwell, on oath states that as stenographer to the Commission to the Five Civilized Tribes, he correctly recorded the testimony and proceedings had in the above entitled cause, and that the foregoing is an accurate transcript of his stenographic notes thereof.

E.C. Bagwell

Subscribed and sworn to before me this August 5, 1902.

PG Reuter
Notary Public.

◇◇◇◇◇

R.

DEPARTMENT OF THE INTERIOR.
Commission to the Five Civilized Tribes.
Muskogee, Indian Territory, July 23rd, 1902.

---

In the matter of the application of Walter Holland for the enrollment of his father, Hugh Holland, as a citizen by intermarriage of the Cherokee Nation.

---

Supplemental to D-2025

---

Walter Holland was listed for enrollment on Cherokee doubtful card #2024 on June 30th, 1902, upon information.

---

Cherokee Nation appears by W. W. Hastings.

---

WALTER HOLLAND, being duly sworn, testified as follows:
Examination by the Commission.

Q. What is your name?    A. My name is Walter Holland.

Q. How old are you, Mr. Holland?    A. Why, I was born in 1873.

Q. What is your post office address?    A. It will be Grove from now on.

Q. What is the name of your father?    A. Hugh Holland.

Q. About how old is he?    A. I don't know. I couldn't say exactly. I have heard him say he was 54.

Q. Is he living? A. Yes, sir.

Q. Where does he reside?    A. Tahlequah.

Q. Is he a Cherokee or white man?    A. White man.

Q. What is the name of the wife through whom he claims the right for enrollment?
A.    Her name was Hatchet.

Q. What is her given name?    A. Peggie. She died before 1880. She would be on the roll back of 1880.

Q. Was she a Cherokee by blood?    A. Yes, sir.

Q. What is the name of your father's father?    A. I don't know.

Q. Do you know the name of your father's mother?    A. No, sir; I couldn't say that They lived in North Carolina.

Q. How long has your father been a resident of the Indian Territory?
A.    Why, I couldn't say that. He has been here as long as I can remember. I heard him say he came here in 1832.

Q. Do you know whether or not he has been out of the territory for the purpose of making his home since?    A. No, sir.

Q.   What is your father's mental condition at this time?      A.  I couldn't say that.  I saw him about a month ago.  You said his mental condition?

Q.   Yes.  A.   His health--he is well so far as I know.  There always has been something the matter with him.  He is deranged.

Q.   Do you know whether or not he has married since the death of your mother?

A.   Not to my knowledge.

Q.   Have you seen him cintinuously[sic]?      A.  I see him once in a while.  He comes to my place ever year three or four weeks.

Q.   Did you live with him up to the time you were grown?      A.  No, I left him after mother died.

Q.   Did he ever state to you that he was remarried?      A.  No, sir; never heard him say.

BY MR. HASTINGS:  Have you any reason to believe that he was remarried?

A.   No, sir; I have not.

Q.   Did you ever hear of him living with anybody as husband and wife?      A.  Never have.

BY THE COMMISSION:  About how old were you when your mother died?

A.   Why I was about 6 years old; some where along there.

Q.   Then she died just about the year 1880?      A.  I was born in 1873.  She died before 1880.  You see there was that Daniel, my little brother, he died before my mother died.

Q.   Your brother Daniel is on the 1880 roll.  A.  Well, is he on the 1880 roll.

Q.   You are over 29 years old.  A.  I think he died before the 1880 roll was taken.

Q.   Are you positive he died before your mother did?      A.  Yes, sir; I remember of his dieing[sic].

Q.   Did you ever hear your mother spoken[sic] of a Margaret?      A.  No, not that I remember of.  Might have been, too.

> Hugh Holland is identified upon the authenticated roll of 1880 in Tahlequah district, page 769, opposite number 1051.  He is not identified on the census roll of 1896.

Q.   Did you ever make any attempt to enroll your father in 1896?   A.  Yes, sir.

Q.   How long has he been deranged?      A.  81 or 82.

Q.   Has he ever been confined to any asylum?      A.  Yes, sir; the insane asylum at Tahlequah.  I asked him if he was going to be put on the roll.  He said no, he didn't think it was necessary.  He was on the 1880 roll and didn't think it was necessary.

Q.   You never heard anything about his remarrying since the death of your mother?

A.   No, sir; I never have.  He lived right around Tahlequah all the time.  He never married that I know of.

Jesse O. Carr, being first duly sworn, states that as stenographer to the Commission to the Five Civilized Tribes he correctly recorded the testimony and proceedings in this case and that the foregoing is a true and correct transcript of his stenographic notes thereof.

Jesse O. Carr

Subscribed and sworn to before me this 24th day of July, 1902.

Bruce C Jones<br>Notary Public.

◇◇◇◇◇

C. D. 2025.

Grove, Indian Territory, May 17, 1905.

DEPARTMENT OF THE INTERIOR ,
COMMISSION TO THE FIVE CIVILIZED TRIBES.

In the matter of the application made for the enrollment of Hugh Holland as a citizen by intermarriage of the Cherokee Nation.

James N. Holland, being first duly sworn, testified as follows:

BY THE COMMISSION:

Q   What is your name?   A  James N. Holland.
Q   Mr. Holland, what is your age?   A  49.
Q   What is your post office address?   A  Grove, I. T.
Q   Are you a citizen by blood of the Cherokee Nation?
A   No, an adopted citizen.
Q   How long have you lived in Delaware District?
A   About 20 years.
Q   Are you acquainted with a man by the name of Hugh Holland?
A   Mighty well.
Q   Do you know the name of his father?
A   No, sir.
Q   Do you know the name of his mother?
A   No, sir.
Q   Is the Hugh Holland to whom you refer a citizen by blood of the Cherokee Nation or a white man?
A   A white man.
Q   About how old is the Hugh Holland you know?
A   He is about 60 years old - 66 or 65.
Q   Was Hugh Holland once married to a recognized citizen by blood of the Cherokee Nation?
A   Yes, sir, I reckon he was.
Q   What was her name?
A   I do not know whether I know her name or not, but I believe her name was Noisewater.
Q   Was she the only Cherokee woman to whom Hugh Holland was ever married?
A   I think so.

Q   Is she living or dead?

A   She is dead.

Q   How long has she been dead?

A   15 or 20 years - between 15 and 20, I have an idea.

Q   Do you know in what district Hugh Holland was living in 1880?

A   In 1880?    I presume the was he is doing now he did not have any home.

Q   Do you know in what district he was enrolled in 1880?

A   I expect in Tahlequah.

Q   Is Hugh Holland living at the present time?

A   He was about three weeks ago; he staid all night with me; he makes trips through here about once a month.

Q   Has Hugh Holland any definite home?

A   I do not think he has.

Q   Where does he live most of the time?

A   He just travels through this country.

Q   Is he a peripatetic preacher?

A   Yes, he claims he is fighting the devil all the time; he tells me about fighting the devil.

Q   Does he claim any rights as a citizen by intermarriage of the Cherokee Nation?

A   Yes, I think he does.

Q   Do you know whether this Cherokee woman to whom you refer as being his wife was his first wife or not?

A   No, I could not say; he was a grown man when I came from North Carolina.

Q   Do you know whether he was her first husband?

A   No, I do not

Q   Was he living with her when the 1880 Roll was made?

A   I guess he was, if she had not died at that time; I do not know positively the date she died.

Q   What is Hugh Holland's post office address?

A   He has not got any post office.

Q   Is Walter Holland at Bluejacket his son?

A   Yes, he's his son.

Hugh Holland is identified on the 1880 Cherokee Tribal Roll, Tahlequah District, as an intermarried white man, number 1051, and is listed from information on Cherokee Doubtful Card number 2025.

W. P. Covington, being duly sworn, states that, as stenographer to the Commissioner to the Five Civilized Tribes, he correctly reported proceedings had in the above and foregoing case on the 17th day of May 1905, and that the above and foregoing is a full and correct transcript of his said stenographic notes taken in said case.

W. P. Covington

Subscribed and sworn to before me, this June 13th 1905.

Fred P Branson
Notary Public.

# Cherokee Intermarried White 1906
## Volume X

*(The Affidavit below was originally handwritten on the microfilm and is typed as given.)*

### Affidavit

Personally appeared before me this 23d day of Feb. 1907, J. H. Dannenberg of Stilwell Ind. Ter. Northern District. Who says I live in Stilwell of the above named Ter. and District. I am 69 years old. That I remember very distinctly when Hugh Holland and wife Peggy were married in the year 1870. I think about one year after I married in 1869 the month and day I don't remember but I know it ~~they~~ was about that time. And they lived together as man and wife until the day of his wifes death ~~Peggy about~~ between the years 1880 and 1890.

Given under my hand this 23d day of Feb. 1907

Signed J H Dannenberg

Sworn to and subscribed before me this 23d day of Feb. 1907.

My Commission expires Nov 21st 1908.
THIRD TERM.

Hugh M. Adair
Notary Public.

◇◇◇◇◇

*(The Affidavit below was originally handwritten on the microfilm and is typed as given.)*

### Affidavit

Personally appeared this 23 day of Feb 1907. W. A. Allen of Stilwell of the Northern Judicial District Ind. Ter. who says: I am 47 years of age - live in the above named District. That I am well acquainted with Hugh Holland, father of Walter Holland. That I reccollect when said Hugh Holland was married about 1869 or 1870, I cant say exactly but I know they the said Hugh Holland and wife Peggy Holland lived together as man and wife until said wife Peggy Holland died ~~in~~ July 5th 1883.

In witness whereof I set my hand this 23 day of Feb. 1907

W. A. Allen

Sworn to and subscribed before me this 23 day of Feb. 1907

Hugh M. Adair
Notary Public.

My Commission expires Nov 21st 1908.
THIRD TERM.

◇◇◇◇◇

E.C.M.                                                Cherokee D 2025.

## DEPARTMENT OF THE INTERIOR,
## COMMISSIONER TO THE FIVE CIVILIZED TRIBES,
## MUSKOGEE, I. T., FEBRUARY 25, 1907.

———————

In the matter of the application for the enrollment of HUGH HOLLAND as a citizen by intermarriage of the Cherokee Nation.

CHEROKEE NATION represented by W. W. Hastings.

WILLIAM J. McKEE being first duly sworn by Walter W. Chappell, a Notary Public, testified as follows:

ON BEHALF OF THE COMMISSIONER:

Q What is your name?     A William J. McKee.

Q What is your age?     A 65.

Q What is your post office address?     A Tahlequah.

Q Do you appear here today for the purpose of giving testimony relative to the right of Hugh Holland to enrollment as a citizen by intermarriage of the Cherokee Nation? A Yes sir.

Q Is Hugh Holland a white man?     A He was always considered a white man.

Q Then he derives his right to enrollment by virtue of his marriage to a citizen by blood of the Cherokee Nation?     A Yes sir.

Q Who was that citizen?     A Peggie Hatchet.

Q Is she a citizen by blood of the Cherokee Nation?     A Yes sir, a full blood Indian.

Q When did he marry her?     A Well, I couldn't say positively whether it was in 1869 or 1870, by either one of those two.

Q Did he secure a license from the authorities of the Cherokee Nation in order to marry her?     A I couldn't say, I dont[sic] remember.

Q Do you know where he was married?     A At Nancy Adair's.

Q What district?     A Flint District.

Q Did he secure a license there?     A I suppose he did.

Q Were you present at their marriage?     A I was not, I was there the night afterward, though, at the chivarri[sic].

Q Was this Peggie Hatchet Hugh Holland's first wife?     A Yes sir.

Q Is she living?     A No sir.

Q When did she die?     A I dont[sic] remember the date of her death, but they had a little family when she died, about five children.

Q Was she the only wife he ever married?     A The only one I ever knew of.

Q Was he her first husband?     A I couldn't say; I suppose so, as she was a young woman when he married her.

Q From the time of their marriage until the death of his wife, Peggie did they reside together as husband and wife, and live in the Cherokee Nation?     A Yes sir.

Q   Since the death of his wife has he remained in the Cherokee Nation?
A   All the time.
Q   Is he living?   A Yes sir.
Q   Is he insane?   A Well, he has as good sense as any common man on some things, but you say Bible to him, and he appears to be perfectly insane.

( Witness excused ).

The undersigned, upon oath, states that, as stenographer to the Commissioner to the Five Civilized Tribes, she correctly reported the above and foregoing testimony, and that the same is a full, true and complete transcript of her stenographic notes thereof.

Sarah Waters

Subscribed and sworn to before me this 25th day of February, 1907.

Frances R Lane
Notary Public.

<><><><><>

C O P Y
Page 108, Book B, Old Marriage Record,
Flint District.

Cherokee Nation   )   By the authority in me vested by the law of the Cherokee Nation

Flint District   )   I do hereby Grant License of Marriage, to Hugh Holland, a citizen of the United States, and a Man of Good Moral Character and of industrious habits, to Marry Miss Margaret Noisy, a Cherokee by Birth and a Daughter of Choo noh zuh kee Noisy Decd. He (Hugh Holland), having complied with the requirements of the law regulating intermarriage with white men. Given from under my hand in office this the 21st day of Aug. 1869

License fee $5.00                              James W Adair   Clk
                                              Dist Ct Flint C.N.

I certify that the above named parties were married by me Aug 22nd A.D. 1869

W. A. Duncan Minst
M.E. C South

I certify the above is a true copy of the original Sept 1st, 1869

James W Adair, Clk
Dist Ct Flint C.N.

# Cherokee Intermarried White 1906
## Volume X

-----------------------

I, Gertrude Hanna, on oath state that the above and foregoing is a true and correct copy of Page 108 of the Book B of Old Marriage Record of Flint District, now in the possession of the Commissioner to the Five Civilized Tribes

Gertrude Hanna

Subscribed and sworn to before me this 26th day of February, 1907.

Frances R Lane
Notary Public.

◇◇◇◇◇

T.W.L.                                                     Cherokee D 2025

## DEPARTMENT OF THE INTERIOR
## COMMISSIONER TO THE FIVE CIVILIZED TRIBES

-----

In the matter of the application for the enrollment of Hugh Holland as a citizen by intermarriage of the Cherokee Nation.

## D E C I S I O N .

THE RECORDS OF THIS OFFICE SHOW: That Emmet Starr appeared before the Commission to the Five Civilized Tribes Five Civilized Tribes on June 30, 1902, at Muskogee, Indian Territory, and made application for the enrollment of Hugh Holland as a citizen by intermarriage of the Cherokee Nation. Further proceedings in the matter of said application were had at Muskogee, Indian Territory, July 23, 1902 Grove, Indian Territory, May 17, 1905 and Muskogee, Indian Territory February 25, 1907.

THE EVIDENCE IN THIS CASE SHOWS: That the applicant herein, Hugh Holland, was married in accordance with Cherokee law August 22, 1869 to Margaret or Peggie Hatchet (or Noisy or Noisewater), since deceased, who was at the time of said marriage a recognized citizen by blood of the Cherokee Nation and who is identified on the Cherokee authenticated tribal roll of 1880, Canadian District, Page 769, No. 1051, as Margaret Holland, a native Cherokee. It is further shown that from the time of said marriage the said Hugh Holland and the said Margaret Holland resided together as husband and wife and continuously lived in the Cherokee Nation, up to and including the death of the latter which occurred July 5, 1883; that said applicant has continuously resided in the Cherokee Nation since his removal thereto about 1832. Said applicant is identified on the Cherokee authenticated tribal roll of 1880, Tahlequah District, No. 1050, as an adopted white.

IT IS THEREFORE ORDERED AND ADJUDGED: That in accordance with the decision of the Supreme Court of the United States, dated November 5, 1906, in the cases of Daniel Red Bird, et al., vs. the United States, Nos. 125, 126, 127, and 128, the said applicant, Hugh Holland is entitled, under the provisions of section 21 of the Act of Congress approved June 28, 1898, (30 Stats. 495), to enrollment as a citizen by intermarriage of the Cherokee Nation, and his application for enrollment as such is accordingly granted.

Tams Bixby

Commissioner.

Dated at Muskogee, Indian Territory,
this    FEB 27 1907

◇◇◇◇◇

Grove, Indian Territory, May 17, 1905.

Commission to the Five Civilized Tribes,
      Cherokee Enrollment Division,
          Muskogee, Indian Territory.

Gentlemen:

Since our last report we have taken testimony in the following cases:

| | |
|---|---|
| C. D. 2480. | Applicant left Deleware[sic] District when an orphan; not heard of since. |
| C. D. 1578. | Applicant died prior to September 1, 1902. |
| C. D. 2782. | Evidence shows these two children are illegitimate; born in State of Kansas; mother not made Cherokee Nation her home since their birth; their reputed father was a recognized and enrolled citizen of Cherokee Nation. |
| C. D. 1578. | Additional testimony in this case. |
| C. D. 1655. | Applicant died prior to September 1, 1902. |
| C. D. 2025. | Intermarried status taken. |
| C. D. 2821. | Applicant was married to his Cherokee wife on August 13, 1896. |

Respectfully,

(Signed)   Fred P. Branson.

◇◇◇◇◇

# Cherokee Intermarried White 1906
## Volume X

-COPY-

E. D. Hicks
Tahlequah, I. T.

Sept. 20, 1905.

B. C. Jones
    Dear Sir:

        In your published list of undermined Cherokee Citizens I find the following in Tahlequah District, which may be of some interest to the Commission

| | |
|---|---|
| Hugh Holland  age 60. | This man is a crippled W. A. and is "Bug house" Saw him about a week ago. |
| Jackson Kelly  age 59. | W. A. and now lives near Hulburt, I. T. |
| Harriet Ross  age 42- | Freedman, and is on '96 rolls as Harried Johnson. Think she must be down twice. |
| Reese, W. A.  age 67. | W. A. lived here in the early 80's, - abandoned his Cherokee wife and moved to Eureka Springs Arks. Died about 2 yrs ago. |
| Mary Wilkerson  age 45 | This is probably Mary Coody wife of Jno H. who now lives at Nowata. |
| Grace Johnson  age 51 | This darkey woman was murdered in 1882 by Willie Pettit. |
| Moss Ross  age 47. | This darkey died here 3/8/1902 |

    "96 Roll

| | |
|---|---|
| Horace Gray  age 39 | Now office deputy marshal at this place. Is W. A. and married after Cherokee Council stopped his kind from having any rights. His wife is dead, and was Mattie Whitewater. |
| Benjamin Laws,  age 32 | W. A. Claimed to be an English Lord. Married John Price daughter Emma, and abandoned her after skinning every body he could. Not been heard of for 6 or 7 years. |

| | |
|---|---|
| McAlester Jas. H. age 57 | This W. A. used to live here, but moved somewhere in Cooweescoowee. He was here about 2 months ago. |
| Maud M. Johnson, age 11 | This darkey is now the [sic] of Andy Kirkum, and is still living. She has filed, and must be on twice. |
| Geo. Webber, age 24, | This coon is around here, and I don't know why he has not been before you. |

Thinking this may be of some use to you, I send it. If it is not- no harm is done.

Yours Very Truly,

(Signed) Ed. D. Hicks.

◇◇◇◇◇

| REFER IN REPLY TO THE FOLLOWING: | **DEPARTMENT OF THE INTERIOR,** |
|---|---|
| Cherokee | **COMMISSIONER TO THE FIVE CIVILIZED TRIBES.** |
| D-2025 | |

Muskogee, Indian Territory, December 28, 1906.

Hugh Holland,
Tahlequah, Indian Territory.

Dear Sir:

November 6, 1906, the United States Supreme Court held that white persons who intermarried with Cherokee citizens according to Cherokee law prior to November 1, 1875, are entitled to enrollment and allotments of land as citizens of the Cherokee Nation.

You are advised that to properly determine your right to enrollment as a citizen by intermarriage of the Cherokee Nation, it will be necessary for you to appear before the Commissioner for the purpose of giving testimony as to the date of your marriage and whether or not your wife, by reason of your marriage to whom you claim the right to enrollment as a citizen of the Cherokee Nation, was a recognized citizen of the Cherokee Nation at the time of your marriage to her, and whether or not you were married to her in accordance with Cherokee laws.

You are, therefore, directed to appear before the Commissioner at Muskogee, Indian Territory, at 9 o'clock A. M., on Saturday, January 5, 1907, and give testimony as above indicated.

Respectfully,
Wm O. Beall
Acting Commissioner.

JMH

◇◇◇◇◇

Form No. 260.

## THE WESTERN UNION TELEGRAPH COMPANY.

INCORPORATED

23,000 OFFICES IN AMERICA.   CABLE SERVICE TO ALL THE WORLD.

ROBERT C. CLOWRY, President and General Manager.

| Receiver's No. | Time Filed | | Check |
|---|---|---|---|
| | | Cherokee No.2025. | ECM |

**SEND** the following message subject to the terms on back hereof, which are hereby agreed to.

February 15, 1907.

Walter Holland,

Grove, Indian Territory.

Intermarried case of father incomplete.

Appear immediately with witnesses to establish his

marriage.

Bixby,

Commissioner.

O.B.G.R.   Paid.

☞ READ THE NOTICE AND AGREEMENT ON BACK. ☜

*(Copy of original document from case.)*

◇◇◇◇◇

REFER IN REPLY TO THE FOLLOWING:

Cherokee 2025.

**DEPARTMENT OF THE INTERIOR,**
**COMMISSIONER TO THE FIVE CIVILIZED TRIBES.**

ECM

Muskogee, Indian Territory, February 15, 1907.

SPECIAL.

Walter Holland,
Grove, Indian Territory.

Sir:-

The Commission sent you this day a telegram as follows:

"Intermarried case of your father incomplete.  Appear immediately with witnesses to establish his marriage".

# Cherokee Intermarried White 1906
## Volume X

The Act of Congress approved April 26, 1906 provides that the Secretary of the Interior shall have no jurisdiction to approve the enrollment of any person as a citizen of the Cherokee Nation after March 4, 1907.
This matter, therefore, demands your immediate attention.

Respectfully,

Commissioner.

GHC

◇◇◇◇◇

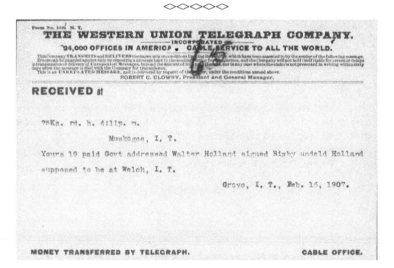

*(Copies of original documents from case.)*

Cherokee
D 2025

Muskogee, Indian Territory, February 19, 1907.

Walter Holland,
    Welch, Indian Territory.

Sir:

      There has been sent you this day a telegram as follows:

      "Intermarried case of father incomplete.  Appear immediately with witnesses to establish his marriage."

      The Act of Congress approved April 26, 1906, provides that the Secretary of the Interior shall have no jurisdiction to approve the enrollment of any person as a citizen of the Cherokee Nation after March 4, 1907.

      This matter therefore demands your immediate attention.

Respectfully,

M.T.M.                                     Commissioner.

◇◇◇◇◇

Form No. 168. M. T.

# THE WESTERN UNION TELEGRAPH COMPANY.
—— INCORPORATED ——
24,000 OFFICES IN AMERICA.    CABLE SERVICE TO ALL THE WORLD.

This Company TRANSMITS and DELIVERS messages only on conditions limiting its liability, which have been assented to by the sender of the following message. Errors can be guarded against only by repeating a message back to the sending station for comparison, and the Company will not hold itself liable for errors or delays in transmission or delivery of Unrepeated Messages, beyond the amount of tolls paid thereon, nor in any case where the claim is not presented in writing within sixty days after the message is filed with the Company for transmission.
This is an UNREPEATED MESSAGE, and is delivered by request of the sender, under the conditions named above.
ROBERT C. CLOWRY, President and General Manager.

**RECEIVED** at

24 KS RD E IO15 am 36 paid ,

                    Stilwell, I.T. Feb. 23 rd

Tams Bixby,

      Commissioner, Muskogee, I.T.

My witnesses are not able to come will two affidavits answer in my person by notary republic both parties are old and feeble and cannot appear before you now answer and tell me what to do ,

                    Walter Holland.

MONEY TRANSFERRED BY TELEGRAPH.             CABLE OFFICE.

*(Copy of original document from case.)*
◇◇◇◇◇

231

# Cherokee Intermarried White 1906
## Volume X

Muskogee, Indian Territory, February 23, 1907.

Special

Walter Holland,
　　　　Stilwell, Indian Territory.

Dear Sir:

The Commissioner sent you this day a telegram as follows:

"Replying your telegram forward immediately affidavits referred to."

The Act of Congress approved April 26, 1906, provides that the Secretary of the Interior shall have no jurisdiction to approve the enrollment of any person as a citizen of the Cherokee Nation after March 4, 1907.

This matter, therefore, demands your immediate attention.

Respectfully,

Commissioner.

MMP

◇◇◇◇◇

Form No, 260.

## THE WESTERN UNION TELEGRAPH COMPANY.
INCORPORATED

23,000 OFFICES IN AMERICA.　　CABLE SERVICE TO ALL THE WORLD.

ROBERT C. CLOWRY, President and General Manager.

| Receiver's No. | Time Filed | Check |
|---|---|---|
| | | |

SEND the following message subject to the terms on back hereof, which are hereby agreed to.

Muskogee, Indian Territory, February 23, 1907.

Walter Holland,

Stilwell, Indian Territory.

Replying your telegram forward immediately affidavits referred to.

Bixby,

O.M.O.M.Paid

Commissioner

☞ READ THE NOTICE AND AGREEMENT ON BACK. ☜

*(Copy of original document from case.)*

◇◇◇◇◇

**THE WESTERN UNION TELEGRAPH COMPANY.**
INCORPORATED
23,000 OFFICES IN AMERICA. CABLE SERVICE TO ALL THE WORLD.
ROBERT C. CLOWRY, President and General Manager.

Form No. 260.

Receiver's No. NS | D | Time Filed | H | 14 Paid | Govt | Check

SEND the following message subject to the terms on back hereof, which are hereby agreed to.

2/23   1907

Received at 2.58 P

Dated Muskogee, I.T.

Walter Holland

Replying your telegram forward immediately affidavits referred to

Bixby

Commissioner

☞ READ THE NOTICE AND AGREEMENT ON BACK. ☜

*(Copy of original document from case.)*
◇◇◇◇◇

Cherokee D
2025.

COPY
Muskogee, Indian Territory, February 27, 1907.

W. W. Hastings,
Attorney for the Cherokee Nation,
Muskogee, Indian Territory.

Dear Sir:

There is enclosed herewith a copy of the decision of the Commissioner to the Five Civilized Tribes, dated February 27, 1907, granting the application for the enrollment of Hugh Holland as a citizen by intermarriage of the Cherokee Nation.

Respectfully,

SIGNED *Tams Bixby*

Encl. HJ-141.
HJC

Commissioner.

◇◇◇◇◇

Cherokee D
2025.

Muskogee, Indian Territory, February 27, 1907.

The Commissioner to the Five Civilized Tribes,
  Muskogee, Indian Territory.

Sir:

Receipt is acknowledged of the testimony and of your decision enrolling Hugh Holland as a citizen by intermarriage of the Cherokee Nation. Time for protesting said decision is waived and I consent that said person may be placed upon the schedule immediately.

Respectfully,

W. W. Hastings
Attorney for the Cherokee Nation.

◇◇◇◇◇

| REFER IN REPLY TO THE FOLLOWING: |
| --- |
| Cherokee D |
| 2025 |

**DEPARTMENT OF THE INTERIOR,
COMMISSIONER TO THE FIVE CIVILIZED TRIBES.**

Muskogee, Indian Territory, February 27, 1907.

Hugh Holland,
  Tahlequah, Indian Territory.

Dear Sir:

There is enclosed herewith a copy of the decision of the Commissioner to the Five Civilized Tribes, dated February 27, 1907, granting your application for enrollment as a citizen by intermarriage of the Cherokee Nation.

You will be advised when your name has been placed upon a schedule of citizens of the Cherokee Nation and approved by the Secretary of the Interior.

Respectfully,

Tams Bixby

Encl. HJ-139.
  HJC

Commissioner.

◇◇◇◇◇

234

# Cherokee Intermarried White 1906
## Volume X

Cherokee
I.W. 285

Muskogee, Indian Territory, June 11, 1907.

Walter Holland,
        Welch, Indian Territory.

Dear Sir:

In reply to your letter of June 5, asking to be advised as to the status of the Cherokee intermarried case of your father, Hugh Holland, you are advised that the records of this office show that the application for the enrollment of Hugh Holland as a citizen by intermarriage of the Cherokee Nation was granted on February 27, 1907, and his name now appears upon a roll of such citizens approved by the Secretary of the Interior.

Respectfully,

L M B                                                   Commissioner

◇◇◇◇◇

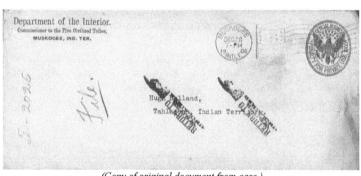

*(Copy of original document from case.)*

---

**Cher IW 286**

◇◇◇◇◇

# Cherokee Intermarried White 1906
## Volume X

COPY

Department of the Interior,
Commission to the Five Civilized Tribes,
Vinita, I.T., October 2, 1900.

In the matter of the application of George W. Walker for the enrollment of himself and children as Cherokees by blood, and his wife as a Cherokee by intermarriage: being sworn and examined by Commissioner Needles, he testified as follows:

Q    What is your name?    A George W. Walker.
Q    What is your post office address?    A Kennison.
Q    What is your age?    A 70 years old.
Q    In what district do you live?    A Cooweescoowee district.
Q    Are you a recognized citizen of the Cherokee Nation?    A Yes, sir.
Q    By blood?    A Yes, sir.
Q    Shawnee, Cherokee or Delaware?    A Cherokee.
Q    For whom do you apply for enrollment?    A I want to enroll my family.
Q    Yourself and wife?    A Yes, sir, and children.
Q    what[sic] is the name of your wife?    A Mary Jane.
Q    what[sic] is her age?    A 57.
Q    when[sic] were you married to her?    A About thirty years ago.
Q    What are the names of your children under 21 years of age?    A Lewis 19 years old.
Q    The name of the next one?    A Henry, 16 years old.
Q    The next one?    A David, 14 years old.
Q    The next child?    A That is all.
Q    These children alive and living with you?    A Yes, sir.
Q    How long have you lived in the Cherokee Nation?    A Always have, I was born here.
(George W. Walker on 1880 roll, page 198, No. 3171, Cooweescoowee district. Mary J. Walker on 1880 roll, page 198, No. 3172, Cooweescoowee district.)
Q    Is your wife a white woman or an indian[sic]?    A She is white.
(George W. Walker on 1896 roll, page 283, No. 5180, Geo. W. Walker, Cooweescoowee district. Mary J. Walker on 1896 roll, page 283, No. 1048, Cooweescoowee district. Lewis Walker on 1896 roll, page 283, No. 5183, Cooweescoowee district. Henry Walker on 1896 roll, page 283, No. 5184, Cooweescoowee district. David Walker on 1896 roll, page 283, No. 5185, Cooweescoowee district.)
The name of George W. Walker and his wife, Mary J. appear upon the authenticated roll of 1880, as well as the census roll of 1896, and the names of his children, Lewis, Henry, and David, appear upon the census roll of 1896, and they all being duly identified according to the page and number of said roll, and having made satisfactory proof as to their residence, the said George W. Walker and his said children will be duly listed for enrollment as Cherokee citizens by blood and his wife, Mary J., as a Cherokee citizen by intermarriage.

-----------------o-----------------

Bruce C. Jones, being duly sworn, says that as stenographer to the Commission to the Five Civilized Tribes he correctly recorded the proceedings and testimony in the above case, and the foregoing is a true and complete transcript of his stenographic notes thereof.                                   Bruce C. Jones

Sworn to and subscribed before me this the 3rd of October, 1900.

                                   T. B. Needles,
Endorsement.                                   Commissioner.
### DEPARTMENT OF THE INTERIOR
COMMISSION TO THE FIVE CIVILIZED TRIBES
FILED
OCT 3 1900
Tams Bixby, Acting Chairman.

◇◇◇◇◇

To be filed in Cherokee 3933.                                   Cherokee 4067.

### DEPARTMENT OF THE INTERIOR,
COMMISSION TO THE FIVE CIVILIZED TRIBES.
Muskogee, I. T., October 16, 1902.

In the matter of the application of Alexander M. Anderson for the enrollment of himself as a citizen by intermarriage, and for the enrollment of his grand-daughter, Rachel C. Anderson, as a citizen by blood, of the Cherokee Nation.

### SUPPLEMENTAL PROCEEDINGS.

CHARLES J. ANDERSON, being sworn, testified as follows:

By the Commission,

Q What is your name?    A What is my name?
Q Yes. A Charles J. Anderson.
Q How old are you?    A Twenty-six.
Q What is your postoffice?    A Kinnison[sic].
Q Do you know Alexander M. Anderson?    A Yes, sir.
Q What relation is he to you?    A He is my father.
Q Is he a white man?    A Yes, sir.
Q How old is he?    A Seventy-four.
Q Seventy-four?    A Yes, sir.
Q Is he physically unable to be here today?    A Yes, sir.
Q What is your mother's name?    A Rachel Anderson.
Q Is she living?    A Yes, sir.

Q  Do you know whether your father and mother have been living together ever since 1880?    A  Yes, sir, they have never been separated at all.

Q  Living together now?    A  Yes, sir.

Q  Who is Rachel C. Anderson?    A  Rachel C. Anderson?

Q  Yes.  A  That's my brother's little child.

Q  Your brother's child?    A  Yes, sir.

Q  Is she living?    A  Yes, sir.

Q  Do you know George W. Walker?    A  Yes, sir.

Q  Do you know his wife, Mary J. Walker?    A  Yes, sir.

Q  Is she a white woman?    A  Yes, sir.

Q  Do you know whether George W. and Mary J. Walker have been living together ever since 1880?    A  Yes, sir, they have.

Q  You have known them all that time, have you?    A  Yes, sir.

Q  Do they live at the same place you do today?    A  They live about a mile and a half from where I do.

Q  Are they both living?    A  Yes, sir.

Q  Never been separated?    A  No, sir.

Q  Do you know how many children they have living at home with them?

Q[sic]  They only have one living at home with them.

Q  What's his name?    A  Lewis.

Q  Where are the others?    A  David is dead and Henry is married.


JAMES F. WALKER, being sworn, testified as follows:


By the Commission,

Q  What is your name?    A  James F. Walker.

Q  How old are you?    A  Twenty-five.

Q  What is your postoffice?    A  Kinnison[sic].

Q  Do you know George W. Walker?    A  Yes, sir.

Q  What relation is he to you?    A  Father.

Q  What is your mother's name?    A  Mary J.

A  Mary J. is a white woman, is she?    A  Yes, sir.

Q  Your father is a Cherokee by blood, is he?    A  Yes, sir.

Q  Do you know whether your father and mother have been living together in the Cherokee Nation ever since 1880?    A  Yes, sir.

Q  They're living together now, are they?    A  Yes, sir.

Q  Have they ever been separated?    A  No, sir.

Q  How many brothers have you living at home?    A  Only one at home.

Q  Lewis?    A  Lewis, yes, sir.

Q  Is your brother, Henry, married?    A  Yes, sir.

Q  And your brother, David, is dead?    A  Yes, sir.

Q  When did David die?    A  The fifth of last December.

Q  When?    A  Fifth of last December.

Q  Do you know Alexander M. Anderson?    A  Yes, sir.
Q  How near to him do you live?    A  About two miles, I guess.
Q  How long have you know him?    A  All my life.
Q  Pretty old man, isn't he?    A  Yes, sir.
Q  What's his wife's name?    A  Rachel.
Q  Do you know whether Alexander M. Anderson and his wife, Rachel, have been living together for the last twenty years?    A  Yes, they have been living together.
Q  Ever since you knew them?    A  Yes, sir.
Q  Have they ever been separated?    A  No, sir.
Q  And have lived all the time in the Cherokee Nation?    A  Yes, sir.

By Mr. Starr,

Q  Have George W. Walker and Mary J. Walker lived in the Cherokee Nation ever since 1880?    A  Yes, sir.
Q  Never been out any time?    A  No, sir.

Retta Chick, being first duly sworn, states that, as stenographer to the Commissioner to the Five Civilized Tribes, she recorded the testimony and proceedings in the matter of the foregoing application, and that the above is a true and complete transcript of her stenographic notes thereof.

Retta Chick

Subscribed and sworn to before me this 12th day of November, 1902.

BC Jones<br>Notary Public.

Copy

◇◇◇◇◇

Cherokee 3933.

## DEPARTMENT OF THE INTERIOR,
## COMMISSION TO THE FIVE CIVILIZED TRIBES.
### Muskogee, Indian Territory, January 4, 1907.

In the Matter of the Application for the Enrollment of Mary J. Walker as a citizen by intermarriage of the Cherokee Nation.

APPEARANCES:

James F. Walker, appearing for Applicant.

Cherokee Nation represent by H. M. Vance, in behalf of W. W. Hastings, Attorney.

James F. Walker being first duly sworn by B. P. Rasmus, Notary Public, testified as follows:

ON BEHALF OF COMMISSIONER.

| | | | |
|---|---|---|---|
| Q | What is your name? | A | James F. Walker. |
| Q | How old are you? | A | 30. |

Q    What is your post office address?
A    Welch.
Q    Are you a citizen by blood of the Cherokee Nation?
A    Yes sir.
Q    What is the name of your father?
A    George W. Walker.
Q    What is your mother's name?
A    Mary J. Walker.
Q    Are both your parents living?
A    No.
Q    Which, if either of them, is dead?
A    Mother.
Q    When did she die?
A    I believe it was 1903.
Q    Your mother was a white woman, was she?
A    Yes sir.
Q    Your father was a Cherokee by blood?
A    Yes sir.
Q    You appear here today for the purpose of giving testimony relative to the right of your mother, Mary J. Walker, to enrollment as a citizen by intermarriage of the Cherokee Nation?
A    Yes sir.
Q    Do you have any knowledge as to when your father and mother were married?
A    Why, not exactly; my father don't recollect, himself.
Q    Couldn't he give about the year that they were married?
A    Well, I can give you about the year that he gives; he says about '63.
Q    Was he a recognized citizen of the Cherokee Nation at the time he married your mother?
A    Yes sir.
Q    He was born in the Cherokee Nation, was he?
A    No, I don't think he was.
Q    Where was he born?
A    Tennessee.
Q    When did he come to the Cherokee Nation?
A    When he was just a boy.
Q    He was living here at the time he married your mother?
A    Yes sir.
Q    Is it your understanding that your mother was your father's first wife?
A    No sir.

Q   You understand that your father was married before he married your mother?
A   Yes sir.
Q   Was his former wife living or dead at the time he married your mother?
A   Dead.
Q   Is it your understanding that your father was your mother's first husband?
A   No sir.
Q   Was your mother married before she married your father?
A   Yes sir.
Q   Was her former husband dead at the time she married your father?
A   Yes sir.
Q   Is it your understanding that from the time of their marriage, they continuously lived together as husband and wife?
A   Yes sir.
Q   Until the death of your mother?
A   Yes sir.
Q   And lived in the Cherokee Nation, did they?
A   Yes sir.
Q   You were born in the Cherokee Nation?
A   Yes sir.
Q   And have lived in the Nation all your life, have you?
A   Yes sir.
Q   Did your father obtain a marriage license and certificate at the time he married your mother?
A   I don't think he did.
Q   You never heard him say as to that?
A   Well, he said that they didn't have to have one at the time they married, and that is what all these old fellows here tell me to-day. I asked about it.
Q   Did you ever see a certificate showing the marriage of your father and mother?
A   No sir.
Q   Your father never had one?
A   Not that I know of.
Q   Is there any reason why your father George W. Walker does not appear here to-day for the purpose of giving testimony in this case?
A   Nothing only his old and bad health.
Q   He is in a feeble condition?
A   Yes sir.

The applicant, Mary J. Walker is identified on the Cherokee Authenticated Tribal Roll of 1880, Cooweescoowee District, 3172. The name of her husband, George W. Walker is included in the approved partial roll of citizens by blood in the Cherokee Nation, opposite No. 9489.

The undersigned being first duly sworn states that as stenographer to the Commission to the Five Civilized Tribes, she correctly recorded the testimony taken in this case and that the foregoing is a full, true and correct transcript of her stenographic notes thereof.

Myrtle Hill

Subscribed and sworn to before me this the 5th day of January, 1907.

John E. Tidwell
Notary Public.

◇◇◇◇◇

C.E.W.                                                                 Cherokee 3933.

### DEPARTMENT OF THE INTERIOR,

### COMMISSIONER TO THE FIVE CIVILIZED TRIBES.

In the matter of the application for the enrollment of Mary J. Walker, as a citizen by intermarriage of the Cherokee Nation.

## D E C I S I O N

THE RECORDS OF THIS OFFICE SHOW: That at Vinita, Indian Territory, October 2, 1900, George W. Walker appeared before the Commission to the Five Civilized Tribes and made application for the enrollment of his wife, Mary J. Walker, as a citizen by intermarriage, and for the enrollment of himself, et al., as citizens by blood of the Cherokee Nation has been heretofore disposed of and their rights to enrollment will not be considered in this decision. Further proceedings in the matter of said application were had at Muskogee, Indian Territory, October 16, 1902, and January 4, 1907.

THE EVIDENCE IN THIS CASE SHOWS: That the applicant herein, Mary J. Walker, a white woman, married about the year 1870 to one George W. Walker, who was at the time of said marriage a recognized citizen by blood of the Cherokee Nation, and whose name appears upon the approved partial roll of citizens by blood of the Cherokee Nation, opposite number 9489; that from the time of said marriage the said George W. Walker and Mary J. Walker resided together as husband and wife and continuously lived in the Cherokee Nation up to and including September 1, 1902. Said Mary J. Walker is identified on the Cherokee Authenticated tribal roll of 1880, and the Cherokee Census Roll of 1896 as an intermarried citizen of the Cherokee Nation.

IT IS, THEREFORE, ORDERED AND ADJUDGED: That in accordance with the decision of the Supreme Court of the United States, dated November 5, 1906, in the cases of Daniel Red Bird, et al., vs. the United States under the provision of Section 21 of the Act of Congress approved June 28, 1898, (30 Stats., 495), Mary J. Walker is entitled to enrollment as a citizen by intermarriage of the Cherokee Nation, and her application for enrollment as such is accordingly granted.

Tams Bixby

Commissioner.

Dated at Muskogee, Indian Territory,
this    JAN 17 1907

◇◇◇◇◇

Cherokee 3933

## DEPARTMENT OF THE INTERIOR,

## COMMISSIONER TO THE FIVE CIVILIZED TRIBES.

————

In the matter of the application for the enrollment of Mary J. Walker as a citizen by intermarriage of the Cherokee Nation.

--:--

## O R D E R .

The Commissioner having been informed by the Attorney for the Cherokee Nation that he has received reliable information that Mary J. Walker, wife of George W. Walker, was married prior to her marriage to said George W. Walker, and that her former husband was living at the time of her marriage to him, and her former marriage had not been annulled by death or divorce, it is hereby ordered that the decision of the Commissioner, dated January 17, 1907, granting the application for the enrollment of said Mary J. Walker, be rescinded, set aside and held for naught, and that the Cherokee Nation and the applicant be permitted to offer such testimony as they desire in order to properly determine the right of said Mary J. Walker to enrollment as a citizen by intermarriage of the Cherokee Nation.

Tams Bixby

Commissioner.

Dated at Muskogee, Indian Territory,
this January 23, 1907.

◇◇◇◇◇

Cherokee 3933

### DEPARTMENT OF THE INTERIOR,
### COMMISSIONER TO THE FIVE CIVILIZED TRIBES.
### MUSKOGEE, I. T., JANUARY 30, 1907.

In the matter of the application for the enrollment of MARY J. WALKER as a citizen by intermarriage of the Cherokee Nation.

JAMES WALKER, being first duly sworn by B. P. Rasmus, a Notary Public, testified as follows:

ON BEHALF OF THE COMMISSIONER:

Q    What is your name?    A James Walker.

Q    Your postoffice address is Welch?    A Yes sir.

Q    You appear here to give some testimony in the matter of the application of Mary J. Walker as a citizen by intermarriage of the Cherokee Nation, do you?    A Yes sir.

Q    You are the son of George W. Walker and Mary J. Walker?    A Yes sir.

Q    Well do you know when George W. Walker and Mary J. Walker were married, or have you any record showing the date of their marriage?    A Why no, I don't know, but just what he said.

Q    What did your father tell you as to the date of their marriage?
A    Well it was somewheres[sic] between,---it was either '63 or '69, I couldn't tell you just exactly which.

Q    Where were they married?    A He was married in the Cherokee Nation.

Q    Is it your understanding that Mary J. Walker was married before she married George W. Walker?    A Yes sir.

Q    How many time had she been married before?    A Why she was supposed to have been married once only.

Q    Was her first husband living at the time she married George W. Walker?
A    Yes sir, I guess he was.

Q    She had been divorced from that first husband?    A I don't know whether she had or not.

Q    Did you ever hear them say whether or not she secured a divorce or the first husband secured a divorce?    A No sir, I never.

Q    Well what is your understanding with reference to the matter, what have you been told concerning that first marriage?    A Well the last few days I understand she was married to a fellow named Davis and after they were married awhile it appears like he was sent to the pen.

Q    They didn't tell you the date he was sent to the penitentiary?    A No sir.

Q    And he was in the penitentiary serving a sentence at the time she was married to George W. Walker?    A Yes sir.

Q    You don't know how long he had been in the penitentiary at that time?    A No sir.

# Cherokee Intermarried White 1906
## Volume X

Q    What is your understanding as to the date of her marriage to the man Davis, her first husband?    A  Well I don't know as ever I heard anybody say anything about the date or the time she was married to him.

Q    Or as to how long they lived together?    A  Well they didn't live together but a short time until Davis was sent to the pen.

Q    You didn't hear them say whether she married Davis before or after the war?    A    I think it was after the war.

Q    You never heard for how long a term Davis was sent up did you?    A    Five years.

Q    You never heard whether or not he was pardoned or served his full term?    A    Well I heard he served his full time.

Q    You never heard when he got out of the penitentiary?    A  No sir.

Q    He didn't get out of the penitentiary until after Mary J. Walker was married to George W. Walker?    A  I don't think so.

Q    You never made any effort did you to find out whether or not any divorce was granted to Mary J. Walker from her first husband?    A  No sir.

Q    You have got no information at all on that?    A  No sir, I haven't got none at all.


(Witness excused).


--------------------------------oOo--------------------------------


Geo. H. Lessley, being first duly sworn states that as stenographer to the Commissioner to the Five Civilized Tribes, he reported the proceedings had in the above entitled cause, and that the above and foregoing is a true and correct transcript of his stenographic notes thereof.

Geo H Lessley


Subscribed and sworn to before me this 31st day of January, 1907.

John E. Tidwell
Notary Public.

E C M                                                     Cherokee 3933.

## DEPARTMENT OF THE INTERIOR,
## COMMISSIONER TO THE FIVE CIVILIZED TRIBES.

---

In the matter of the application for the enrollment of MARY J. WALKER as a citizen by intermarriage of the Cherokee Nation.

## D E C I S I O N

THE RECORDS OF THIS OFFICE SHOW:  That at Vinita, Indian Territory, October 2, 1900 application was received by the Commission to the Five Civilized Tribes for the enrollment of Mary J. Walker as a citizen by intermarriage of the Cherokee Nation.  Further proceedings in the matter of said application were had at Muskogee, Indian Territory, October 16, 1901, January 4 and January 30, 1907.

THE EVIDENCE IN THIS CASE SHOWS:  That the applicant herein, Mary J. Walker, a white woman, married about the year 1870 one George W. Walker, who was at the time of said marriage a recognized citizen by blood of the Cherokee Nation, who is identified on the Cherokee authenticated tribal roll of 1880, Cooweescoowee District No. 3171 as a native Cherokee, and whose name is included on the approved partial roll of citizens by blood of the Cherokee Nation opposite No. 9489.  It is further shown that from the time of said marriage the said George W. Walker and Mary J. Walker resided together as husband and wife and continuously lived in the Cherokee Nation up to and including September 1, 1902.  The evidence further shows that the said Mary J. Walker was married prior to her marriage to the said George W. Walker to one _____ David, who, it appears, was living at the time she married George W Walker, and from whom, it is not affirmatively shown, she was divorced.

The Cherokee Nation, after having been given ample opportunity to prove that said Mary J. Walker was never divorced from said _____ Davis, has failed to do so, and it is a presumption in favor of the validity of the second marriage that said Mary J Walker was divorced from her said husband, _____ Davis, prior to her second marriage.

IT IS, THEREFORE, ORDERED AND ADJUDGED:  That in accordance with the decision of the Supreme Court of the United States, dated November 5, 1906, in the cases of Daniel Red Bird, et al. vs. the United States, Nos. 125, 126, 127, and 128, the said applicant, Mary J. Walker is entitled under the provisions of Section Twenty-one of the Act of Congress approved June 28, 1898 (30 Stats., 495), to enrollment as a citizen by intermarriage of the Cherokee Nation, and her application for enrollment as such is accordingly granted.

Tams Bixby
Commissioner.

Dated at Muskogee, Indian Territory,
this     FEB 28 1907

◇◇◇◇◇

DEPARTMENT OF THE INTERIOR,
COMMISSIONER TO THE FIVE CIVILIZED TRIBES.

In the matter of the application for the enrollment of Mary J. Walker as a citizen by intermarriage of the Cherokee Nation, Cherokee 3933.

Protest of the Cherokee Nation.

The record in this case shows that Mary J. Walker was married previous to her marriage to George W. Walker through whom she claims citizenship by intermarriage in the Cherokee Nation, and it is contedned[sic] on behalf of the Cherokee Nation that the burden is upon the applicant to show that she was free to contract a lawful marriage with George W. Walker at the time she was alleged to have married him.

The Cherokee Nation cannot subscribe to the dostrine[sic] set forth in the opinion of the Commissioner to the Five Civilized Tribes that the burden is upon the Cherokee Nation to show that Mary J. Walker was not divorced from George Walker. In said decision the following language is used:

"The Cherokee Nation after having been given ample opportunity to prove that said Mary J. Walker was never divorced from said _____ Davis has failed to do so."

Now, as above asserted, we contend that the burden was upon Mary J. Walker to prove every material point necessary to be proven in her case, and when it is shown in the testimony that she had been previously married and that her former husband was alive, then it was incumbent upon her to show that she was divorced from her first husband prior to her marriage to her second husband.

The Cherokee Nation of course cannot in the rush of the last few days of enrollment search over every county throughout the United States to find whether or not Mary J. Walker was divorced, but the burden was upon her and not having shown it, we protest against her enrollment.

Respectfully submitted,

Signed W. W. Hastings
Attorney for the Cherokee Nation.

Muskogee, I. T., Feb. 28, 1907.

Copy

◇◇◇◇◇

Cherokee
3933

Muskogee, Indian Territory, January 17, 1907.

W. W. Hastings,
       Attorney for the Cherokee Nation,
              Muskogee, Indian Territory.

Dear Sir:

There is enclosed herewith a copy of the decision of the Commissioner to the Five Civilized Tribes, dated January 17, 1907, granting the application for the enrollment of Mary J. Walker as a citizen by intermarriage of the Cherokee Nation.

Respectfully,

Encl. H-41                                                          Commissioner.
   JMH

◇◇◇◇◇

---

Form No. 2.

## THE WESTERN UNION TELEGRAPH COMPANY.
————— INCORPORATED —————
**24,000 OFFICES IN AMERICA.   CABLE SERVICE TO ALL THE WORLD.**
ROBERT C. CLOWRY, President and General Manager.

| Receiver's No. | Time Filed | Check |
|---|---|---|
|  |  |  |

**SEND** the following message subject to the terms on back hereof, which are hereby agreed to.        January 23, 1907           190

To   James F. Walker

              Welch, Indian Territory.

       You can introduce evidence before the Commissioner January

29 as to right of your mother Mary J. Walker to enrollment as

citizen by intermarriage.  Cherokee Nation will be permitted to

introduce testimony on that date.

                                                        BIXBY,
   O B C R Paid                                         Commissioner

☞ READ THE NOTICE AND AGREEMENT ON BACK. ☜

---

*(Copy of original document from case.)*

◇◇◇◇◇

Cherokee
3933

Muskogee, Indian Territory, January 23, 1907

James F. Walker,
    Welch, Indian Territory.

Dear Sir:

      In connection eith[sic] the application for the enrollment of your mother, Mary J. Walker, as a citizen by intermarriage of the Cherokee Nation, you are directed to appear before the Commissioner at Muskogee, Indian Territory, on Tuesday, January 29, 1907, and introduce such testimony as you desire relative to her right to enrollment.

      The Cherokee Nation will also be permitted to appear on that date and introduce such testimony as it desires in her case.

Respectfully,

L M B                                           Commissioner

Register

◇◇◇◇◇

Cherokee
3933

Muskogee, Indian Territory, January 23, 1907

W. W. Hastings,
    Attorney for the Cherokee Nation,
        Muskogee, Indian Territory.

Dear Sir:

      You are hereby advised that James F. Walker has this day been notified that he will be permitted to appear before the Commissioner at Muskogee, Indian Territory, on Tuesday, January 29, 1907, and introduce such testimony as he desires in the matter of the application for the enrollment of his mother, Mary J. Walker, as a citizen by intermarriage of the Cherokee Nation.

      The Cherokee Nation will also be permitted to appear on that date and introduce such testimony as it desires in said case.

Cherokee Intermarried White 1906
Volume X

Respectfully,

L M B                                                    Commissioner

◇◇◇◇◇

Form No. 1511.          **NIGHT MESSAGE.**
**THE WESTERN UNION TELEGRAPH COMPANY.**
------- INCORPORATED -------
24,000 OFFICES IN AMERICA.     CABLE SERVICE TO ALL THE WORLD.
ROBERT C. CLOWRY, President and General Manager.

| Receiver's No. | Time Filed | Check |
|---|---|---|
| | | Cherokee No.3933.     ECM |

**SEND** the following night message subject to the
terms on back hereof, which are hereby agreed to.          February 22, 1907.

James Walker,

Welch, Indian Territory.

Intermarried case of Mary J. Walker incomplete. Produce
witnesses immediately to establish divorce from Davis.

BIXBY,

Commissioner.

O.B.G.R.   Paid.

☞ READ THE NOTICE AND AGREEMENT ON BACK. ☚

*(Copy of original document from case.)*
◇◇◇◇◇

Cherokee 3933.

ECM                          Muskogee, Indian Territory, February 22, 1907.

SPECIAL.

James Walker,
        Welch, Indian Territory.

Sir:

The Commission sent you this day a telegram as follows:

"Intermarried case of Mary J. Walker incomplete.  Produce
witnesses immediately to establish divorce from Davis."

The Act of Congress approved April 26, 1906 provides that the
Secretary of the Interior shall have no jurisdiction to approve the enrollment of

any person as a citizen of the Cherokee Nation after March 4, 1907. This matter, therefore, demands your immediate attention.

Respectfully,

Commissioner.

GHC

◇◇◇◇◇

Cherokee
   3933

Muskogee, Indian Territory, February 28, 1907

W. W. Hastings,
      Attorney for the Cherokee Nation,
            Muskogee, Indian Territory.

Dear Sir:

There is enclosed a copy of the decision of the Commissioner to the Five Civilized Tribes, dated February 28, 1907, granting the application for the enrollment of Mary J. Walker as a citizen by intermarriage of the Cherokee Nation.

The record of proceedings had in your case, together with the Commissioner's decision has been this day forwarded to the Department for review. You will be advised of any further action taken in the case.

Respectfully,

Encl. B-4                                              Commissioner

◇◇◇◇◇

Muskogee, Indian Territory, February 28, 1907

The Honorable
      The Secretary of the Interior.

Sir:

There is transmitted herewith the record of proceedings had in the matter of the application for the enrollment of Mary J. Walker for enrollment as a citizen by intermarriage of the Cherokee Nation, together with the Commissioner's decision of this date granting her application.

The Attorney for the Cherokee Nation protests against the Commissioner's decision in this case, and his protest, filed this day, is also enclosed.

There is enclosed a schedule containing the name of said Mary J. Walker, and in event the Department concurs in the Commissioner's decision therein, the approval of this schedule is recommended. It will be noted that no number has been given the name of this person on the schedule herewith transmitted. This action is taken in accordance with the procedure reported by me to the department on January 28, 1907, and approved by the Department's telegram of February 9, 1907.

In case of the approval of this schedule, it is recommended that a number be placed thereon by Mr. McGarr, the employe[sic] of my office now in Washington.

Respectfully,

Commissioner.

Through the
Commissioner of Indian Affairs.

Encl. W-2.
S.W.

◇◇◇◇◇

Land                                    (COPY)
Reference in
body of letter.

DEPARTMENT OF THE INTERIOR,
OFFICE OF INDIAN AFFAIRS,
WASHINGTON/[sic]

March 2, 1907.

The Honorable,
The Secretary of the Interior.

Sir:

There are forwarded herewith several reports from Commissioner Bixby, transmitting the records in certain citizenship cases, with the recommendation that the persons involved in each case be enrolled, as follows:

CHEROKEE CITIZENS BY INTERMARRIAGE

21684.     Mary J. Walker.

CHEROKEE FREEDMEN.

21685.        John Humphrey.

21686        Eugene French.

The Office has examined the record in each of the above cases, together with the protest filed by the attorney of the Cherokee Nation in each case, and finds the conclusions of the Commissioner granting the applications for the enrollment of the above named persons to be correct, and recommends that they be enrolled, and that the protests of the Cherokee Nation be disregarded.

There are also inclosed herewith schedules containing the names of these persons, the approval of which is recommended.

It will be noted that no numbers are placed opposite the names of the persons on these schedules, and the Commissioner suggests that this be done by Mr. McGarr, an employe[sic] of his Office now in Washington.

Very respectfully,

C R. LARRABEE,

AJW:LM.                                          Acting Commissioner.

◇◇◇◇◇

Y.P.

D.C. 14851-1907.                (COPY)
I.T.D. 7926-1907.

LRS
Direct.

DEPARTMENT OF THE INTERIOR        FHE
WASHINGTON.

March 4, 1907.

Commissioner to the Five Civilized Tribes,
        Muskogee, Indian Territory.
Sir:

In accordance with the recommendation made in Indian Office letter of March 2, 1907 (Land 21684- et al.,) copy inclosed, your decisions in the Cherokee intermarried case of Mary J. Walker, and the Cherokee freedmen cases of John Humphrey and Eugene French, in favor of the applicants, are affirmed, and the schedules submitted with your letters of February 28, 1907, bearing their names, have been approved this day and will be disposed of in the usual manner, with the papers in the case.

Respectfully,

E. A. Hitchcock,
Secretary.

7 inc. and
15 for Ind. Of. with
copy hereof.
AFMc.
3-5-07.

◇◇◇◇◇

Cherokee
　　3933

Muskogee, Indian Territory, March 5, 1907

George W. Walker,
　　Kinnison[sic], Indian Territory.

Dear Sir:

There is enclosed herewith a copy of the decision of the Commissioner to the Five Civilized Tribes, dated February 28, 1907, granting the application for the enrollment of your wife, Mary J. Walker, as a citizen by intermarriage of the Cherokee Nation. The Cherokee Nation protests against her enrollment.

The record of proceedings had in this case, together with the Commissioner's decision, has been this day forwarded the Secretary of the Interior for review. You will be advised of any further action in the case.

Respectfully,

Encl. B-3

Commissioner.

◇◇◇◇◇

Cherokee
3933

COPY

Muskogee, Indian Territory, March 20, 1907.

W. W. Hastings,
     Attorney for the Cherokee Nation,
        Muskogee, Indian Territory.

Dear Sir:

You are hereby advised that the decision of the Commissioner to the Five Civilized Tribes, dated February 28, 1907, granting the application for the enrollment of Mary J. Walker, as a citizen by intermarriage of the Cherokee Nation, was affirmed by the Department March 4, 1907.

For your information there is enclosed herewith a copy of Departmental decision referred to.

Respectfully,

Encl. HJ-32.
HJC

SIGNED *Tams Bixby*
Commissioner.

◇◇◇◇◇

Cherokee
3933.

COPY

Muskogee, Indian Territory, March 20, 1907.

Mary J. Walker,
     Kinnison[sic], Indian Territory.

Dear Madam:

You are hereby advised that the decision of the Commissioner to the Five Civilized Tribes, dated February 28, 1907, granting your application for enrollment as a citizen by intermarriage of the Cherokee Nation, was affirmed by the Department March 4, 1907.

For your information there is enclosed herewith a copy of Departmental decision referred to.

Respectfully,

Encl. HJ-32.
HJC

SIGNED *Tams Bixby*
Commissioner.

**Cher IW 287**

Department of the Interior.
Commission to the Five Civilized Tribes.
Claremore, I. T., October 22, 1900.

In the matter of the application of Charles M. Beavers for the enrollment of himself and his wife as Cherokee citizens; he being sworn and examined by Commissioner T. B. Needles, testified as follows:

Q   What's your name?    A  Charles M. Beavers.
Q   What's your age?    A  53.
Q   What's your postoffice address?    A  Claremore, I.T.
Q   What district do you live in?    A  Cooweescoowee.
Q   Are you a recognized citizen of the Cherokee Nation?    A  Have been.
Q   By blood or intermarriage?    A  Intermarriage.
Q   For whom do you apply for enrollment?    A  Myself and my wife.
Q   What's your wife's name?    A  Sarah M. Beavers.
Q   When did you marry her?    A  In '72.
Q   What's her age?    A  45. (49)
Q   Is your wife living?    A  Yes sir.
Q   You and her been living together since you married?    A  Yes sir.
Q   Livin[sic] together now?    A  Yes sir.
Q   Alwats[sic] lived in the Cherokee Nation?    A  Yes sir, ever since I have been married.
1880 roll:  page 3,  #71,  C. M. Beavers, Canadian Dist.
1880 roll:  page 3,  #72,  S. M. Beavers, Canadian Dist.
1896 roll:  page 294,  #69,  Charles M. Beavers, Cooweescoowee.
1896 roll:  page 110,  #333, Sarah M. Beavers, Cooweescoowee.
Commissioner-
    The name of Charles M. Beavers and his wife, Sarah, appears upon the authenticated roll of 1880, he as C. M. and she as S.M.  Their names also appear upon the Census roll of 1896 as Charles M. and Sarah M.  Having made satisfactory proof as to the residence and being duly identified, the said Charles M. Beavers will be duly listed for enrollment as a Cherokee citizen by intermarriage:  his wife Sarah M., as a Cherokee citien[sic] by blood.

    E.G. Rothenberger, being duly sworn, states that as stenographer to the Commission to the Five Civilized Tribes, he reported in full all proceedings in the above case, and that the foregoing is a true and complete translation of his stenographic notes in said case.

                                        E.G. Rothenberger

Subscribed and sworn to before me this 23rd day of October, 1900.

TB Needles
Commissioner.

◇◇◇◇◇

Statement of Applicant Taken Under Oath.

## CHEROKEES BY BLOOD AND ADOPTION."

Name *Charles M. Beavers*          Date OCT 23 1900          *Claremore*          1900.

District          CANADIAN.          Year *1880*          Page *3*          No. *91*

Citizen by blood *7 8*          Mother's citizenship ____

Intermarried citizen *yes*

Married under what law ____          Date of marriage ____

License *19*          Certificate ____

Wife's name *Sarah M Beavers*

District ____          Year *1880*          Page *3*          No. *92*

Citizen by blood *yes*          Mother's citizenship ____

Intermarried citizen *no*

Married under what law ____          Date of marriage ____

License ____          Certificate ____

Names of Children :

| | Dist. | Year | Page | No. | Age |
|---|---|---|---|---|---|
| | Dist. | Year | Page | No. | Age |
| | Dist. | Year | Page | No. | Age |
| | Dist. | Year | Page | No. | Age |
| | Dist. | Year | Page | No. | Age |
| | Dist. | Year | Page | No. | Age |
| | Dist. | Year | Page | No. | Age |
| | Dist. | Year | Page | No. | Age |
| | Dist. | Year | Page | No. | Age |
| | Dist. | Year | Page | No. | Age |

*1 on 1880 roll as          C. M. Beavers*
*2 "    "    "    "          S. M. Beavers*

*(Copy of original document from case.)*

◇◇◇◇◇

Cherokee 4712.

Department of the Interior,
Commission to the Five Civilized Tribes,
Muskogee, I. T., October 14, 1902.

In the matter of the application of Charles M. Beavers for the enrollment of himself as a citizen by intermarriage, and for the enrollment of his wife, Sarah M. Beavers, as a citizen by blood of the Cherokee Nation; he being sworn and examined by the Commission, testified as follows:

Q    What is your name?    A  Charles M. Beavers.
Q    How old are you?    A  About fifty-six.
Q    What is your postoffice?    A  Claremore.
Q    You are a white man?    A  Yes sir.
Q    You are on the 1880 roll as an intermarried white?    A  Yes sir.
Q    What is your wife's name?    A  Sarah M.
Q    Was she your wife in 1880?    A  Yes sir.
Q    Have you and your wife, Sarah, been living together since 1880?
A    Yes sir.
Q    Living in the Cherokee Nation?    A  Yes sir.
Q    Never made your home outside of the Cherokee Nation?    A  No sir.
Q    You were living together on the first day of last September, were you?
A    Yes sir.

The undersigned, being duly sworn, states that as stenographer to the Commission to the Five Civilized Tribes he correctly recorded the testimony and proceedings in this case, and that the foregoing is a true and correct transcript of his stenographic notes thereof.

E.G. Rothenberger

Subscribed and sworn to before me this 7th day of November, 1902.

BC Jones
Notary Public.

◇◇◇◇◇

Cherokee-4712.

## DEPARTMENT OF THE INTERIOR,
## COMMISSION TO THE FIVE CIVILIZED TRIBES.
### Muskogee, Indian Territory, March 1, 1905.

------------------

In the matter of the application for the enrollment of Charles M. Beaver as a citizen by intermarriage of the Cherokee Nation.

------------------

Charles M. Beaver, being duly sworn, testified as follows:

Q. What is your name?    A. Charles M. Beaver.
Q. What is your post office address?    A. Claremore, I.T.
Q. How old are you?    A. About 57.
Q. Are you a white man?    A. Yes sir.
Q. You claim no right as a Cherokee by blood?    A. No sir.
Q. Are you an intermarried citizen?    A. Yes sir.
Q. What is the name of the Cherokee wife through whom you claim you intermarried right?    A. Sarah Ann Cannon.
Q. Was she your first wife?    A. Yes sir.
Q. Were you her first husband?    A. No sir.
Q. Was her former husband living at the time of your marriage to her?    A. No sir.
Q. Did she have a living husband at the time of her marriage to you from whom she had not been divorced?    A. Not that I know of.
Q. You are on the '80 roll?    A. Yes sir.
Q. When were you married?    A. I think it was the 22nd. day of February, 1872.
Q. Were you married in the Cherokee Nation?    A Yes sir.
Q. Did you have a tribal license?    A. Yes sir.
Q. Since your marriage in 1982 where have you and she lived?
    A.    In the Cherokee Nation.
Q. Have you lived anywhere else than in the Cherokee Nation from the time of your marriage to her up to and including September 1, 1902?    A. No sir.
Q. Any separation, abandonment, or divorce?    A. No sir.

### WITNESS EXCUSED.

Eula Jeanes Branson, being duly sworn, states that, as stenographer to the Commission to the Five Civilized Tribes, she reported the proceedings had in the above entitled cause on the 1st. day of March, 1905, and that the above and foregoing is a full and complete transcript of her stenographic notes taken in said cause on said date.

Eula Jeanes Branson

Subscribed and sworn to before me this the 2nd day of March, 1905

Myron White
Notary Public.

Cherokee 4712

## DEPARTMENT OF THE INTERIOR
## COMMISSIONER TO THE FIVE CIVILIZED TRIBES
Muskogee, Indian Territory
January 4, 1907

In the matter of the application for the enrollment of Charles M. Beavers as a citizen by intermarriage of the Cherokee Nation.

The applicant being first duly sworn, testified as follows

Q   What is your name?   A  Charles M. Beavers the way its[sic] on the roll
Q   How old are you Mr. Beavers?   A  59
Q   What is your postoffice address?   A  Claremore
Q   Do you claim to be a citizen by intermarriage of the Cherokee Nation?  A  Yes sir.
Q   Through whom do you claim your intermarried rights?
A   My wife was Sarah M. Beavers.
Q   When were you married to Sarah M. Beavers?   A  In 1872
Q   Where?   A  Goingsnake District.
Q   Got a license?   A  Yes sir

The applicant offers in evidence license issued to him on the 17th day of January, 1872 by Joseph M. Starr to marry Miss Sarah Cannon, also certificate of Harry Crittenden judge of Goingsnake District, that they were married under said license.

Q   Were you ever married before you married Sarah M. Beavers?
A   No sir
Q   Was she ever married before?   A  I suppose she was--she was married in Georgia
Q   What was her husband's name?   A  I think it was Crane
Q   Was he living at the time you married her?   A  No sir, - I don't know--she was a widow here
Q   Didn't she ever tell you whether her husband was living or dead?
A   She supposed he was dead--that's something I don't know.
Q   Well what did she say, that he was living or dead?   A  She said he was dead.
Q   Have you lived together continuously as husband and wife since your marriage in 1872 in the Cherokee Nation?   A  Yes sir
Q   Was your wife a recognized citizen of the Cherokee Nation in 1872?   A  Yes sir.
Q   When was she admitted?   A  Sometime in '71--I was not here.  She was admitted before I came here.
Q   Was her people living here at that time?   A  Yes sir

Q    Were they recognized citizens?    A Yes sir
Q    Have you always been recognized as a citizen of the Cherokee Nation since your marriage in 1872?    A Yes sir.

The applicant is identified on the 1880 Cherokee roll Canadian District opposite No. 71. His wife, through whom he claims his right to enrollment is identified on said roll opposite No. 72. She is also identified on the final roll of citizens by blood of the Cherokee Nation opposite No. 11297.

Witness excused.

Gertrude Hanna, being duly sworn, states that as stenographer to the Commission to the Five Civilized Tribes she reported the proceedings had in the above numbered case on January 4, 1907, and that the above and foregoing is a true and correct transcript of her stenographic notes taken thereof.

Gertrude Hanna

Subscribed and sworn to before me this __5__ day of January, 1907

Walter W. Chappell
Notary Public.

◇◇◇◇◇

F. R.                                                                                  Cherokee 4712.

## DEPARTMENT OF THE INTERIOR,
## COMMISSIONER TO THE FIVE CIVILIZED TRIBES.
### Muskogee, Indian Territory, January 22, 1907.

In the matter of the application of Charles M. Beavers for enrollment as a citizen by intermarriage of the Cherokee Nation.

### SUPPLEMENTAL.

Sarah M. beavers being first duly sworn by B. P. Rasmus, Notary Public, testified as follows:

Q    What is your name?                       A    Sarah M. Beavers.
Q    What is your age?                         A    54.
Q    What is your post office address?
A    Claremore.
Q    You are the wife of Charles M. Beavers?
A    Yes sir.

| Q | When were you married to Charles M. Beavers? |
|---|---|
| A | January, 1872. |
| Q | What was your name before you became Sarah M. Beavers? |
| A | Crane; I have been married twice. |
| Q | When were you married the first time? |
| A | 1868. |
| Q | The marriage in 1868 was to a man named Crane? |
| A | Yes sir. |
| Q | Where were you married to this man Crane? |
| A | In Georgia. |
| Q | How long did you live with Crane? |
| A | 6 months; something thereabout. |
| Q | Then you separated, did you?      A Yes sir. |
| Q | Did you ever secure a divorce from him? |
| A | No sir; he was suing for a divorce when I left there. |
| Q | Do you know whether or not he was dead at the time you married Charles M. Beavers? |
| A | I do not; I got a letter he was dead but I can't swear to that. He was married. |
| Q | When did you get the letter saying he was dead? |
| A | I can't tell you whether it was before or after I married Mr. Beavers. |
| Q | Who was the letter from? |
| A | A lady by the name of Barrett. |
| Q | Was she related to you in any way? |
| A | No sir; just a neighbor. |
| Q | Did you write and ask her? |
| A | No sir; never wrote nothing about it. |
| Q | You are unable to testify positively then as to whether Crane was living or dead at the time you married Charles M. Beavers? |
| A | Yes sir. |
| Q | At the time you married Charles M. Beavers, were you a recognized citizen by blood of the Cherokee Nation? |
| A | I was a recognized citizen by blood of the Cherokee Nation when I married him. |
| Q | When were you admitted to citizenship? |
| A | In '70; the year I came here. |
| Q | By what tribal authority were you admitted? |
| A | I don't know; my parents went to Tahlequah and proved my rights. |
| Q | What was the name of your parents? |
| A | Cannon. |
| Q | What was your father's name?      A Irbie Cannon. |
| Q | Is it your understanding that you were admitted to citizenship at the same time he was admitted in 1870? |
| A | Yes sir; I wasn't there but he went to enroll the whole family just after we came to the Nation. |
| Q | How soon after you came to the Nation was it? |
| A | We got here along the last of November, '70, and they went on to Tahlequah. |

Q  Then it was within a few days after you reached the Nation?

A  Yes sir; just 3 or 4 days.

Q  You don't know whether any papers showing the admission of your family to citizenship, were issued to our parents at that time?

A  No sir; I don't know.

Q  You say you separated from your husband, Crane, about six months after your marriage to him in '68?

A  I was married to him in August '68 and he went off the last day of April in '69.

Q  Did you continue to reside in Georgia until the time you came to the territory in '70?

A  Yes, I stayed right there.

Q  Did he return to that country during the time you stayed there?

A  He was born and raised there and stayed there in his own settlement and I stayed in mine.

Q  Die he make any effort to secure a divorce from you?

A  I can't tell whether that's so or not but people said he was suing me for a divorce at the time I left there.

Q  You never had any papers served upon you? You never appeared in court in any divorce proceedings?

A  No sir; if they ever served any papers, they never reached me.

Q  You never heard after you came here whether he secured a divorce?

A  No; but I heard that he was married,- about two years before I was married,- and he couldn't have married and lived there without a divorce.

Q  Is there anyone living in the Indian Territory at this time who knows any of the facts with reference to your first marriage; or that is would know whether or not Crane was living or dead at the time you married Charles M. Beavers, or would know whether or not he secured a divorce?

A  If there is, I don't know it.

Q  Did you ever attempt to get copies of any of the court records back in Georgia to show whether or not he secured a divorce from you?

A  No sir; I never tried. When I came here they said I couldn't get a divorce; they said I was from here and would have to marry over. The Judge that married them told me that,- ma and pa married over after we came here.

Q  You and Charles M. Beavers have resided together as husband and wife and lived continuously in the Cherokee Nation since your marriage in 1872?

A  Yes sir.

Q  You have been regarded by your neighbors as having been married in accordance with the laws of the Cherokee Nation?

A  Yes sir.

Q  You have never lived anywhere else than in the Cherokee Nation from the time of your marriage up until the present time?

A  No sir.

Q  You don't think that you could be mistaken as to the time that you were admitted to citizenship in the Cherokee Nation,- that is as to the date; you say it was just a few days after you came to the Cherokee Nation?

A  No sir; I couldn't.

Q    Do you know when your father first voted in the elections of the Cherokee Nation?
A    No sir; I don't.

---

The undersigned being first duly sworn stated that as stenographer to the Commissioner to the Five Civilized Tribes, she recorded the testimony in this case and that the foregoing is a full, true and correct transcript of her stenographic notes thereof.

Myrtle Hill

Subscribed and sworn to before me this the 26th day of January, 1907.

John E. Tidwell

◇◇◇◇◇

T.W.L.                                                                 Cherokee-4712.

DEPARTMENT OF THE INTERIOR,
COMMISSIONER TO THE FIVE CIVILIZED TRIBES.

In the matter of the application for the enrollment of Charles M. Beavers as a citizen by intermarriage of the Cherokee Nation.

## D E C I S I O N.

THE RECORDS OF THIS OFFICE SHOW:  That at Claremore, Indian Territory, October 22, 1900, application was received by the Commission to the Five Civilized Tribes for the enrollment of Charles M. Beavers as a citizen by intermarriage of the Cherokee Nation.   Further proceedings in the matter of said application were had at Muskogee, Indian Territory, October 14, 1902, March 1, 1905, January 4, 1907 and January 22, 1907.

THE EVIDENCE IN THIS CASE SHOWS:  That the applicant herein, Charles M. Beavers, a white man, was married in accordance with Cherokee law in January or February, 1872, to one Sarah M. Beavers, formerly Crane, nee Cannon, who was at the time of said marriage a recognized citizen by blood of the Cherokee Nation, who was admitted to citizenship in the Cherokee Nation by the duly constituted authorities thereof in 1870, is identified on the Cherokee authenticated tribal roll of 1880, Canadian District page 3, number 72, as an adopted Cherokee, and whose name is included in the approved partial roll of citizens of the Cherokee Nation, opposite number 11297.  A letter from the Executive Secretary of the Cherokee Nation, attached to the record, states that no record of an act admitting Sarah M. cannon, or Crane, to citizenship in the Cherokee Nation could be found, but it is considered that the positive testimony of the said Sarah M. Crane nee Beavers, together with the circumstances that in the marriage license, which is a part of the record, the clerk who issued the license recited that the said person, "Mrs. Sarah Cannon" was a Cherokee citizen and that the said Sarah M. Cannon, or Crane, is identified upon the 1880 and subsequent tribal rolls of the Cherokee Nation, is fully sufficient not only to show that the said Sarah M. Cannon was lawfully admitted to citizenship in the Cherokee Nation but that such admission took place prior to the date of her marriage with the applicant herein. If further appears from the evidence that prior to her marriage to the applicant herein, the said Sarah M. Cannon had been married to a name named Crane, in Georgia. There is some testimony that the said crane was divorced from the said Sarah M. Cannon, or Crane, and had re-married prior to the date of the marriage of the applicant herein, and also some testimony tending to show that the said Crane was dead at the time of the marriage in question. Although the said death may not be established by the evidence, it is clear that it is not affirmatively shown that the said Crane was living and undivorced[sic] at the time of the applicant's marriage to his Cherokee spouse, the presumptions are all in favor of the subsequent marriage and to sustain a subsequent marriage either the divorce or death of the former spouse would be presumed, and the burden of proof transferred to the party whose interest it is to show the subsequent marriage void. It is further shown that from the time of the said marriage of the applicant herein to the said Sarah M. Cannon, or Crane, he and she resided together as husband and wife and continuously lived together in the Cherokee Nation up to and including September 1, 1902. Said applicant is identified on the Cherokee authenticated tribal roll of 1880, Canadian District, page 3, number 71, and on the Cherokee census roll of 1896, Cooweescoowee District, page 294, number 69.

IT IS, THEREFORE, ORDERED AND ADJUDGED: That in accordance with the decision of the Supreme Court of the United States, dated November 5, 1906, in the cases of Daniel Red Bird, et al., vs. the United States, Nos. 125, 126, 127, and 128, the said applicant, Charles M. Beavers, is entitled, under the provisions of Section 21 of the Act of Congress approved June 28, 1898 (30 Stats. 495), to enrollment as a citizen by intermarriage of the Cherokee Nation, and his application for enrollment as such is accordingly granted.

Tams Bixby

Commissioner.

Dated at Muskogee, Indian Territory,
this      FEB 26 1907

◇◇◇◇◇

Cherokee 4712.

DEPARTMENT OF THE INTERIOR,
Commissioner to the Five Civilized Tribes.

In the matter of the application for the enrollment of Charles M. Beavers as a citizen by intermarriage of the Cherokee Nation.

Protest of the Cherokee Nation.

The representative of the Cherokee Nation does not believe that the applicant, Charles M. Beavers, is entitled to be enrolled as a citizen by intermarriage of the Cherokee Nation for two reasons:

First, the record in this case shows that the wife through whom he claims had been previously married in the State of Georgia, and there is no sufficient testimony that she was ever divrced[sic] from her first husband and if not divorced she was not free to contract a lawful marriage with the applicant Charles M. Beavers, and he therefore acquired no rights by virtue of his marriage to her.

Second, there is no sufficient testimony showing that Sarah M. Beavers, the wife through whom Charles M. Beavers, the applicant, claims was admitted to citizenship in the Cherokee Nation prior to November 1, 1875.

It is true she states that she was admitted to citizenship in 1870, but the record is the best testimony, and the certificate of the Executive Secretary attached to the papers shows that he is unable to find any record of the admission of the said Sarah M. Beavers, and there is no evidence whatever that any of the records were destroyed, but upon the contrary the Commissioner to the Five Civilized Tribes is aware that all records of the admission of all parties to citizenship in the Cherokee Nation since 1866 are preserved and are either upon file now with the Commissioner to the Five Civilized Tribes or are in the Executive Office at Tahlequah, and it certainly is a dangerous precedent to establish to accept the unsupported testimony of the wife of the applicant as sufficient to prove the date of her admission. But it will be argued that her name appears upon the 1880 authenticated roll of the Cherokee Nation; that is true, and she is entitled now to be enrolled as a citizen by blood of the Cherokee Nation by virtue of the fact that she was enrolled in 1880, and not upon her unsupported testimony which is contradicted by the record to the effect that she was admitted prior to that time.

Again it is stated in the decision that the Clerk of the District where the marriage license issued said that the woman was a Cherokee by blood. The Commissioner to the

266

Five Civilized Tribes knows that the clerks of the several districts were not the custodians of the rolls and that marriage licenses was[sic] issued at the suggestion of the applicant, which was Charles M. Beavers in this case, and upon his statement as to the citizenship of his wife.

The applicants have had years within which to secure a record from Georgia which would prove a divorce if one were ever secured and of course it is now too late for the Cherokee Nation to send back to the State of Georgia to have the records searched and the burden is upon the applicant to show that his wife was free to contract the marriage relation with him when he married her and he should be required to show that his wife was divorced from her first husband, and although she was upon the stand on January 22, 1907, and had ample time to have the records in the State of Georgia searched, yet no certified copy of divorce is presented and filed with the papers in this case. His wife, Sarah M. Beavers, admits that she was never served with any summons or citation in the case, and we submit that the applicant in this case should not be enrolled unless it is shown:

First, that his wife was free to contract the marriage with him in 1872, and,

Second, that she was then, in 1872, at the time of the of the marriage an admitted and recognized citizen of the Cherokee Nation by blood.

Respectfully,

Attorney for the Cherokee Nation

◇◇◇◇◇

Chrokee[sic]
    4712.

Muskogee, Indian Territory, December 27, 1906.

Charles M. Beavers,
    Claremore, Indian Territory.

Dear Sir:

November 6, 1906, the United States Supreme Court held that white persons who intermarried with Cherokee citizens according to Cherokee law prior to November 1, 1875, are entitled to enrollment and allotments of land as citizens of the Cherokee Nation.

## Cherokee Intermarried White 1906
## Volume X

You are advised that to properly determine your right to enrollment as a citizen by intermarriage of the Cherokee Nation, it will be necessary for you to appear before the Commissioner for the purpose of giving testimony as to the date of your marriage and whether or not your wife, by reason of your marriage to whom you claim the right to enrollment as a citizen of the Cherokee Nation, was a recognized citizen of the Cherokee Nation at the time of your marriage to her, and whether or not you were married to her in accordance with Cherokee laws.

You are therefore directed to appear before the Commissioner at Muskogee, Indian Territory, at 9 o'clock A. M., on Friday, January 4, 1907, and give testimony as above indicated.

Respectfully,

H.J.C.                                                                Acting Commissioner.

◇◇◇◇◇

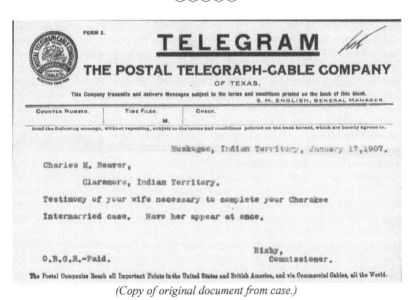

*(Copy of original document from case.)*

◇◇◇◇◇

Cherokee
4712

Muskogee, Indian Territory, January 22, 1907

Charles M. Beavers,
Claremore, Indian Territory.

Dear Sir:

Referring to your letter of December 17, 1906, relative to your right to enrollment as a citizen by intermarriage of the Cherokee Nation, you are advised that the Supreme Court of the United States by its decision of November 5, 1906, held that white persons who intermarried, according to Cherokee law, with Cherokee citizens, prior to November 1, 1875, are entitled to enrollment as citizens by intermarriage of the Cherokee Nation.

If you claim to be entitled to enrollment under the Court's decision, you should appear before the Commissioner at Muskogee, Indian Territory, at once, and introduce such testimony as you desire relative to your marriage to your Cherokee wife, by reason of your marriage to whom you claim the right to enrollment as a citizen by intermarriage of the Cherokee Nation, and as to the date of your marriage to him[sic].

The Act of Congress approved April 26, 1906, provides that the Secretary of the Interior shall have no jurisdiction to approve the enrollment of any person as a citizen of the Cherokee Nation after March 4, 1907, and the matter of your enrollment should therefore receive your immediate attention.

Respectfully,

L M B

Commissioner

◇◇◇◇◇

Cherokee 4712.

Muskogee, Indian Territory, January 30th, 1907.

Executive Secretary of the Cherokee Nation,
Tahlequah, Indian Territory.

Sir:-

You are requested to forward this office at once, certified copy of the Act admitting Sarah M. Cannon, or Crane, to citizenship in the Cherokee Nation.

Respectfully,

GHC.                                                                 Commissioner.

Muskogee, Indian Territory, February 28, 1907

The Honorable,
       The Secretary of the Interior.

Sir:

There is enclosed the record of proceedings had in the matter of the application for the enrollment of Charles M. Beavers as a citizen by intermarriage of the Cherokee Nation, together with the decision of the Commissioner dated February 26, 1907, granting his application.

You are advised the attorney for the Cherokee Nation protests against his enrollment, and his protest, filed this day, is enclosed.

There is also enclosed a schedule containing the name of Charles M. Beavers, and in the event of the approval of the Commissioner's decision in this case, the approval of the schedule is also recommended.

It will be noted that no roll number has been given the person whose name appears upon the schedule herewith transmitted. This action is taken in accordance with procedure reported by me to the Department on January 28, 1907. It is recommended that a number be placed upon this schedule by Mr. McGarr, the employe[sic] of my office now in Washington.

Respectfully,

Commissioner.

Through the Commissioner of
       Indian Affairs.

Encl. B-70

L M B

Cherokee
4712          COPY

Muskogee, Indian Territory, February 28, 1907.

Charles M. Beavers,
      Claremore, Indian Territory.

Dear Sir:

There is inclosed herewith a copy of the decision of the Commissioner to the Five Civilized Tribes, dated February 28, 1907, grnating[sic] your application for enrollment as a citizen by intermarriage of the Cherokee Nation.

You are advised that the Attorney for the Cherokee Nation protests against your enrollment as a citizen by intermarriage of the Cherokee Nation. Said protest, together with the record of proceedings, and the Commissioner's decision in your case has this day been transmitted to the Secretary of the Interior for his decision.

Respectfully,

SIGNED *Jams Bixby*
Incl. GL-3.                                    Commissioner.
GHL

◇◇◇◇◇

Reference              COPY
in body of letter

### DEPARTMENT OF THE INTERIOR,
### OFFICE OF INDIAN AFFAIRS,
### WASHINGTON.

March 2, 1907.

The Honorable,
      The Secretary of the Interior.

Sir:-

There are transmitted herewith several reports of Commissioner Bixby, forwarding the records of proceedings in the matter of applications for enrollment of the following persons:-

21796-07,    Su-ba-tah Flint as a citizen by blood of the Cherokee Nation.

21805-07,    Charles M. Beavers as a citizen by intermarriage of the Cherokee Nation.

21803-07,    Referring to Departmental decision of January 26, 1907 (I.T.D. 1392-07), affirming decision of Commissioner Bixby of January 10, 1907, denying the enrollment of James M. Price as a citizen by intermarriage of the Cherokee Nation.

Commissioner Bixby reports under date of February 27, 1907, that further proceedings were had in this case and that his decision of January 10 was erroneous, and now recommends that James M. Price be enrolled as a citizen by intermarriage of the Cherokee Nation.

The decision of Commissioner Bixby favorable to the applicants herein have been considered and found correct and their approval is recommended.

There are also enclosed three schedules containing the names of Su-ba-tah Flint, a citizen by blood of the Cherokee Nation; Charles M. Beavers, a citizen by intermarriage of the Cherokee Nation; and James M. rice, also a citizen by intermarriage of the Cherokee Nation. It is recommended that if the enclosed decisions be approved that the schedules transmitted herewith also receive the approval of the Department.

Very respectfully,

C. F. Larrabee,

Acting Commissioner.

EBM-HJS.

◇◇◇◇◇

D.C.14856                    COPY                    Y.P.

DEPARTMENT OF THE INTERIOR,        FHE.

WASHINGTON.

I.T.D. 7894-1907.                        March 4, 1907.

LRS    DIRECT.

Commissioner to the Five Civilized Tribes,
        Muskogee, Indian Territory.

Sir:

In accordance with the recommendation contained in your letter of February 27, 1907, the decision of the Department of the Interior January 26, 1907, affirming your decision denying, among others, the application for the enrollment of James M. Price as a citizen by intermarriage of the Cherokee Nation, is hereby rescinded as to him, and his application is granted. The Indian Office, submitting your report March 2, 1907 (Land 21796 et al), copy inclosed, concurred in your recommendation.

The schedule bearing the name of this person, received with your letter, has been approved this day.

The Indian Office transmitted two other schedules, one bearing the name of Charles M. Beavers as a citizen by intermarriage of the Cherokee Nation, and the other that of Su-ba-tah Flint as a citizen by blood of the Cherokee Nation, and recommended their approval and the decisions of your office in their favor. In accordance therewith the schedules have been approved. Al[sic] three schedules will be disposed of in the usual manner.

The papers in the cases will be sent to the Indian Office with a copy hereof.

Respectfully,

(Signed) E. A. Hitchcock,
Secretary.

7 inc. and
12 for Ind. Of. with
copy hereof.

McM 3-5-07

◇◇◇◇◇

Cherokee
4712.

Muskogee, Indian Territory, March 26, 1907.

Charles M. Beavers,
Claremore, Indian Territory.

Dear Sir:

You are hereby advised that the decision of the Commissioner to the Five Civilized Tribes, dated February 26, 1907, granting your application for enrollment as a citizen by intermarriage of the Cherokee Nation was affirmed by the Department March 4, 1907.

For your information there is enclosed herewith a copy of Departmental decision referred to.

Respectfully,

Encl. HJ-11.                                          *Geo. D. Rodgers.*
HJC                                                    Acting Commissioner.

◇◇◇◇◇

Cherokee
4712.

Muskogee, Indian Territory, March 26, 1907.

W. W. Hastings,
      Attorney for the Cherokee Nation,
          Muskogee, Indian Territory.

Dear Sir:

You are hereby advised that the decision of the Commissioner to the Five Civilized Tribes, dated February 26, 1907, granting the application for the enrollment of Charles M. Beavers, as a citizen by intermarriage of the Cherokee Nation was affirmed by the Department March 4, 1907.

For your information there is enclosed herewith a copy of Departmental decision referred to.

Respectfully,

Encl. HJ-12.                                          *Geo. D. Rodgers.*
HJC                                                    Acting Commissioner.

---

**Cher IW 288**

◇◇◇◇◇

E. C. M.                                                    Cherokee 1033.

DEPARTMENT OF THE INTERIOR,
COMMISSIONER TO THE FIVE CIVILIZED TRIBES.
Muskogee, Indian Territory, February 26, 1907.

In the matter of the application for the enrollment of James M. Price as a citizen by intermarriage of the Cherokee Nation.

Mack E. Price for applicant.

APPEARANCES:

W. W. Hastings for Cherokee Nation.

274

# Cherokee Intermarried White 1906
## Volume X

Mack E. Price being first duly sworn by Walter W. Chappell, Notary Public, testified as follows:

ON BEHALF OF COMMISSIONER:

| Q | What is your name? | A | Mack E. Price. |
|---|---|---|---|
| Q | What is your age? | A | 24. |
| Q | What is your postoffice address? | A | Salisaw |
| Q | Are you the son of James M. Price? | A | Yes sir. |

Q  You appear here today for the purpose of giving testimony relative to his right to enrollment as a citizen of the Cherokee Nation?

A  Yes sir.

| Q | Was he a white man? | A | Yes sir. |
|---|---|---|---|
| Q | He possessed no Cherokee blood? | A | No sir. |

Q  Through whom did he claim his right to enrollment as a citizen of the Cherokee Nation?

A  Mary Starr was her maiden name.

| Q | Is she a Cherokee? | A | Yes sir. |
|---|---|---|---|
| Q | When were they married? | A | '73. |

Q  Have you any documentary evidence of their marriage?

A  I suppose the license and certificate are here; I had them telegraph for them the last time I was here,-- or a copy of them.

Q  You appear here for the purpose of making application for your father?

A  Yes sir.

| Q | Are you the executor of the estate? | A | Yes sir. |
|---|---|---|---|

The witness here presents in evidence a marriage certificate issued by James W. Adair, Clerk of the District Court of Flint District, authorizing the marriage of Mr. James M. Price to Miss Mary Starr; said license was issued on the 26th day of November, 1873.

| Q | Is your father dead now? | A | Yes sir. |
|---|---|---|---|
| Q | Your mother? | A | Yes sir. |

Q  When did you father die?

A  25th of December, 1905.

| Q | When did your mother die? | A | 1901 I believe. |
|---|---|---|---|

Q  Was Mary Price, James M. Price's first wife?

A  Yes sir.

| Q | Was he her first husband? | A | Yes sir. |
|---|---|---|---|

Q  Has James M. Price remarried since the death of your mother, Mary Price?

A  No sir.

Q  From the time of their marriage until the death of Mary Price, did James M. Price and Mary Price continuously reside together as husband and wife and live in the Cherokee Nation?

A  Yes sir; so far as I know.

# Cherokee Intermarried White 1906
## Volume X

Witness Excused.

----------------------

Ellis Starr being first duly sworn by Walter W. Chappell, a Notary Public, testified as follows:

ON BEHALF OF COMMISSIONER.

Q   What is your name?                          A   Ellis Starr.
Q   What is your age?                           A   53.
Q   What is your post office address?                A   Salisaw.
Q   You appear here today for the purpose of giving testimony relative to the right to enrollment of James M. Price as a citizen by intermarriage of the Cherokee Nation?
A   Yes sir.
Q   Through whom does he claim his right to enrollment?
A   Through his wife, Mary.
Q   When were they married?
A   They were married in '73.
Q   You were acquainted with them at the time they were married?
A   Yes sir.
Q   Had James M. Price ever been married prior to his marriage to his wife, Mary?
A   I can't say that; I can only say about Mary.
Q   Was she ever married prior to her marriage to James M. Price?
A   No sir.
Q   From the time of their marriage until the death of Mary Price, did they continuously reside in the Cherokee Nation as husband and wife?
A   Yes sir.
Q   After the death of Mary Price, did James M. Price re-marry?
A   No.
Q   He died in 1905?                            A   Yes sir.

Witness Excused.

----------------------

John Price being first duly sworn by Walter W. Chappell, a Notary Public, testified as follows:

ON BEHALF OF COMMISSIONER.

Q   What is your name?                          A   John Price.
Q   What is your age?                           A   52.
Q   What is your postoffice address?                A   Salisaw.

Q   You appear here today for the purpose of giving testimony relative to the right of James M. Price to enrollment as a citizen of the Cherokee Nation?

A   Yes sir.

Q   He is a white man?        A   Yes sir.

Q   Through whom does he claim his right to enrollment?

A   Through his wife.

Q   What was the name of his wife?        A   Mary Starr.

Q   When were they married?        A   In '73.

Q   Was Mary Starr a Cherokee by blood?

A   Yes sir.

Q   Was James M. Price ever married prior to his marriage to Mary Starr?

A   No sir.

Q   Was she ever married prior to her marriage to him?

A   I don't know; I never knew it.

Q   After the death of Mary Price, did James Price re-marry?

A   No sir.

Q   From the time of their marriage until the death of Mary Price, they continuously resided together as husband and wife and lived in the Cherokee Nation?

A   Yes sir.

Mary Price, the wife of the applicant, James M. Price, is identified on the Cherokee authenticated tribal roll of 1880, Sequoyah District, No. 964, as a native Cherokee. James M. Price, the applicant in this case, is also identified on the 1880 roll, Sequoyah District, opposite No. 963, as an adopted white.

------------------------------

The undersigned on oath states that she reported the testimony taken in this case and that the foregoing is a true and correct transcript of her stenographic notes thereof.

Myrtle Hill

Subscribed and sworn to before me this the 26th day of February, 1907.

Walter W. Chappell
Notary Public.

◇◇◇◇◇

# Department of the Interior.
## COMMISSIONER TO THE FIVE CIVILIZED TRIBES.

*In the matter of the death of* **James M. Price**

a citizen of the **Cherokee** Nation, who formerly resided at or near **Sallisaw** , Ind. Ter., and died on the **25** day of **Dec 25** , **1905**

### AFFIDAVIT OF RELATIVE.

Western Dist
Ind. Ter.

I, **Mack E Price** , on oath state that I am **24** years of age and a citizen by **blood** , of the **Cherokee** Nation; that my postoffice address is **Sallisaw** , Ind. Ter.; that I am **Son** **Intermarriage** of **James M Price** who was a citizen, by **blood** , of the **Cherokee** Nation and that said **James M Price** died on the **25** day of **December** , **1905**

**Mack E Price**

WITNESSES TO MARK:

Subscribed and sworn to before me this **27th** day of **May** , 1907

**Walter W Chappell**
Notary Public.

### AFFIDAVIT OF ACQUAINTANCE.

I, , on oath state that I am
years of age, and a citizen by of the Nation;
that my postoffice address is , Ind. Ter.;
that I was personally acquainted with
who was a citizen, by , of the Nation;
and that said died on the day of
, 1

WITNESSES TO MARK:

Subscribed and sworn to before me this ———— day of ———————, 190—

————————————————————
Notary Public.

◇◇◇◇◇

## Department of the Interior.
### COMMISSIONER TO THE FIVE CIVILIZED TRIBES.

*In the matter of the death of*     **James M. Price**

a citizen of the     **Cherokee**     Nation, who formerly resided at or near **Sallisaw** , Ind. Ter., and died on the     **25th**     day of **December** , 1905

————————————————————

### AFFIDAVIT OF RELATIVE.

I, ——————————————————, on oath state that I am ————— years of age and a citizen by ———————, of the ————————— Nation; that my postoffice address is ——————————————————, Ind. Ter.; that I am ————————— of ————————————— who was a citizen, by ——————, of the ————————— Nation and that said ——————————————— died on the ————— day of ———————————, 1———

WITNESSES TO MARK:

{ ————————————————————
————————————————————

Subscribed and sworn to before me this ———— day of ——————, 190—

————————————————————
Notary Public.

————————————————————

### AFFIDAVIT OF ACQUAINTANCE.

**Indian Territory**
**Northern District** }

I,     **W.W. Wheeler and J.B. Adair**     , on oath state that I am **59** years of age, and a citizen by **blood** of the **Cherokee** Nation; that my postoffice address is **Sallisaw** , Ind. Ter.; that I was personally acquainted with **James M Price** who was a citizen, by **Marriage** , of the **Cherokee** Nation; and that said **James M. Price** died on the **25th** day of **December** , 1905

279

WITNESSES TO MARK:

$\left\{\rule{0pt}{24pt}\right.$

**W.W. Wheeler**

**J B  Adair**

Subscribed and sworn to before me this  **1**   day of  **June**   , 1907

**My Com Ex**
**Dec 14 - 1908**

**Joseph Willoughby**
Notary Public.

◇◇◇◇◇

Cherokee
1033

Muskogee, Indian Territory, January 10, 1907.

James M. Price,
        Hanson, Indian Territory.

Dear Sir:

        There is inclosed a copy of the decision of the Commissioner to the Five Civilized Tribes, dated January 10, 1907, rejecting, among others, the application for your enrollment as a citizen by intermarriage of the Cherokee Nation.   The Commissioner's decision has this day been forwarded to the Secretary of the Interior for review.  You will be advised of the Secretary's action as soon as this office is informed of same.

                                Respectfully,

Incl. Decn. ___A___                                Commissioner.

◇◇◇◇◇

Muskogee, Indian Territory, February 27, 1907.

The Honorable,
        The Secretary of the Interior.

Sir:

        January 10, 1907 the Commissioner to the Five Civilized Tribes rendered his decision denying, among others, the application for the enrollment of James M. Price as a citizen by intermarriage of the Cherokee Nation.

        Said decision was on January 26, 1907, (I.T.D. 1392-1907), affirmed by the Department.

Further proceedings had in this case at the request of the applicant at Muskogee, Indian Territory, February 25, 1907, show the decision of the Commissioner to be erroneous.

The records show that James M. Price, a white man, was married in accordance with Cherokee law November 26, 1873 to Mary Price, nee Starr, since deceased, who was at the time of said marriage a recognized citizen by blood of the Cherokee Nation, who is identified on the Cherokee authenticated tribal roll of 1880, Sequoyah District No. 964 as a native Cherokee marked "Dead". It is further shown that from the time of said marriage until the death of the said Mary Price, which occurred on November 25, 1901, the said James M. Price and Mary Price resided together as husband and wife and continuously lived in the Cherokee Nation; that after the death of said Mary Price the said James M. Price remained unmarried and continuously lived in the Cherokee Nation up to and including September 1, 1902. Said applicant is identified on the Cherokee authenticated tribal roll of 1880 and the Cherokee census roll of 1896 as an intermarried citizen of the Cherokee Nation.

In view of the decision of the Supreme Court, dated November 5, 1906, in the cases of Daniel Red Bird, et al. vs. the United States, Nos. 125, 126, 127 and 128, it is respectfully recommended that the Department rescind its said decision of January 26, 1907, so far as it related to this applicant, and that the application for the enrollment of James M. Price as a citizen by intermarriage of the Cherokee Nation be granted. The record of proceedings had in the case is inclosed.

It will be noted that no roll number has been given the person whose name appears upon the schedule herewith transmitted. This action is taken in accordance with the procedure reported by me to the Department on January 28, 1907 and approved by the Department by its telegram of February 9, 1907. If the Department concur in my recommendation I further recommend that a number be given this applicant, and that said number be placed upon this schedule in order by Mr. McGarr, the employee of my office now in Washington, and that the schedule receive the approval of the Department.

Respectfully,

Through the Commissioner
    of Indian Affairs.                    Commissioner.

ECM - GHC

# Cherokee Intermarried White 1906
## Volume X

Muskogee, Indian Territory, February 28, 1907.

Commissioner to the Five Civilized Tribes,
Muskogee, Indian Territory.

Sir:

I am in receipt of a copy of the testimony taken in the matter of the application for the enrollment of James M. Price as a citizen by intermarriage of the Cherokee Nation. I do not desire to protest against his enrollment, and I consent to his name being placed immediately upon a schedule of intermarried white citizen[sic] of the Cherokee Nation and forward to the Department for approval.

Respectfully,

(Signed)  W W Hastings

Attorney for Cherokee Nation.

◇◇◇◇◇

Reference                    COPY
in body of letter

DEPARTMENT OF THE INTERIOR,
OFFICE OF INDIAN AFFAIRS,
WASHINGTON.

March 2, 1907.

The Honorable,
The Secretary of the Interior.

Sir:-

There are transmitted herewith several reports of Commissioner Bixby, forwarding the records of proceedings in the matter of applications for enrollment of the following persons:-

21796-07,   Su-ba-tah Flint as a citizen by blood of the Cherokee Nation.

21805-07,   Charles M. Beavers as a citizen by intermarriage of the Cherokee Nation.

21803-07,   Referring to Departmental decision of January 26, 1907 (I.T.D. 1392-07), affirming decision of Commissioner Bixby of January 10, 1907, denying the enrollment of James M. Price as a citizen by intermarriage of the Cherokee Nation.

Commissioner Bixby reports under date of February 27, 1907, that further proceedings were had in this case and that his decision of January 10 was erroneous, and now recommends that James M. Price be enrolled as a citizen by intermarriage of the Cherokee Nation.

The decision of Commissioner Bixby favorable to the applicants herein have been considered and found correct and their approval is recommended.

There are also enclosed three schedules containing the names of Su-ba-tah Flint, a citizen by blood of the Cherokee Nation; Charles M. Beavers, a citizen by intermarriage of the Cherokee Nation; and James M. rice, also a citizen by intermarriage of the Cherokee Nation. It is recommended that if the enclosed decisions be approved that the schedules transmitted herewith also receive the approval of the Department.

Very respectfully,

C. F. Larrabee,

Acting Commissioner.

EBM-HJS.

◇◇◇◇◇

D.C.14856             COPY            Y.P.

DEPARTMENT OF THE INTERIOR,      FHE.<br>WASHINGTON.

I.T.D. 7894-1907.            March 4, 1907.

LRS    DIRECT.

Commissioner to the Five Civilized Tribes,
     Muskogee, Indian Territory.

Sir:

In accordance with the recommendation contained in your letter of February 27, 1907, the decision of the Department of the Interior January 26, 1907, affirming your decision denying, among others, the application for the enrollment of James M. Price as a citizen by intermarriage of the Cherokee Nation, is hereby rescinded as to him, and his application is granted. The Indian Office, submitting your report March 2, 1907 (Land 21796 et al), copy inclosed, concurred in your recommendation.

The schedule bearing the name of this person, received with your letter, has been approved this day.

The Indian Office transmitted two other schedules, one bearing the name of Charles M. Beavers as a citizen by intermarriage of the Cherokee Nation, and the other that of Su-ba-tah Flint as a citizen by blood of the Cherokee Nation, and recommended their approval and the decisions of your office in their favor. In accordance therewith the schedules have been approved. Al[sic] three schedules will be disposed of in the usual manner.

The papers in the cases will be sent to the Indian Office with a copy hereof.

Respectfully,

(Signed) E. A. Hitchcock,

Secretary.

7 inc. and
12 for Ind. Of. with
copy hereof.

McM 3-5-07

◇◇◇◇◇

Cherokee
1033

COPY

Muskogee, Indian Territory, March 22, 1907.

James M. Price,
    Sallisaw, Indian Territory.

Dear Sir:

You are hereby advised that your application for enrollment as a citizen by intermarriage of the Cherokee Nation was granted by the Department March 4, 1907.

For your information there is enclosed herewith a copy of Departmental decision referred to.

Respectfully,

SIGNED *Tams Bixby*

Commissioner.

Encl. HJ-82.
  HJC

◇◇◇◇◇

Cherokee
1033.                          COPY

Muskogee, Indian Territory, March 22, 1907.

W. W. Hastings,
        Attorney for the Cherokee Nation,
                Muskogee, Indian Territory.

Dear Sir:

        You are hereby advised that the application for the enrollment of James M. Price as a citizen by intermarriage of the Cherokee Nation was granted by the Department March 4, 1907.

        For your information there is enclosed herewith a copy of Departmental decision referred to.

                        Respectfully,

                                SIGNED *Tams Bixby*
                                Commissioner.

Encl. HJ-83.
    HJC

◇◇◇◇◇

*J.H. No 288*

*James M. Price*

*Record and Decision Not
in No. 1033 — 4/17/07*

Index

FOREMAN
   Johnson.................................178
   Preacher................................18
   Samuel..............................102,175
   Steve.................................... 2
   Steven.................................19
FRENCH, Eugene ...........................253
GAGE, Sarah F.............................14,15
GIDEON....................................135
GRAY
   George R ..............................127
   Horace ................................227
GREEN, M D .....................87,100,143
GULAGER, William M .................180
GULLIGER, William M.................168
HAMILTON, Nancy ......................164
HANKS
   Mr....................................198
   Robert T..............................197,198
HANNA, Gertrude ..................225,261
HANNAH, John .............................95
HARMON, Daniel.......................14,15
HARRIS
   Minta ..................................99
   Phirena................................14,15
HARRISON, David W ....................131
HASTINGS
   Mr.....................14,107,176,209,219
   W.....................................51
   W W ......5,12,13,15,16,23,24,26,39,
   52,62,64,65,68,74,84,88,91,97,111,
   112,122,128,140,141,142,150,158,159
   ,160,161,165,166,175,182,183,191,
   192,194,202,208,215,218,223,233,234
   ,239,247,248,249,251,255,274,282,
   285
HATCHET, Peggie............218,223,225
HAWKINS, W S ...........................207
HENDERSON.................................20
HEREFORD, L P ...........................150
HICKS
   E D ..................................227
   Ed D..................................228
HILL, Myrtle .............105,108,125,211,
242,264,277
HINKLE, Oliver C ........................198
HITCHCOCK

E A ......................9,72,254,273,284
I B...............................149
Mr...............................148
HOLLAND
   Daniel ................................219
   Hugh.............217,218,219,220,221,
   222,223,224,225,226,227,228,233,234
   ,235
   James N ..............................220
   Margaret ..............................225
   Peggy.................................222
   Walter ............218,221,222,229,230,
   231,232,233,235
HOWELL....................................210
   Beckey................................204
   Beckie................................204
   Emmett L.....................204,205,206
   Emmett Lee ............................204
   Isaac.................................204,210
   Isaac P ..........203,204,205,206,207,
   208,209,211,212,213,214,215,216
   Lee H.................................207
   Rebecca .........204,205,206,207,208,
   209,210,211,212
HUDSON, V W, MD .......................90
HUMPHREY, John ........................253
HUTCHINSON, Wm ...........46,78,133
IRONSIDES, Emma L .................14,15
JEFFREY
   Daniel H ..............................43
   Jehu..................................45,47
   John M................................43
   Nancy .......37,43,44,45,46,47,48,49,
   51,52,53,64
   Nancy J...............................43
JEFFRIES
   Jayhu.................................46
   Maggie................................46
   Nancy ................................43,44,46
JOHNSON
   Dovie ................................14,15
   Grace ................................227
   Harried................................227
   Maud M ...............................228
JONES
   B C .............29,88,118,133,145,163,
   172,186,206,227,239,258

Lightning Source UK Ltd.
Milton Keynes UK
UKHW010635270920
370609UK00001B/114